Praise for

Matriarchs
OF THE MESSIAH

"Skousen reimagines the stories of the biblical matriarchs, the women through whom Jesus Christ was born, reading the scriptures as real life. These women take daring steps, making wisdom and virtue out of what has been considered weakness and trickery. They use sex to good ends. From these thoughtful essays, informed by learned biblical scholarship and close scriptural reading, the Bible's women emerge anew."
—Claudia L. Bushman, author of *Building the Kingdom*

"Believers and nonbelievers alike will be fascinated and inspired by the women whose stories are skillfully told here by Jo Ann Skousen. Their trials, triumphs, strengths, and shortcomings will speak to both women and men today. Skousen's knowledge of the times in which they lived is particularly impressive."
—Steve Forbes, editor-in-chief of *Forbes Magazine*

"This is a book that opens the Bible and reveals its riches. Jo Ann Skousen shows fine insight in gathering the stories of the Bible's women, tracing their relationships, and establishing their value for modern readers. No book that I know does a better job with this important subject. The book is crisp, clear, and engaging through-out—a thoughtful and inspiring work."
—Stephen Cox, professor of literature at University of California, San Diego, and author of *The New Testament and Literature, American Christianity,* and other books

"In her well-written and readable *Matriarchs of the Messiah*, Jo Ann Skousen rescues several interesting and important women from their relative biblical obscurity. Retelling their stories with empathy and a trained literary eye, she shows how, despite the constraints of their culturally imposed roles, they acted as free and fully three-dimensional human beings.

"Sometimes, indeed, forced to choose priorities and to decide between competing values, they went directly against those cultural (and other) constraints to make courageous decisions—decisions that powerfully affected not only the narrative of the Bible but, in pivotal ways, the general history of humankind. Most notably, through their choices these women became ancestors of Christ or, in one case, His close and supportive associate and the first witness to His Resurrection.

"These are fascinating stories, worthy of our reflection. In *Matriarchs of the Messiah*, Jo Ann Skousen has given them some of the attention they deserve."

—Daniel Peterson, professor of Islamic Studies and Arabic
at Brigham Young University and author of
Abraham Divided and other books

"Reading *Matriarchs of the Messiah* was eye-popping to me. Stories and lessons came into focus with the prose. The analysis of these women, their motivations, their ambitions, their strengths, their weaknesses, and their skills as *ezerim kenegdo* provided so many 'aha' moments for me it was almost embarrassing. . . . Whether it was because it enhanced my rudimentary understanding of the topic and my natural inclination to love learning, or because it spoke to my inherent love for the Savior, I'm not sure. But I LOVED IT."

—Gary Burnett, attorney-at-law

Matriarchs
OF THE MESSIAH

May 2016

To Jim & Lynne Doti —
Valiant truth seekers,
and good friends!
Thank you for your
support & encouragement —

Matriarchs OF THE MESSIAH

VALIANT WOMEN *in the* LINEAGE *of* JESUS CHRIST

JO ANN SKOUSEN

CFI
An Imprint of Cedar Fort, Inc.
Springville, UT

ISBN 13: 978-1-4621-1783-3

Published by CFI, an imprint of Cedar Fort, Inc.
2373 W. 700 S., Springville, UT 84663
Distributed by Cedar Fort, Inc., www.cedarfort.com

Library of Congress Cataloging-in-Publication Data

Names: Skousen, Jo Ann, author.
Title: Matriarchs of the Messiah : valiant women in the lineage of Jesus
  Christ / Jo Ann Skousen.
Description: Springville, UT : CFI, an imprint of Cedar Fort, Inc., [2016] |
  "2016 | Includes bibliographical references.
Identifiers: LCCN 2015038456 | ISBN 9781462117833 (perfect bound : alk. paper)
Subjects: LCSH: Women in the Bible.
Classification: LCC BS575 .S46 2016 | DDC 220.9/2082--dc23
LC record available at http://lccn.loc.gov/2015038456

Cover design by Shawnda T. Craig
Cover art, "Valiant Women," by Mandy Jane Williams
Cover design © 2016 Cedar Fort, Inc.
Edited by Sydnee Hyer
Typeset by Jessica B. Ellingson

Printed in the United States of America

10 9 8 7 6 5 4 3 2 1

Printed on acid-free paper

CONTENTS

PREFACE

ANY YEARS AGO, I was taking a Bible literature course in college while also teaching a daily Bible study class for high school students. This nearly total immersion in the scriptures was enlightening and inspiring. In the literature class we studied the stories the way we might study a Shakespeare play or a Victorian novel, by looking for character foils, juxtapositions, plot twists, metaphors, and overarching themes. In the Church setting, we discussed our relationship with God and applied principles of righteous living to our own lives. These diverse experiences, one focusing on literary archetypes and the other focusing on devotion, opened my eyes to the richness of the stories and characters found in the scriptures.

One day, I happened to be studying the story of Ruth for my literature class while also preparing to teach the genealogy of Christ for my seminary class. *Pharez*, a name I had not noticed before, stood out in both readings. Matthew listed him in the genealogy of Christ: "And Judas [Judah] begat Phares and Zara of Thamar" (Matthew 1:3). Meanwhile, I had just read that when Boaz and Ruth were married, the well-wishers toasted them by saying, "Let thy house be like the house of Pharez, whom Tamar bare unto Judah" (Ruth 4:12).

Who was this Pharez? I wondered. Why had I never noticed this man who was apparently so noble that the good people of Bethlehem would wish his luck upon a newlywed couple? Further reading revealed that Pharez was one of the twin children born to Tamar and Judah. *Twins.* I remembered the story of twins changing position during their birth, and the midwife tying a scarlet thread around the wrist of the hand that emerged first. I also remembered the story of twins who had "struggled together within [the womb]" (Genesis 25:22). But like that scarlet thread that had been entwined about the baby's wrist, the two stories of twins had become entwined in my memory. Jacob and Esau were the struggling twins born to Isaac and Rebekah, while Pharez and his brother Zarah (about whose wrist the thread had been tied) had been born to the twice-widowed Tamar, who had dressed as a harlot in an elaborate plot to have a baby with Judah, the son of Israel. Their child Pharez was an ancestor of Jesus Christ.

This discovery of what appeared, at my first reading, to be an immoral relationship in Jesus's mortal genealogy surprised and even disturbed me. How different Tamar seemed from the near-perfect image we have of Jesus's mother, the virtuous virgin Mary. As I studied more, I discovered a common thread of barrenness and fertility— of the struggle to become mothers—running through these stories. Sarah, Rebekah, Leah, and Rachel all endured heartbreaking years of barrenness; Tamar and Ruth experienced the sorrow of childless widowhood; Rahab and Bathsheba knew the shame of sexual sin; and even Eve's dilemma centered on obeying the commandment to multiply and replenish the earth by having children.

In many ways, the trials of these individual women echo the trials of their collective posterity and the land of Canaan itself. The desert between Egypt and Palestine (now known as the Fertile Crescent) depends on seasonal rains for survival; one dry spring could create a famine that would last more than a year. In fact, famine would frequently drive these nomadic shepherds to Egypt for food until the promise of God's blessings enticed them back. Consequently, they would look to the heavens for relief—relief in the form of rain and divine intervention in their everyday lives, including opening closed wombs. God, who could make the desert blossom like the rose (Isaiah 35:1–2), could also make a woman blossom with a child.

Within Jesus's mortal ancestry, I discovered fascinating tales of dynamic women who acted boldly to make things happen. Mary's submission to God's plan required tremendous strength and courage, but Jesus's maternal ancestors demonstrated just as much strength and courage. And their paths were not as clear-cut and well marked as hers, so they had to use wit and inspiration to figure out how to accomplish God's goals. Like Tamar, they are remembered for the moments when they faced difficult dilemmas and took unusual steps to set things right, often using disguises and elaborate plots.

It's quite a list: Sarah, who pretended to be her husband's sister in the court of Pharaoh; Rebekah, who dressed her son Jacob in the guise of his older twin, Esau, to claim the birthright; Leah, who wore her sister Rachel's wedding veils to claim that same Jacob as her groom; Tamar, who dressed as a harlot; Rahab, a harlot from the city of Jericho who fooled the Jericho guards; Ruth, who put on her best clothes and covered herself with Boaz's cloak to elicit a marriage proposal from him; Bathsheba, who dressed hurriedly when she was discovered bathing on her rooftop; and of course it all began with Eve, who covered herself with fig leaves when she felt the first rush of mortal modesty.

Theologians have criticized these women for their moments of decisive, daring, and sometimes deceptive action. They have often been maligned and misunderstood in books with titles like *Bad Girls of the Bible* (Liz Curtis Higgs) or *How 8 Scandalous Women Changed the World* (Carol Cook). These titles garner attention, to be sure, but they unfairly misjudge these heroic and intelligent women. In fact, this theme of putting on new clothing at turning points in their lives can be seen as a symbol of the transformation each woman experienced on her path to becoming an ancestor—and ultimately a disciple—of Jesus Christ.

The more I studied the scriptures and the culture of the time period, the more my understanding of Jesus's maternal ancestors grew. Their stories demonstrate courage, resourcefulness, and resolve. They lived in a society where women often had to employ roundabout methods to influence those who had greater power or authority. Francine Klagsbrun writes, "Lacking direct power, women use[d] other means to achieve their goals—shrewdness, verve, wit, and just plain smarts."[1]

These roundabout methods were not limited to women; Israelite men also employed cunning plots when necessary for their protection. Abraham and Isaac both asked their wives to masquerade as their sisters when they were traveling through foreign lands to protect themselves, and they were prophets. Similarly, Esther's uncle

Mordecai instructed her in how to wile the king and outwit the wicked Haman to rescue the Israelites from annihilation, and she is heralded as a great heroine of the Bible. Biblical scholar Susan Niditch explains, "One of the biblical authors' favorite narrative patterns is that of the trickster. Israelites tend to portray their ancestors and thereby to imagine themselves as underdogs, as people outside the establishment who achieve success in roundabout, irregular ways. One of the ways marginals confront those in power and achieve their goals is through deception and trickery. . . . In Genesis, tricksters are found among Israelites sojourning in foreign lands, among younger sons who would inherit, and among women."[2] Sylvia Barack Fishman adds, "Biblical narratives, however, approve of women who plot—and control the plot—outwitting historical circumstance or defying human authority in the service of Jewish destiny. They include Tamar, who uses her sexuality to take her rightful place in the lineage of the tribal dynasty through a complex scenario, . . . Hannah, who rejects her husband's insistence that his love should compensate for their infertility and prays to God on her own behalf most effectively; and Esther, the secretive beauty who . . . plots to outwit a powerful monarch and a Machiavellian villain. Each of these women . . . is challenged by destiny to come out and do battle. And each courageously follows her own personal, inner-directed yet divinely ordained goals."[3]

In short, biblical writers respected a woman's ability to act cleverly as much as they respected a man's ability to fight courageously. It was only later generations who began to interpret the creative plotting of these women as a weakness or a flaw. As Carolyn Custis James concludes, "Biblical writers admired these women and held them up as outstanding examples of godliness even though their conduct broke with accepted convention. They were daring, took the initiative, and courageously exercised leadership, even in their interactions with men."[4]

In many of these stories the woman faces some sort of danger, but she is ultimately protected from harm. Terryl and Fiona Givens suggest that, even more than their underdog status, it is their willingness to risk their own safety and happiness that makes these characters appealing; being risk-takers makes them vulnerable, compassionate, and sympathetic. "Only by opening themselves to the possibility of paramount harm to themselves, do they serve as vehicles of [God's] grace. That vulnerability is both the price of the power to save, and that which saves."[5]

Significantly, these women in the lineage of Christ were not motivated by personal glory, gain, or revenge. They acted within the patriarchal order to perpetuate their lineage—a worthy goal, even though they were frequently compelled by cultural restrictions to use roundabout methods to accomplish this. They became skilled in persistence, quick-wittedness, and kindness. Often their actions served to rescue or protect those who were dear to them. "When the posterity of their house [was] in peril, these women act[ed] unconventionally, even contra-conventionally, to preserve it."[6] Clearly, they had faith in a Heavenly Father who loved them and watched over them, and they nurtured their personal relationship with God. Their goal was to create a better world for you and me, a world in which agency could be exercised, consequences accepted, and weaknesses overcome.

Their specific stories are quite different. Many of them were personally acquainted with grief; many had to wait long years to see promises fulfilled. Some were Canaanites and outsiders, whose ancestors were grafted into the Abrahamic covenant through their posterity. Nevertheless, their images were indeed engraved in the palms of God's hands (see Isaiah 49:15–16). He knew them. Their stories include the aching sorrow of widowhood and barrenness, the stress of single motherhood, the creativity of elaborate plots and disguises, the giddy joy of pregnancy, and some of the greatest love stories ever told. Who has not sighed with vicarious delight when reading the account of Rebekah jumping impetuously from her camel to run into Isaac's waiting arms? Or Jacob, working seven years and then seven years more for his beloved Rachel? Or Ruth, whose story is like a fairy tale: through patience and good works the humble peasant girl finds her Prince Charming and lives happily ever after.

Most of all, we discover that, regardless of how they started out in life, these women became wise and loving mothers who guided their sons and daughters to honor God and fulfill their missions in life. Mary did not raise Jesus on her own; surely she was influenced by the wisdom and experience of the matriarchs who came before her, passed down from generation to generation. God chose these imperfect women to be the mortal ancestors of His perfect Son because He knew that He could trust them. This book focuses on the ten women identified specifically in the lineage found in Matthew, but we know that countless other unnamed women also form the branches of Jesus's maternal family tree. We have much to learn from their stories of courage, ingenuity, and sacrifice.

NOTES

1. Francine Klagsbrun, "Ruth and Naomi, Rachel and Leah: Sisters under the Skin," in *Reading Ruth: Contemporary Women Reclaim a Sacred Story*, edited by Judith A. Kates and Gail Twersky Reimer (New York: Random House, 1994), 268.

2. Susan Niditch, quoted in Alice Ogden Bellis, *Helpmates, Harlots, and Heroes: Women's Stories in the Hebrew Bible* (Louisville, KY: Westminster/John Knox Press, 1994), 69–70.

3. Sylvia Barack Fishman, "Soldiers in an Army of Mothers," in *Reading Ruth: Contemporary Women Reclaim a Sacred Story*, 261–62.

4. Carolyn Custis James, *Lost Women of the Bible: Finding Strength and Significance through Their Stories* (Grand Rapids, MI: Zondervan, 2005), 18–19.

5. Terryl L. Givens and Fiona Givens, *The God Who Weeps: How Mormonism Makes Sense of Life* (Salt Lake City: Ensign Peak, 2012), 31.

6. Tikva Frymer-Kensky, *Reading the Women of the Bible* (New York: Schocken, 2002), 263.

INTRODUCTION:
HEROINES AND SAVIORS

*B*IBLICAL COMMENTARIES TRADITIONALLY focus on God's dealings with the prophets, kings, and heroes who led His people, yet women often played profoundly important roles as well. Noted historian Paul Johnson observes, "One of the most remarkable facts about the Bible—in some ways *the* most remarkable fact—is that it is history with the women left in. . . . From the very beginning, women are part of the Bible story, acting, reacting, talking, scheming, suffering and comforting."[1]

This is especially true of the dozen women who are identified specifically as direct ancestors of Jesus Christ through His mortal mother, Mary. As mothers they received guidance for their families just as surely as the prophets received guidance for the Church. These women also managed businesses, oversaw domestic manufacturing, negotiated major migrations, and gave counsel in political affairs. Jesus Himself would shatter the customs of the culture in which He was born when He encouraged women to come out of the kitchen and join in the gospel discussions (see Luke 10:38–42). He treated every woman—even those who were outcasts—with the utmost dignity and compassion, thus establishing the proper standard of acceptance and respect for women.

Ezer Kenegdo—the Saving Power

Women are endowed from their creation with the power to succor and save. As recorded in Genesis, when God created the earth, He paused at the end of each day and remarked that "it was good"

(Genesis 1:10, 12, 18, 21, 25). The earth was beautiful and glorious, fit for a king. But it was not good for the king to remain without a queen. God had created light, water, mountains, valleys, plants, fish, birds, and animals. He gave Adam dominion over all the earth. But as God admired His final creation—Adam—He remarked, "It is not good" (Genesis 2:18). Something was missing. That something was Eve.

Specifically, God said, "It is not good that the man should be alone" (Genesis 2:18). Samuel Terrien explains in *Till the Heart Sings* that ancient cultures "considered aloneness as the negation of authentic living," not only "not good" but also *not appropriate* for humankind. He adds, "The Hebrew word translated as 'alone' carries an overtone of separation and even of alienation."[2] Indeed, it foreshadows the aloneness of Christ on the cross, when, separated for the first time from His Father's Spirit, He cried out in despair, "My God, my God, why hast thou forsaken me?" (Matthew 27:46). No, it is definitely not good to be alone.

"I will make him an help meet for him," God says in Genesis 2:18, according to the King James Version of the Bible,[3] and so woman was formed from Adam's rib. Modern versions have retranslated the archaic sounding "help meet" to "help mate" (Darby Bible Translation), "helper" (New American Standard Bible), or "companion" (New English Translation). However, a closer look at the original Hebrew word provides insights into the nature and calling of women. When God notes that "it is not good for man to be alone," and then says He would provide a companion for Adam, He uses the phrase *ezer kenegdo* to describe her in the Hebrew Bible. Recent scholarship focusing on the original language of the earliest texts of the Old Testament has restored the true and majestic meaning of this important name. Samuel Terrien explains, "The verb *azar,* from which the noun *ezer* derives, means 'to succor,' (at the existential level of being), 'to save from extremity,' 'to deliver from death.'"[4] What a powerful definition of woman at the moment of her creation! She is so much more than a mere helper. In fact, the authors of *Eve and Adam: Jewish, Christian, and Muslim Readings on Genesis and Gender* contend that the word "*ezer* should be translated as 'power' and [coupled with the adjective *kenegdo*] the verse should read: 'a power equal to him.'"[5] In *Rediscovering Eve*, Carol Meyers agrees: "*Ezer* can be derived from a Hebrew root meaning 'to be strong, powerful' rather than the one meaning 'to help.' . . . Because women had considerable power in agrarian Israelite households in the Iron Age, this reading is compelling."[6] Other characteristics associated with *ezer kenegdo* include royalty, achievement, pioneering, and risk taking.[7]

These heroic characteristics fit the women whose stories are written in *Matriarchs of the Messiah*. Carolyn Custis James concludes, "Eve and all her daughters are *ezers*—strong warriors who stand alongside their brothers in the battle for God's kingdom."[8] It is not only in motherhood or wifehood that women exercise this great endowment from God. James adds, "We do not have to wait until we're grown to become *ezers*. The doctor who announces the birth of a girl might just as well exclaim, 'It's an *ezer!*' for we are *ezers* from birth."[9] I would suggest that it happens even before mortality. The essence of womanhood is to be a powerful savior and rescuer. It is inherent in a woman's character and essential spirit.

In sum, an *ezer* is indeed a helper, but not in an inferior sense of the word; an *ezer* does not exist merely to hand Adam the screwdriver or bring him his lunch. In fact, the word is most often used in the Bible in reference to a king, an army, or even, as we shall see, to God Himself. It is a word that connotes superior benevolence or godly help from above, not inferiority or servitude. The role of women can be compared to the role of Israel itself: "Weaker than the empires, vulnerable to them and ultimately their victim, Israel never considered herself inferior to the nations. Knowing that weakness and even subordination do not imply inferiority, Israel could see herself in the savior-victors who can rise to victory, in the daughter-victims in their texts of terror, and in the oracle-women in their knowledge of God."[10] David wrote in the Psalms that God Himself "who dwelleth on high, . . . humbleth himself to behold the things that are in heaven, and in the earth!" (Psalm 113:5–6). A true *ezer* knows that there is no humiliation in humility.

One meaningful reference to the godly nature of an *ezer* occurs in the book of 1 Samuel. For twenty years, the Israelites had suffered crushing defeats at the hands of the Philistines. Finally they turned to the Lord in fasting and prayer. "Cease not to cry unto the Lord our God for us, that he will save us out of the hand of the Philistines," they pleaded with Samuel the prophet. And he did. "As Samuel was offering up the burnt offering, the Philistines drew near to battle against Israel: but the Lord thundered with a great thunder on that day upon the Philistines, and discomfited them; and they were smitten before Israel" (1 Samuel 7:8, 10). After the Israelites prevailed so resoundingly in this third battle, Samuel acknowledged and commemorated God's protection and deliverance from their enemies. He "took a stone, and set it between Mizpeh and Shen, and called the name of it Eben-Ezer, saying, Hitherto hath the Lord helped us" (1 Samuel 7:12). The name Ebenezer is thus translated in the Bible Dictionary as "the stone (*eben*) of help (*ezer*)" or "stone of my support," and refers directly to God as an *ezer*.

The name *Ebenezer* has unfortunately become associated in modern times with mean-spirited and miserly behavior because of the early actions of Ebenezer Scrooge in Charles Dickens's beloved story, *A Christmas Carol*. But Dickens seemed to have understood the deeper meaning of this name when he chose it for his protagonist. He saw in his character Scrooge what God sees in each of us: the image not of what we are, but of what we can become. God sees, in fact, the image of Himself (Genesis 1:26–27). Similarly, Ebenezer Scrooge is endowed by his creator (Dickens) with the innate power to become a "stone of help" to all those around him. He can save Tiny Tim from an early death, give Bob Cratchit a raise in pay, and bring comfort and peace of mind to those who work for him and live near him. But Ebenezer is not forced to do good works; instead, Dickens gives Ebenezer a glimpse into the past and the future, and then allows him the right to choose what he will do in the present. In the end, Scrooge chooses to live up to the true meaning of his name. He becomes an Ebenezer, a stone of support to his entire community, and he becomes a happy man because of it.

The second verse of the beloved hymn "Come Thou Fount of Every Blessing" also refers to the story of the Israelites' deliverance from the Philistines and reinforces the divine nature of the term *ezer*. The repentant narrator of the hymn praises the redeeming power of the Atonement: "Here I raise my ebenezer, hither by thy help I'm come; and I hope by thy good pleasure, safely to arrive at home." In this song, the *ezer* is so much more than a mere helper; He is the Savior Himself. The hymn continues: "Jesus sought me when a stranger, wandering from the fold of God; he, to rescue me from danger, interposed his precious blood."[11] In this song, Jesus actively seeks out the sinner to bring him safely home. Metaphorically, we all face defeat as we wander through the Philistine world. But by turning to the Savior for help and strength, we can be redeemed. This is the name and title God gave to women in the beginning, because He knew that women would do all in their power to bring their children "safely home."

A wise husband will also "raise his *eben ezer*" in praise of the wife on whom he leans for comfort, counsel, and support. Many years ago, I was serving in a volunteer community outreach program that met in the evenings. The man who was conducting the meeting was running late after a long day at his job and did not have time to go home to pick up the materials he would need for the meeting, so he had asked his wife to bring them to him. It was a simple task—the kind of thing that ordinary helpers and assistants do. But this wife turned it into something much more. Just as our meeting was starting, she breezed in with his briefcase in one hand and a pan full of soft, warm, gooey homemade cinnamon rolls in the other. Before we could even adequately thank her, she smiled, waved, and breezed out again. As she reached the door, her husband sighed loudly and said, with a tone of wonder, love, and respect, "Isn't she wonderful!" She smiled again, and the look that passed between the two of them was magical. He had raised his *eben ezer*, right there in that room, and she had responded with a love that transcended mere "helper" status.

This happened almost forty years ago, but it is a moment I have never forgotten. It inspired me to become that kind of spouse—not the kind who bakes cinnamon rolls per se, but the kind who knows what is needed to lift and support a sagging spirit. It requires that same kind of spouse to make it work—the kind who raises an *eben ezer* of sincere appreciation and understanding. Today, this couple is still a team, leading and supporting in turn. Often she is the one running an event, while he wields the screwdriver and hefts the boxes. Each is still a pillar of support to the other. And that magical look still passes between them. "Aren't you wonderful!" their actions continue to say. True marriage is a partnership of superiors. Samuel Terrien sums it up this way: "Far from being a subordinated or menial servant, woman is the savior of man."[12]

A PARTNERSHIP OF EQUALS

The adjective *kenegdo* that follows the noun *ezer* is also significant in understanding Eve's role and the role of all women. The word appears only once in the entire Hebrew Bible,[13] so there is only one context in which it is used biblically; it occurs when Eve is introduced to Adam in the Garden of Eden. That makes it the alpha and omega of true marriage, as it both introduces and sums up the relationship between Adam and Eve. The word *kenegdo* has complex meanings and has been interpreted in multiple and seemingly conflicting ways. It has been used to suggest "less than," "greater than," "parallel with," "against," "in opposition to," or "complementary," for example.[14] In English Bibles, it is most often translated as "meet" (King James Version, American Standard), "mate" (Darby Bible Translation), "suitable for" (multiple translations), and "like unto" (Douay-Rheims Bible). The tension implied in the words "against" and "opposite" can be cleared up by considering the opposition of looking into a mirror or placing two hands together in prayer—they are opposite and against, but equal.

In Eastern religions, it might be called the "yin and yang" of masculine and feminine characteristics. In modern parlance, one might say of the other, "You complete me" (*Jerry Maguire*, 1996). Benjamin Franklin compared marriage to a pair of scissors, pointing out that one blade is useless without the other. Carolyn Custis James extends the meaning outside the marriage relationship to our personal and individual relationship with God when she writes, "The mirror effect of the Bible will work on us, for we will find ourselves in the stories . . . of the Bible."[15] Even more to the point, we find ourselves reflected in the image of God (Genesis 1:26–27).

In sum, men and women in the Old Testament had different roles and functions, but this does not mean that women were inferior to men. Carol Meyers explains that "*kenegdo* means 'corresponding to' or 'on a par with.' The two people will be neither superior nor subordinate to each other; the phrase connotes a non-hierarchical relationship."[16] To understand this concept better, I often think of a house or a temple. The roof is on the top, covering and sheltering all who are inside. The columns or pillars stand in what might be considered a subordinate position, supporting the roof. However, these columns are not inferior to the roof; in fact, they are absolutely essential. Without them, the roof would fall. Remove the roof, and the pillars are still pillars. But remove the pillars, and the roof is nothing but a floor. Together, the roof and the columns shelter and protect the family inside the house; each complements or completes the other. In ancient architecture, the columns became an expression of beauty and creativity as well as support, from the plain and simple Doric columns to the regal and elegant Ionic design and to the ornate and intricate Corinthian pedestals.[17] In fact, it is the columns, not the roof, which we notice in Greek architecture.

By the same token, in a traditional home, a wife supported and held up her husband as his complement and partner, while he sheltered and protected her. She could stand alone as a column, but they functioned more completely as a house. Paul wrote to the Corinthians, "Neither is the man without the woman, neither the woman without the man, in the Lord" (1 Corinthians 11:11). Each is a necessary and complementary component of the whole. As Tikva Frymer-Kensky writes in *Reading the Women of the Bible,* "Contrary to all assumptions—my own included—the Hebrew Bible, unlike other ancient literature, does not present any ideas about women as the 'Other.' The role of woman is clearly subordinate, but the Hebrew Bible does not 'explain' or justify this subordination by portraying women as different or inferior. The stories do not reflect any differences in goals and desires between men and women. Nor do they point out any strategies or methods used by women that are different from those used by men who are not in positions of authority."[18]

An even more profound argument can be seen in the relationship between Jesus Christ and God the Father. John MacArthur explains, "The relationships within the Trinity illustrate perfectly how headship and submission can function within a relationship of absolute equals. Christ is in no sense inferior to the Father. . . . Three divine

Persons (Father, Son, and Holy Spirit) constitute the one true God of Scripture. All three are fully God and fully equal. *Yet the Son is subordinate to the Father.* Jesus said, 'I do not seek My own will but the will of the Father who sent Me.' "[19]

"Women are the compassionate, self-sacrificing, loving power that binds together the human family," Richard G. Scott concludes in *21 Principles: Divine Truths to Help You Live by the Spirit.*[20] Sheri Dew, author of *Are We Not All Mothers?* puts it this way: "Loving and leading—these words summarize not only the all-consuming work of the Father and the Son, but the essence of [the labor of women], for [their] work is to help the Lord with His work."[21]

LOVING AND LEADING

"Loving and leading" was also the work of the women of the Bible, and they often accomplished that work in remarkably creative ways. We see in their stories the founding principles of agency, faith, and repentance. This profound gift—the freedom to choose—would be exercised judiciously and sometimes aggressively by the women who led the way as they became the foremothers of Christ. Through their choices they would learn to know the bitter from the sweet. In each of the stories in this book, the women act boldly and creatively to become mothers and ensure the continuation of their posterity. They also gently and ingeniously guide the fathers of their children to become better men as well. In that respect, they were true *ezerim*, saviors of their own families.

Eve was the first to transgress God's commandment. In partaking of the forbidden fruit, she would open the path to mortality for all of humankind. Sacrificing the ease and comfort provided in the Garden of Eden, she accepted the consequences that came with her choice, including the sorrow and hard work that accompany motherhood. She set the standard for women who willingly sacrifice their own comfort and ease to bring children into the world and nurture them in every way. Together, Adam and Eve learned that God would not abandon them, but would provide a Savior to guide them back home to Him.

Mother Noah. Noah's wife is mentioned only four times in the scriptures, and never by name; twice we are told that she entered the ark and twice we are told that she exited it. And yet in those simple acts we can recognize her character and her faith. When the Lord said to do something, she did it. She was a second Eve, trusted by God to become "the mother of all living."

Sarah led the way in suggesting that Abraham take Hagar as his wife, even though the relationship would bring her personal sorrow. She knew that Abraham was foreordained to be the father of many nations. She believed that his posterity would be as numerous "as the stars of the heaven." Naturally, she believed that this prophetic blessing extended to her as his wife. For sixty years, she waited to have a child. But when she saw that her childbearing years were ended, Sarah urged her husband to take her bondwoman and have children through her. Sarah willingly sacrificed her own peace and comfort to fulfill her husband's destiny. She earned the name of "princess" because she possessed the nobility of a queen.

Rebekah knew the power of personal prayer. When she entreated the Lord for guidance, she received a revelation that Jacob, the second-born of her twin boys, would be the birthright son. Guided by that personal revelation, Rebekah acted quickly and boldly to make sure Isaac blessed the correct son when it became apparent that Isaac was planning to give the birthright blessing to Esau. Dressing Jacob in Esau's clothing, she guided Jacob to receive the blessing that had been foreordained for him by God.

Leah disguised herself to accomplish her goal of marriage and motherhood. Obeying her father, she dressed in Rachel's veils and stood in Rachel's place to become Jacob's first wife. Sadly, Jacob did not love Leah the way he loved Rachel. But as Leah turned to the Lord and nurtured her relationship with Him, her relationship with her husband gradually strengthened, and harmony with her sister was restored. Leah led the way to a loving relationship with them both. Her son Judah would be the ancestor of David, and thus of Jesus Christ.

Tamar discovered a way to help Judah, the future leader, keep his pledge and his word of honor when he deviated temporarily from the right path. Disguising herself as a harlot, Tamar sacrificed her temporal reputation and comfort to secure the eternal blessings of motherhood. She accepted the scorn of public opinion and the possibility of execution at the hands of her father-in-law in order to bring a child into the world. But Tamar was not really a harlot, as we shall see. And moreover, through her, Judah would be guided back to the right path so that the great Kingdom of Judah would be born. She, too, became a direct ancestor of Jesus Christ.

Rahab literally led the way to safety for Israelite strangers whom the Spirit told her she could trust. She is a powerful example of how a person's life can change. Regardless of how she may have spent her early years, when Rahab heard the word of God, she embraced it wholeheartedly. She then risked her life to protect the elders of her newfound faith and earned her place as one of only four women listed by name in Matthew's genealogy of Jesus Christ. She, too, was a matriarch of the Messiah.

Ruth is the ideal example of loyalty and love. Given the choice to stay in Moab with her family and friends or move to Bethlehem, where she would be a stranger, with her grieving and disheartened mother-in-law, she chose to remain loyal to Naomi. In Bethlehem, under Naomi's direction and advice, Ruth boldly persuaded the shy older gentleman Boaz to marry her. It is a story worthy of a fairy tale ending, and they indeed lived happily ever after. Their great-grandson would be David, the greatest king of Israel. Ruth's marriage to Boaz would also restore Lot's family, once lost through the worldly influence of Sodom, to the lineage of Jesus Christ, as Ruth was a descendant of Lot through his grandson, Moab.

Bathsheba was washing herself within the boundaries of her own home when King David sent for her. She would experience the grief of widowhood, the shame of illegitimate motherhood, and the anguish of losing a baby as the result of submitting to adultery with King David. But she would also become a noble queen and trusted counselor to her husband. Her son Solomon would become the crown prince of Israel, through whom the Savior would be born. Moreover, through the gift of the Atonement, Bathsheba could be forgiven of her adultery. The stain of her sin could be wiped clean by the blood of her own Lamb.

Mary is the literal mother of Jesus Christ in the flesh. She leads the way for all women as an example of virtue, nobility, courage, and strength. Presented with this responsibility when she was just a young girl, she accepted this mission despite the great sacrifice it might mean for her: her betrothed husband, Joseph, might be hurt, ashamed, or angry; as an unwed mother she could be shunned, scorned, and even stoned; her Son's destiny on the cross would pierce her own heart. Even though all of history had been building toward this one moment, Mary had the right to choose. She bowed her head. "So be it unto me," she vowed. Her Son would accept His mission with the same humble certainty. The blood of sacrifice ran in His veins. It came from the noble blood of His maternal ancestors.

Mary Magdalene was not a "matriarch of the Messiah," but she holds a special place in history. She was the first person to see the resurrected Lord. His chief Apostles, Peter and John, had raced to the tomb and, finding it empty, had gone home (John 20:3–10). Other women, including perhaps Jesus's own mother, had also been on the scene that morning. Nevertheless, the Lord withheld Himself in a shadow of the Garden Tomb until the others had gone. Finally He showed Himself to her— to her alone. Clearly there is something special about the relationship between Jesus and this woman who is mentioned only once by name prior to the Crucifixion scene. I believe she represents the Church itself and our own personal, individual relationship with Him. Traditionally, she is connected with the sinner who washed Jesus's feet with her tears. Thus the story of the Bible begins with a woman in a Garden who falls, and it ends with a woman in a Garden who is redeemed.

A Garden with Many Paths

Recently, I had the opportunity to explore a lovely botanical garden that covered many acres. I strolled along the peaceful lakeside where trees and flowers were reflected in its placid waters. Enjoying my walk, I turned away from the main trails to climb a rocky hillside, wander through a maze of shrubbery, and detour onto an unused path. Eventually I realized that I was lost. I wasn't sure which path would take me back to the lodge, and it was starting to thunder and rain. The way became arduous as I kept my eyes on the unfamiliar path and held my coat over my head, trying to avoid the puddles and the downpour. But when I finally looked up, I could see the cupola of the lodge beckoning me to safety. Keeping that lodge in sight, my confidence grew, and I was soon back within the safety of the lodge. From that lofty vantage point, I looked down into the garden I had explored. There were many paths in that garden, some of them rocky and others pleasant. It was up to the traveler to choose which path to take and how long to stay on each path. Significantly, all of them led back home.

Jesus Christ stands at the center of our earthly garden. He is the Mediator and Redeemer for us all. This garden we call earth life has many paths. Some lead to safe and relaxing lakesides, while others lead to risky and arduous climbs. We are free to choose which paths we will take, but His plan is always in place. He is watching over all. Even when we wander into rocky terrain or forbidden fields, He is there to guide us gently back to that Garden House toward which all paths lead, if we will just look up. He wants us to lodge in His bosom. And, like Mary Magdalene, when we arrive there, He will call us by name.

The righteous matriarchs of the Bible were *ezerim kenegdo*—saviors fit for their callings and equal to their tasks. They were given extraordinary missions, and they often rose to the occasion by using extraordinary means. They learned to do hard things as they discovered that nothing is "too hard for the Lord" (Genesis 18:14). God chose these women carefully for the times in which they lived and the missions to which they were called, just as He has chosen each of us for the times and missions to which we are called. He knows us by name and will come to us in our times of sorrow and need (Isaiah 43:1–28; Jeremiah 1:5; John 10:14–15).

My hope is that the readers of this book will come to know the women of the Bible as closely as they know the men. After all, the God of Abraham, Isaac, and Jacob is also the God of Sarah, Rebekah, and Leah. They are equally important in this grand epic of families who face challenges together.

As we shall see, these women embodied many of the gospel principles Jesus Himself would teach during His earthly ministry, and they manifest the Lord's loving kindness and patient persuasion as portrayed in the hymn "Know This, That Every [One] Is Free": "He'll call, persuade, direct aright, / And bless with wisdom, love, and light, / In nameless ways be good and kind, / But never force the human mind" (*Hymns*, no. 240).

Far from being inferior, these valiant women in the lineage of Jesus Christ employed the same persuasive methods as the Savior to accomplish their goals and fulfill their roles as rescuers and saviors. They faced the same kinds of trials and struggles that believers in every generation have encountered, and they did so with courage, faith, and noble sacrifice. We have much to learn from their examples about overcoming adversity, establishing strong families, developing personal relationships with God, and accepting the redeeming gift of the Atonement.

NOTES

1.   Paul Johnson, *The Quest for God: A Personal Pilgrimage* (New York: HarperCollins, 1996), 57.

2.   Samuel L. Terrien, *Till the Heart Sings: A Biblical Theology of Manhood and Womanhood* (Philadelphia: Fortress Press, 1985), 9.

3.   Author's note: I use the King James Version as my primary biblical text throughout this book.

4.   Terrien, *Till the Heart Sings*, 10.

5.   *Eve & Adam: Jewish, Christian, and Muslim Readings on Genesis and Gender*, edited by Kristen E. Kvam, Linda S. Schearing, and Valarie H. Ziegler (Bloomington, IN: Indiana University Press, 1999), 28.

6.   Carol Meyers, *Rediscovering Eve: Ancient Israelite Women in Context* (Oxford: Oxford University Press, 2013), 74.

7.   Terrien, *Till the Heart Sings*, 11.

8.   Carolyn Custis James, *Lost Women of the Bible: Finding Strength and Significance through Their Stories* (Grand Rapids, MI: Zondervan, 2005), 36.

9.   Ibid. (emphasis included in quote).

10.   Tikva Frymer-Kensky, *Reading the Women of the Bible* (New York: Schocken, 2002), 338.

11. Robert Robinson, "Come, Thou Fount of Every Blessing," *Come Thou Fount of Every Blessing: Vocal Score*, edited by Mack Wilberg (Oxford: Oxford University Press, 1998).

12. Terrien, *Till the Heart Sings*, 10.

13. *Eve & Adam*, edited by Kvam, Schearing, and Ziegler, 28.

14. Ibid., 29.

15. James, *Lost Women of the Bible*, 24.

16. Meyers, *Rediscovering Eve*, 73.

17. The Apostle Paul made this same point when he described the essential function of each part of the body: "The eye cannot say unto the hand, I have no need of thee: nor again the head to the feet, I have no need of you. Nay, much more those members of the body, which seem to be more feeble, are necessary: And those members of the body, which we think to be less honourable, upon these we bestow more abundant honour; and our uncomely parts have more abundant comeliness. For our comely parts have no need: but God hath tempered the body together, having given more abundant honour to that part which lacked: that there should be no schism in the body" (1 Corinthians 12:21–25).

18. Frymer-Kensky, *Reading the Women of the Bible*, xv.

19. John MacArthur, *Twelve Extraordinary Women: How God Shaped Women of the Bible and What He Wants to Do with You* (Nashville, TN: Thomas Nelson, 2005), 7–8.

20. Richard G. Scott, *21 Principles: Divine Truths to Help You Live by the Spirit* (Salt Lake City: Deseret Book, 2013), 64.

21. Sheri Dew, *Are We Not All Mothers?* (Salt Lake City: Deseret Book, 2011), 2.

EVE ACCEPTS THE BITTER CUP

"These things have I spoken unto you, that
my joy might remain in you, and that
your joy might be full" (John 15:11).

EVE SIGHED WITH contentment as she strolled through the Garden of Eden. The sun warmed her skin, and a slight breeze lifted her hair. It was so lovely to be alive, to have a body and experience its sensations. She could hear the melody of birds in the air, accompanied by the babble of the nearby brook. She delighted in the colors of the flowers that grew along her path and the shapes of the mountains in the distance. The sweet taste of plums lingered on her lips from the meal she had enjoyed with Adam that morning. It was so peaceful here in the Garden, so quiet and so . . . nice.

She breathed deeply. There was that fragrance again, so sweet and enticing. What was it? Oh yes. The intoxicating smell of that fruit they weren't allowed to eat—the fruit that would make them wise. It was such a delicious aroma. She wanted to taste it, but she had been told it was forbidden. How many times had she passed by this tree, planted in the middle of the Garden? A dozen times? A hundred? Thousands? Time meant nothing in the Garden of Eden. Nothing aged and nothing died. Yes, it was so nice. Perfect, in fact. And yet. . . .

Eve wanted more than just "nice." She wanted knowledge. She wanted children. She wanted to multiply and replenish the earth, as they had been commanded to do. But she needed to know how it was done. Suddenly, a strange hissing voice joined the warble of the bird and the babble of the brook. The voice beckoned her. She remembered what Father had said after telling Adam not to eat that special fruit: "Nevertheless, thou mayest choose for thyself, for it is given unto thee" (Moses 3:17). Eve would take Him at His word. She was ready to act—to choose for herself and for all humankind.

Eve turned in the direction of the hissing sound. It was coming from that tree, the one whose aroma was so enticing. As she neared the tree, she recognized the sibilant sounds as actual words coming from the mouth of a strange beast that had curled itself among the branches of the tree. It looked like a serpent, but it spoke as a man. His voice had a somnambulant quality about it, the hissing soft and hypnotic.[1] He beckoned to her and engaged her in conversation. "Hasn't God told you that you shall eat of every tree of the Garden?" he purred.

Eve felt emboldened to speak with this creature. "We may eat of all the other trees," she explained, "but God said that if we eat from this one, or even touch it, we shall die."

The serpent shook his head with a patronizing smile and hissed reassuringly, "You shall not surely die. God Himself knows that if you eat this fruit, your eyes will be opened, and you shall be as the gods, knowing good from evil."

Drawing closer, Eve "saw that the tree was good for food, and that it was pleasant to the eyes, and a tree to be desired to make one wise" (Genesis 3:6). Its promise of wisdom and knowledge was powerful. She instinctively feared this thing called "death," but the serpent beguiled her, reassuring her that they would not die. Carefully considering the consequences, Eve made her decision. She and Adam had been obedient to all that God had commanded them; they had never actively broken a law. But they had passively violated the first commandment—they would not be fully obedient until they had multiplied and replenished the earth. Eve could think of no other way to accomplish this great goal. In her mind and in her heart, it was a risk worth taking. She would transgress the second commandment they were given in the Garden to obey the first.

Eve reached for the fruit. Its flesh felt ripe and pliant to her touch. Its aroma was so sweet it nearly made her dizzy. She hesitated as she looked once more at the nice, lovely Garden. Then she thought of her holy calling of motherhood. Those children—all of humankind—could only come to earth as a result of this transgression. Courageously she forged ahead and bit into the fruit that would transform her body and plunge her into mortality. She swallowed the succulent juice. It truly was delicious, but it came with a price. Already her mind began to understand the consequences of her action. She would no longer be allowed to live in Eden. Because of her choice, she would be cast out.

Her thoughts turned to Adam. His body was still Edenic. Adam needed to partake of the fruit as well, or they would be separated forever, he remaining in Eden and she cast out of the Garden. Without Adam, her sacrifice would be for nothing. Already she was discovering that choices have consequences and that consequences lead on to further choices.

Eve glared at the serpent. Only moments before his voice had sounded soft and reassuring, but now its hiss seemed sinister. She plucked another piece of the fruit and carried it to her husband.

It is just so peaceful here in the Garden, Adam sighed as she approached. *Such a nice place to live.* But Eve did not look content. She was covering her body in an awkward stance, and there was something new about her complexion, a ruddier glow in her cheeks and lips. Even her scent was different—sweeter, earthier—and in her hand. . . . Suddenly, Adam knew what had happened. He was dismayed to see what Eve had done. He had intended always to obey Father's commandment to avoid that fruit. Nevertheless, Eve was his treasured companion. How could he remain comfortably here in the Garden while abandoning her to roam the wilderness alone? With courage that matched hers, Adam bit into the fruit Eve offered him and accepted the consequences of mortality. Whatever lay ahead of them, they would face it together.

And they would face it right now. God was calling to them. In their pre-fallen condition, it had been His custom to visit them in the Garden. In fact, they had often "heard the voice of the Lord God walking in the garden in the cool of the day" (Genesis 3:8). But how would He react to their choices? What should they do now? Adam looked at Eve. Her cheeks blushed scarlet, and he knew why. They were suddenly aware of, and astonished by, their own nakedness

(Genesis 3:10). Quickly, they grabbed some of the large fig leaves growing nearby and fashioned aprons to cover themselves. The fruit was already having an effect. They were beginning to recognize right from wrong, good from evil. A sense of modesty came with it.

As they hid among the trees of the Garden, Adam and Eve heard the voice of God calling, "Where are you?"

Covering themselves with their makeshift clothing, man and woman stepped forward meekly to meet with God. They were ready to confess. Eve hid her newfound nakedness, but she did not hide her actions. She trusted God. She loved Him. She knew He would not abandon them. Her heart was full of sorrow and apprehension, but her eyes were full of hope. This new life was going to be hard, but it was going to be worth it.

"Who told you that you were naked?" God asked, gesturing at their fig leaves, but knowing the answer in advance. "Have you eaten from the tree that I commanded you not to touch?"

As the first to be created, Adam responded first. He explained not only what he did, but why. "The woman gave me some of the fruit, and I did eat it," he explained.

God turned to the woman. "What have you done?" He asked.

Following Adam's example, she too gave her reasons. "The serpent beguiled me with his flattering charms, and I did eat the fruit," she confessed.

God banished the serpent first. "Because you have done this, you will be cursed above all other creatures," He commanded. "You will slither on your belly, eating the dust of the earth throughout all time. And I will place hostility between you and the descendants of the woman. They will crush your head, and you will bruise their heel." Cowering, the serpent slithered away. But he would not go far.

Now God turned to the couple. It was time for them to hear the consequences of their actions. He began with the woman. "I will greatly multiply your sorrow and your conception," He told her. "In sorrow you will bring forth children. Your desire shall be to your husband, and he shall rule over you" (see Genesis 3:9–17).

The consequences pronounced upon Adam and Eve as they were expelled from the Garden were just that: consequences and instructions, not punishments or condemnations. God's explanation to

Eve about the pain and sorrow of motherhood was a consequence of mortality, and a temporary one at that. Christ Himself would clarify this during His ministry when He said, "Your sorrow shall be turned into joy. A woman when she is in travail hath sorrow, because her hour is come: but as soon as she is delivered of the child, she remembereth no more the anguish, for joy that a man is born into the world" (John 16:20–21). Jesus understands deeply the role of sorrow, and that it is not a punishment for sin. Moreover, Eve would find joy and pleasure in her relationship with her husband. God's instruction that Eve's "desire shall be to thy husband" (Genesis 3:16) was a wonderful gift. It should not be interpreted as a punishment or a demeaning subjugation of her own will or accomplishment, but rather as God's sanctioning of the physical marital relationship, which is given for the pleasure and enjoyment of both spouses. This physical, spiritual, and emotional desire would create a strong bond between them, cementing their relationship and bringing them joy.

God turned to Adam to pronounce His next judgment. "The ground will be cursed, for your sake," He said to Adam. "In sorrow you will eat of it all the days of your life. It will bring forth thorns and thistles to you, so you will have to work to make it produce. Through sweat and hard work you shall eat bread, until you return to the ground in death" (see Genesis 3:17–19). Thus, Adam too would experience sorrow as he entered the mortal world. But it was the *ground* God cursed, not Adam. Adam and his descendants would learn that work is a blessing. Honest, productive work is good for the body, good for the family, and good for the soul. Without it, we die a little inside.

Adam and Eve bowed their heads in sorrow and acquiescence as they heard these pronouncements. Then the most wonderful thing happened. As she passed through the veil into mortality, Eve heard her name and understood its significance for the first time. "Adam called his wife's name Eve; because she was the mother of all living" (Genesis 3:20). She knew then that everything was going to be all right. God still trusted her. Through her transgression, physical death had indeed become a reality, but so had life. Eve smiled at her name. It did not signify the end of their days in the Garden, but the eve, or beginning, of their life in the world. She would indeed become the mother of all living—of the entire human race. And she would literally be "saved in childbearing" (1 Timothy 2:15), for through her posterity a Savior would be born with the power to redeem them all from the Fall into mortality.

Eve took one long, last, lingering look at the beautiful Garden before turning away to cross with Adam into the wilderness that would become their new home. She could see the Garden clearly now. It was so much more than just "nice." How had she not been able to see that before? The Garden was magnificent. But so was the world in front of them. They would till the earth and build a house and bring children into it. There would be much sorrow in Eve's life as a consequence of her choice. She would experience physical exertion, pain, and fatigue as they built their home and tended their new fields. She would endure the pain of childbirth and the sorrow of watching her children suffer the trials of this world. But she would also know the joy of her children's accomplishments and the sweetness of their caresses. Life would be so much more than just "nice."

Years later, she would also know the pain of inconsolable grief as she and Adam discovered the crumpled and lifeless body of their beloved son Abel, killed by his own brother, their firstborn son, Cain, in an act of jealous greed. Two kinds of death came into the world on the day they ate the forbidden fruit: physical death, which is the separation of the spirit from the body, and spiritual death, which is the separation of the spirit from the presence of God. Cain would suffer that spiritual death as a consequence when he chose to align himself with Satan to kill his brother. In that moment, Eve would also understand the anguish that would be felt by a loving Heavenly Father whose own Son—His only begotten Son—would be hated, despised, and ultimately killed in a world influenced by the misery and bitterness of His other, once-beloved son, Lucifer. She would know the agony contained in the phrase, "How art thou fallen from heaven, O Lucifer, son of the morning!" (Isaiah 14:12). Eve too would lose two sons who had been her shining stars, one to physical death and the other to spiritual darkness.

But as they stood poised on the edge of Eden on the eve of their mortality, that grief was still far in their future. For now, Eve took

Adam's hand, and together they walked into the world that had been created for them and their posterity.

APPLICATION FOR TODAY: THE GIFT OF AGENCY

The four great purposes of earth life are to love God, to experience the pleasures and pains of a physical body, to establish eternal family relationships, and to recognize right from wrong by exercising agency. David O. McKay taught, "Next to the bestowal of life itself, the right to direct that life is God's greatest gift to man." The importance of free will can be summed up in the words of the hymn "Know This, That Every Soul Is Free":

> Know this, that ev'ry soul is free
> To choose his life and what he'll be;
> For this eternal truth is giv'n:
> That God will force no man to heav'n.
>
> He'll call, persuade, direct aright,
> And bless with wisdom, love, and light,
> In nameless ways be good and kind,
> But never force the human mind.
>
> Freedom and reason make us men;
> Take these away, what are we then?
> Mere animals, and just as well
> The beasts may think of heav'n or hell.
>
> May we no more our pow'rs abuse,
> But ways of truth and goodness choose;
> Our God is pleased when we improve
> His grace and seek his perfect love.
>
> (Anon. circa 1805)

Mother Eve is the first of the great heroines of the Bible—the first human on earth to exercise will and self-determination by deliberately choosing which of two paths she would take. Like the traveler depicted by Robert Frost, whose "roads diverged in a yellow wood," Eve knew that this choice or "way" would "[lead] on to way," and that it would "[make] all the difference"[2] not just for herself, but for all humankind. By choosing to eat the fruit of knowledge of good and evil, she closed the gate to Eden but opened the door to mortality and earthly experience for the entire human family.

But the door to mortality was also the door to disease, pain, corruption, and evil. Because she was the first to eat the fruit, Eve has been despised and rejected for many centuries as the "weaker sex." She has been likened to Pandora, the first mortal woman in Greek mythology. In that myth, Pandora was created from clay as a companion for Epimetheus, the first human man. They were given an alabaster box, which they were instructed not to open. Unable to resist, however, Pandora opened the box and out rushed all the evils, sorrows, and pains of the world, followed at last by Hope. This story has long been used to demonstrate woman's uncontrolled curiosity and impetuous disobedience. But as we have seen, Eve was not overcome by curiosity; she made a deliberate choice based on desired outcomes. She wanted to have children and she wanted to become more like God.

The Traditional View of Eve

Eve's actions have also been equated with the sin of sexual immorality and temptation, but this is not a fair or true characterization of Eve or of the Fall. In fact, the view of Eve as a cosmic villain is a relatively recent development that began to take hold during the Hellenistic period, between the writings of Malachi that ended the Old Testament in the fifth century BC and the writings of the four Gospels half a millennium later. In fact, it was an apocryphal writer, Ben Sira, who removed the blame for the Fall from Adam and placed it squarely on the shoulders of Eve when he wrote in the *Ecclesiasticus* during the second century before Christ: "From a woman was the beginning of sin, and because of her we all died."

In contrast to the author of Proverbs, who wrote that the value of a virtuous woman was "far above rubies" (Proverbs 31:10), many Greek philosophers and writers taught that women were inferior creatures by nature. The story of Pandora is a case in point. As the similarities between Pandora and Eve became mythologically entwined, blaming Eve became the "fallback position" for the Fall.

Even Paul used it to justify in his letter to Timothy that a woman should "learn in silence . . . for . . . Adam was not deceived, but the woman being deceived was in the transgression" (1 Timothy 2:11, 13–14).[3] Building on Paul's writings, in the fifth century AD Saint Augustine further developed the concept of original sin in *City of God*, blaming both Adam and Eve for the transgression but focusing more particularly on Eve as being "inferior" to Adam in her weakness against temptation. Eve's vilification would eventually become codified in Milton's *Paradise Lost*, where the anonymous fruit becomes an apple, the serpent becomes a phallic symbol of lust, and the image of Eve as a weak and fallen temptress would take almost permanent hold. As Alice Ogden Bellis notes, "The story of Eve has been used more than any other as a theological base for sexism."[4]

However, biblical scholarship in recent years has shattered many traditional misconceptions about the role of women in general and Eve in particular. These scholars have taken a fresh historical look at the Bible to discover what is really there and what is not. They often ask different literary and historical questions than their predecessors did and have uncovered truths that were there all along. For example, Kristen E. Kvam, Linda S. Schearing, and Valarie H. Ziegler discovered that "Eve plays a different role in Jewish theological reflection than she does in other traditions," in their research for *Eve & Adam: Jewish, Christian, and Muslim Readings on Genesis and Gender*. "The Jewish Eve . . . is remarkably free from the doctrinal baggage that accompanies the Christian Eve. While Christian doctrine developed concepts of 'sin' and a 'Fall' based on Eve's disobedience, the corresponding rabbinical traditions of Israel's 'pollution' after Eden was never, to any degree, central to Jewish thought."[5] Carol Meyers adds in *Rediscovering Eve: Ancient Israelite Women in Context*, "So well known is the Eden narrative of Genesis that it is somewhat surprising to find that the story of Eden is not a prominent theme elsewhere in the Hebrew Bible. Neither are the actions of Eve and Adam ever mentioned as examples of disobedience and punishment, although the long story of Israel's recurrent rejection of God's word and will provides ample opportunity for citing the Eden case."[6]

In fact, the early record does not suggest that Eve gave in to temptation in a moment of weakness; significantly, "the word 'tempted' is not used in the early Hebrew Bible and begins creeping in through various later translations, from 'persuaded' to 'beguiled' to 'tempted' "[7] to fit and even shape the changing cultural definition of womanhood. Instead, it is apparent that Eve had an intellectual conversation with the serpent, thought long and hard about the potential consequences of her actions, and then deliberately chose wisdom over ignorance. Indeed, if Eve is to be associated with any of the classical Greek goddesses, it should be Athena, goddess of wisdom, not Pandora, bringer of evil.

Biblical scholar Carol Meyers acknowledges that "in eating the appealing fruit the first couple makes a decidedly unwise move. They disobey God. The consequence is not only mortality but also the reality of agrarian life anticipated at the beginning of the Eden episode and prescribed in its closing section."[8] Yet Meyers praises Eve's role in the story: "Rather than a blot on her character, her dialog with the reptile is a function of her intellect. . . . The interaction between Eve and the serpent also gives her a speaking part that . . . exceeds Adam's."[9] Terryl and Fiona Givens agree, pointing out that the Fall into mortality was precipitated by a conscious decision, not by a moment of weakness. "At Eve's courageous instigation, they opt to lose paradise, hoping to eventually regain heaven—but transformed and ennobled by the schoolhouse of experience that comprises mortality."[10]

One Garden, Two Commandments

When Adam and Eve were placed in the Garden of Eden, they were given two conflicting commandments. The first was to multiply and replenish the earth; the second was to avoid eating the fruit of the tree of knowledge of good and evil. The problem was that they needed to eat this forbidden fruit to gain the mortal ability to have children. Because they could not keep one commandment without breaking the other, transgression was inevitable. They could put off the commandment to multiply while keeping the commandment to avoid the fruit, but it was impossible to keep both commandments forever. Metaphorically, "the fruit of paradise perched precariously between sets of demands held in dynamic tension."[11] Free will and accountability are such important concepts for humankind that God introduced them from the beginning, and then deliberately stood back while Adam and Eve made their choice. If there was any force at all in the Garden of Eden, it was that they were forced to choose for themselves which path they would take, and when.

At first, Adam and Eve chose to wait patiently for the Lord to resolve this conflict. They were happy being instructed by the Lord and obeying His law. This choice led to a comfortable lifestyle surrounded by peaceful waters and lovely trees that produced fruits spontaneously. They might have lived forever in that innocent, blissful state. But Eve was the catalyst for change, and when she chose to transgress the injunction against eating the fruit, Adam chose to join her. Both understood the consequences of their actions and accepted what would come next. This choice should not be interpreted as rebellion against authority but as a step forward, together.

Was God angry at their choice? Did Eve's action destroy His plan? This question has vexed philosophers and theologians for centuries. The traditional Christian view is that Adam and Eve sinned grievously and should not have eaten the fruit. The fifth century theologian and bishop Saint Augustine taught forcefully that "through an act of will Adam and Eve *did* change the structure of the universe; that their single, willful act permanently corrupted human nature as well as nature in general."[12] However, "Augustine's position is paradoxical in that he attributes virtually unlimited power to the human will but confines that power to an irretrievable past—to a lost paradise."[13]

Surely God was concerned when Adam and Eve ate the fruit that would make them wise. He was anxious, perhaps. Probably stern. But He does not seem angry. He asks them what happened, giving them an opportunity to speak for themselves. And they do. He tells them the consequences of their actions, which are severe. But mortality for all of humankind was the plan from the beginning. Consider how a pregnant woman is anxious, apprehensive, and a bit afraid of the pain she is about to experience when the time for her baby's birth draws near. But she is also wonderfully alive and excited. A new life is about to begin. Consider also how she feels a few years later, when that child is ready to strike out on his or her own. Similarly,

God must have waited patiently and expectantly for the inevitable moment when His chosen children would choose mortality. One can almost imagine Him standing in the woods and nodding at the folly of the serpent playing right into His hands. Surely this is exactly what He expected to happen. God must have been pleased with Eve's choice. This was His plan all along.

Historian Paul Johnson, a devout Catholic, came to this same conclusion. He writes, "[Traditional Christianity] asks us to believe that God altered his plan for mankind in a fundamental respect, when his new creatures behaved more badly than he had intended. It tells us, in effect, that the almighty, all-seeing, all-foreseeing God had not expected Adam to sin, and in his surprise and anger at Adam's disobedience, revoked his edict of bodily immortality and so recreated the earth as a vale of tears. All this seems very strange. Why had God not foreseen Adam's weakness—or Eve's propensity to listen to temptation and to tempt in her turn—and made his male creature stronger? And why did God permit Satan, in serpent-guise, to upset his carefully considered plan to create a paradisal Garden of Eden with sinless and deathless inhabitants, and settle instead for a world full of sin and suffering? . . . It seems to me far more likely that God knew perfectly well what he was doing when he gave Adam free will—that he knew his creatures would sin and thus invoke misery on themselves—but that he wished to create a moral drama in which sinful man would be redeemed by the passion and death of his own divine son made man. . . . Death is an indispensable element in it, a crucial function of the mechanism of salvation and redemption. If this argument is valid, the fact of death is not an accident, a modification of God's original plan, but absolutely central to his concept of creation."[14]

Mormon theology also embraces this revisionist view of the fall into mortality as a necessary good, not a disastrous mistake. As early as 1830, the Church proclaimed this refreshing doctrine:

"If Adam had not transgressed he would not have fallen, but he would have remained in the garden of Eden. And all things which were created must have remained in the same state in which they were after they were created; and they must have remained forever, and had no end. And they would have had no children; wherefore they would have remained in a state of innocence, having no joy, for they knew no misery; doing no good, for they knew no sin. But behold, all things have been done in the wisdom of him who knoweth all things. Adam fell that men might be; and men are that they might have joy" (2 Nephi 2:22–25).

In sum, Eve was neither rebellious nor impetuous, but a noble woman making a heroic choice for the good of all humankind. In choosing to eat the fruit, Eve did not choose between good and evil but rather between two good paths with different consequences, both leading to God. Her choice was "between the safety and security of the Garden, and the goodness, beauty, and wisdom that come at the price—and only at the price—of painful lived experience. Her decision is more worthy of admiration for its courage and initiative than reproach for its rebellion."[15] By eating the fruit, she learned to *recognize* good and evil, but eating the fruit was not itself an evil act.

Sheri Dew concurs. "Eve set the pattern. In addition to bearing children, she mothered all of mankind when she made the most courageous decision any woman has ever made and with Adam opened the way for us to progress. She set an example of womanhood for men to respect and women to follow, modeling the characteristics with which . . . women have been endowed: heroic faith, a keen sensitivity to the Spirit, an abhorrence of evil, and complete selflessness."[16] Eve developed these characteristics through the experience of mortality. Through trial and error, choice and consequence, she and her children would learn to recognize good from evil and choose which path to follow. Jewish author David S. Ariel offers a similar interpretation: "God gave this world to Adam and Eve in order that they and their descendants might make of it something heavenly."[17]

In sum, the Fall should not be considered a "fall" at all. God ended His conversation with Adam and Eve by saying, almost triumphantly, "Behold, the man [and woman too, for the Hebrew word for Adam is gender-inclusive] is become as one of us, to know good and evil" (Genesis 3:22). To become more like God is to step *up* in existence, not to fall downward. Humans had finally entered mortality. The plan could begin.

In the Midst of the Garden

If there is any doubt that God expected and wanted Adam and Eve to eat the fruit of knowledge, one need only consider where God planted the forbidden tree. It was located "in the midst of the garden" (Genesis 3:3), where Adam and Eve could not avoid seeing it and smelling its sweet aroma every day. When a mother doesn't want her children to eat her freshly baked cookies, she does not leave them on the table "in the midst of the kitchen." She hides them in a cupboard. By contrast, as soon as Adam and Eve became mortal and susceptible to death, God placed "Cherubims, and a flaming sword which turned every way, to keep [them from] the way of the tree of life" (Genesis 3:24). Then He banished Adam from the Garden, "lest he put forth his hand, and take also of the tree of life, and eat, and live for ever" in his sins (Genesis 3:22). That's what God does when He really doesn't want someone to touch something. He would take no chance that His children might eat the fruit of immortality on this earth and thereby become stranded in mortality with no way to return to His presence. There are indeed some fates worse than death, and immortality without resurrection and eternal life is one of them. By contrast, He placed the tree of knowledge right in the middle of the Garden. He wanted them to choose mortality. Eternal life would come later.

The serpent's role, too, was for the good of mankind. God could have destroyed or banished him completely, restoring the perfection of His Eden to the earth. But opposition is essential to choice. As argued in Coleridge's *Biographia Literaria,* "Man cannot be a moral human being without having had the choice of good and evil, and he cannot choose good without being able to choose evil."[18] Satan does his best to bring misery to God's children, but through the Light of Christ, they can resist him. He can "bruise their heels" and misdirect their paths, but they can outwit him and return to the right path through the gospel of Jesus Christ. Sheri Dew said of this relationship, "Satan has declared war on motherhood and on the family. . . . He well knows that those who rock the cradle are perhaps in the best possible position to rock his diabolical earthly empire. . . . He knows that without righteous mothers loving and leading the rising generation, the kingdom of God will fail."[19] Casting Eve as a villain rather than as a hero has long been a part of that war against women.

Mother Eve is an *ezer kenegdo*. Through her we learn of the divine nature of women and of the glorious, though often painful and sorrowful, plan that God has for His beloved daughters.

A Partnership of Equals

Adam was created from the dust of the earth; in fact, his name, *Adamah*, means "earth" (and is gender-inclusive). Eve was created from Adam's rib, making her "bone of [his] bones, and flesh of [his] flesh" (Genesis 2:23). It has been said poetically that Eve was "not made out of his head to top him, nor out of his feet to be trampled upon by him, but out of his side to be equal with him, under his arm to be protected, and near his heart to be beloved,"[20] and to be part of his very breathing. While this is a lovely thought, it is somewhat patronizing as it still places Adam in the primary position. A closer look at the word *rib* in its original Hebrew, *sela'*, sheds further light and suggests a more balanced relationship. It is used most often in an architectural sense, as the ribs that support a boat or a building or a temple, or the chest cavity that protects the heart.

Carol Meyers discovered another fascinating use of the word in 1 Kings 6:34, where it describes the double doors in Solomon's temple. "Used for large entryways," she writes, "a double door consists of two doors, each about half the width of the door frame, each hinged to the door from on its outer edge. . . . Together they form a wide door; alone they . . . have no value. . . . The imagery is remarkably apt for Eve and Adam. They are virtually the same, and their combination produces humanity; but a male or a female 'side' without the other could never produce the whole."[21] This definition of the "rib" from which Eve was taken correlates well with her founding designation as *ezer kenegdo,* a power complementing and corresponding to Adam, at once opposite to him and yet equal to him. Together, they opened the doors to mortality for all humankind.

Early writers used the fact that Adam was created first to attribute superiority to him; Eve entered the Garden second, so she must have been second rate, second place, the runner-up, the afterthought—or so they argued. "Not only is Eve associated with sin; her creation is viewed as secondary and, by implication, of lesser importance," Carol Meyers laments of this theological history.[22] However, modern interpretations are beginning to rethink the hierarchical implications of the order of creation. Woman was formed after Adam not because she was second best, but because the best was saved for last.

Richard G. Scott writes, "If there is any woman reading these words who wonders about how valuable you are, would you remember that you are the last created, you are the best. He saved womanhood for the final magnificent creation."[23] Lawrence and Sue Richards make this point even clearer, reminding readers, "In spiritual essence Adam and Eve were the same; both were created in the image of God. But in all creation, Eve alone was created from what God had already refined. Adam and all the rest were made from the earth; Eve alone was fashioned by the hand of God from the living tissue of Adam."[24]

Because "they shared the same essential nature, . . . she was in no way an inferior character . . . but . . . his spiritual counterpart, his intellectual coequal, and in every sense his perfect mate and companion."[25] Adam himself recognized the difference. He had already named all the animals God had created, but only when he was presented with Eve did he exclaim with joy, "This is now bone of my bones, and flesh of my flesh" (Genesis 2:23). This was the companion for whom he had been searching. No longer would he be alone.

GOD INTRODUCES A MEDIATOR
FOR A FALLEN WORLD

Writers such as Augustine and Milton shaped Christian thinking for centuries with the belief that the choice made by Eve in the Garden brought mortality and sexual desire to the human race, which paradoxically deprived Adam's posterity of the freedom to choose not to sin. By contrast, we have seen that choice and accountability were gifts designed for humankind even before the fall into mortality, because they are essential to the great plan of salvation. Learning to choose right from wrong, good from evil, and even to "better" from "good" is one of the profound purposes of earth life.

This great gift leads to one that is even greater. Because mortality came through transgression, humans would now need a Savior to bring them back home. This was the most significant part of God's plan. Humans could choose from the gamut of earthly experiences, but they would not be able to save themselves from their sins. They would need a Mediator, an Advocate, a Savior, a Friend. They would turn to Him for His tender mercies, and He would bestow those tender mercies abundantly. They would endeavor to teach their children the same principles.

Thus, Eve should not be remembered as the source of all our sorrow, pain, and evil, but as the chosen vessel through whom the Savior of the world and all His mortal ancestors would come. Even death is a blessing, a consequence of the Fall, rather than a punishment. Without it, humankind would be stranded here on earth, unable to return to "God, who is our home."[26] Eve is the first hero of the Bible. Like the mythical Pandora, whose name means "all-gifted," Eve brought Hope into the world.

Eve Foreshadows the Teachings of Jesus Christ

Jesus would also exercise the characteristics of agency, acceptance, and sacrifice. Just as Eve had to eat the fruit and accept the consequences of mortal death to bring humankind into the world, Jesus would have to drink the bitter cup of Gethsemane and die to bring humankind back into the presence of God. Yet despite His glorious mission to rescue humankind, Christ would be "despised and rejected of men; a man of sorrows, and acquainted with grief" (Isaiah 53:3). Similarly, generations who followed Eve would revile her unfairly in art and theology. They would blame her for their own sorrows and anguish.

Eve courageously accepted her role in the great plan. She was a woman of wisdom, strength, and love. "Like the Savior, 'who for the joy that was set before him endured the cross' (Hebrews 12:2), Eve, for the joy of helping initiate the human family, endured the Fall. She loved us enough to help lead us."[27] Let us ever remember that in the beginning, God created woman as an *ezer*, whose mission is to rescue, strengthen, and save. Every woman is endowed by her Creator with this powerful and benevolent characteristic, not only in the role of wife and mother, but in every way that she touches the world. It is her birthright from Mother Eve.

Notes

1. According to Daniel Peterson, professor of Islamic Studies and Arabic at Brigham Young University and author of *Abraham Divided,* the words of the serpent when spoken in Arabic have a hissing, sibilant sound.

2. Robert Frost, "The Road Not Taken," *Robert Frost: Collected Poems, Prose, and Plays*, edited by Richard Poirier and Mark Richardson (New York: Penguin Putnam, 1995), 103.

3. My interpretation of this verse is that Paul was speaking of silencing a specific woman in the congregation who had been causing trouble, not all women. He says, "the woman," not "women."

4. Alice Ogden Bellis, *Helpmates, Harlots, and Heroes: Women's Stories in the Hebrew Bible* (Louisville, KY: Westminster/John Knox Press, 1994), 45.

5. *Eve & Adam: Jewish, Christian, and Muslim Readings on Genesis and Gender*, edited by Kristen E. Kvam, Linda S. Schearing, and Valarie H. Ziegler (Bloomington, IN: Indiana University Press, 1999), 3.

6. Carol Meyers, *Rediscovering Eve: Ancient Israelite Women in Context* (Oxford: Oxford University Press, 2013). Abraham, Isaac, and Jacob are referenced throughout the writings of the Old Testament. Moses and the Exodus is another recurrent reminder to the Israelites. But Adam and Eve are never mentioned again in the Old Testament after Cain's murder of Abel and the birth of their son Seth. Meyers continues, "Only in the writings of early Judaism and Christianity, in the last centuries BCE and the first centuries CE, do Eve and Adam emerge into the mainstream of religious literature and theological discussion" (Ibid., 1).

7. Ibid., 63–64.

8. Ibid., 80.

9. Ibid.

10. Terryl L. Givens and Fiona Givens, *The God Who Weeps: How Mormonism Makes Sense of Life* (Salt Lake City: Ensign Peak, 2012), 59. Tikva Frymer-Kensky asserts that the Old Testament "does not claim that women need to be controlled because they are wild, or need to be led because they are foolish, or need to be directed because they are passive, or any of the other justifications for male domination that have been prevalent in Western culture."

11. Givens and Givens, *The God Who Weeps*, 4.

12. Elaine Pagels, *Adam, Eve, and the Serpent* (New York: Random House, 1988), 133.

13. Ibid.

14. Paul Johnson, *The Quest for God: A Pilgrimage* (New York: HarperCollins, 1996), 131–32.

15. Givens and Givens, *The God Who Weeps*, 57.

16. Sheri Dew, *Are We Not All Mothers?* (Salt Lake City: Deseret Book, 2011), 8.

17. David Ariel, *What Do Jews Believe?: The Spiritual Foundations of Judaism* (New York: Schocken, 1995), 127.

18. Johnson, *The Quest for God*, 160.

19. Dew, *Are We Not All Mothers?* 4.

20. Matthew Henry, *An Exposition of the Old and New Testament* (Philadelphia: Barrington and Haswell, 1828), 36.

21. Meyers, *Rediscovering Eve*, 74–75.

22. Ibid., 62.

23. Richard G. Scott, *21 Principles: Divine Truths to Help You Live by the Spirit* (Salt Lake City: Deseret Book, 2013), 64.

24. Lawrence Richards and Sue Richards, *Women of the Bible: The Life and Times of Every Woman in the Bible* (Nashville, TN: Thomas Nelson, 2003), 66.

25. John MacArthur, *Twelve Extraordinary Women: How God Shaped Women of the Bible and What He Wants to Do with You* (Nashville, TN: Thomas Nelson, 2005), 5.

26. William Wordsworth, "Ode: Intimations of Immortality from Recollections of Early Childhood," stanza 5, line 8, 1804.

27. Dew, *Are We Not All Mothers?* 8.

MOTHER NOAH BEGINS ANEW

*"Which of these two did the will of his
father?" (see Matthew 21:31).*

ALMOST NOTHING IS written in the scriptures about the wife of Noah. We don't know whether she was a willing partner in building the ark, or if she resisted the idea of saving themselves while everyone else they knew was drowned. Hers is the most exciting story ever lived but never told. Similar to the wives of many powerful and celebrated men, she has been relegated to the shadow of her more famous husband. We don't even know her name.

Sadly, Noah's wife is often parodied in art as a shrewish wife and critical mother-in-law. In medieval mystery plays, her story provided comic relief between the more serious acts. It is far more likely, however, that she was a deeply spiritual, nurturing, and insightful woman. After all, the Lord trusted her to become the mother of all humankind! The descendants of Adam and Eve had become so evil that "every imagination of the thoughts of [their] heart was only evil continually" (Genesis 6:5). God had to cleanse the earth of this vile wickedness and start anew. Surely He would not have risked His new generation of children on a woman who was not morally and spiritually grounded. It stands to reason that God selected the new "grandmother of all living" as carefully as He had selected Noah.

We know nothing of her life or personality. So we wonder: Like Eve, did this unnamed matriarch step willingly toward the catastrophe that would cleanse the earth? Like Sarah, was she prepared to take the next difficult step commanded by the Lord? Like Rebekah, did she receive personal revelation from God confirming His will regarding her family? Like Mary, did she bow her head humbly and respond, "So be it unto me"? The record is silent on the details of her life. We only know that in the end, she entered the ark with her husband, three sons, and three daughters-in-law, plus two of every kind of beast and bird on earth, plus seven of each of the edible beasts. She did what was asked of her.

When Noah and his wife walked the earth, crime, lust, greed, patricide, and fraud were so rampant that it was impossible for children to be reared in righteousness. The light and truth that were naturally born in them soon flickered and sputtered out, before they could learn to choose for themselves between right and wrong. "God saw that the wickedness of man was great in the earth, and . . . it grieved him at his heart" (Genesis 6:5–6). His wonderful plan of salvation would fail if children could not grow up with true choice and accountability.

Mother Noah must have grieved as well. Her children and grandchildren needed the example of choosing the righteous path, but that would not happen if every living example was greedy, lazy, vile, and hateful. "The earth was also corrupt before God, and the earth was filled with violence" (Genesis 6:11). God had to start over.

A Necessary Cleansing

With this dark chaos as a backdrop, Noah was instructed to build an ark. God was the master planner, giving Noah specific directions about size, materials, and workmanship. Noah was the master builder, following those directions precisely. Parodies and stereotypes aside, we can assume that Noah's wife and their sons and their sons' wives were supportive and helpful. Noah could not have completed a task like this on his own. It required strong shoulders and extra hands. When the time came, Noah and his family loaded up the animals, seven "of every clean [edible] beast . . . and of beasts that are not clean by two, the male and his female. [And] fowls also of the air by sevens" (Genesis 7:2–3). They also gathered seeds and supplies. Then they, too, entered the ark.

And they waited. For seven long days and nights, they sat in the ark with great faith, even while the sun shone. They believed that the rain would come, simply because God told them it would. We don't know what they thought or what they said to one another. We don't know how they felt about their friends, neighbors, and cousins outside the ark. Once the rains came, did they cover their ears against the cries of people and animals scrabbling to get in? Were they filled with fear that the doors might break? Did they long to open those doors and let just a few people in? Did they pray for the souls of those who were dying outside—neighbors and acquaintances who had squandered their time on earth in lewd and lascivious living?

The daughters-in-law in particular were leaving behind their own parents, siblings, and cousins; how must they have felt? What great faith they exhibited toward their father-in-law! Surely they were comforted and strengthened by the faith and love of their mother-in-law. We only know that they believed the word of God regarding the catastrophe that was about to occur, and that they chose to obey His word. It must have been a long and challenging week.

Finally, the sky darkened and the waters came. It rained from the sky, and it flooded from below, as "all the fountains of the great deep [were] broken up, and the windows of heaven were opened" (Genesis 7:11). For forty days it rained, and the ark was pushed by the storm toward its eventual resting place on Mount Ararat in Mesopotamia. Meanwhile, there was work to be done. Animals had to be fed and their stalls cleaned. Food and provisions had to be carefully apportioned. Surely Noah's wife oversaw the work and led the way in their daily chores. The rain finally stopped, but the floodwaters remained for nearly half a year. The earth had been cleansed and baptized. She was ready to start anew.

As Noah and his wife left the ark, it was almost like Eden—just a man and his wife and their children, starting out to populate a new world and trying to make the right choices. Once again, God gave them two commandments. The first was identical to the commandment that had been given to Adam and Eve: "Be fruitful, and multiply, and replenish the earth" (Genesis 9:1). He also gave them dominion over the animals, just as He had given to Adam. Then He gave them a new dietary law. In the Garden of Eden it had been,

"Of every tree of the garden thou mayest freely eat: but of the tree of knowledge of good and evil, thou shalt not eat of it," and He had given them a consequence: "For in the day thou eatest thereof thou shalt surely die" (Genesis 2:16–17). The dietary law given to Noah and his family was different: "Every moving thing that liveth shall be meat for you; even as the green herb have I given you all things. But flesh with the life thereof, which is the blood thereof, shall ye not eat." Again, He included a consequence: "Whoso sheddeth man's blood, by man shall his blood be shed: for in the image of God made he man" (Genesis 9:4, 6).

Two important truths were established in this dietary law: first, animals are intended as food for humans; and second, humans are not merely animals. They are not to be eaten as food, and for them, food would be more than mere animal sustenance; they would prepare their foods and eat together in a civilizing and unifying manner.

Soon, Noah and his wife would say good-bye to their children. According to legend, Ham and his wife would travel southward to populate the land of Africa. Japheth and his wife would travel eastward to populate Asia. Shem and his wife would remain near his parents and populate what would become the Middle East and Europe. A common ancestor would unite them: all were the children of Noah and his wife, who is an unnamed matriarch of the Messiah.

SYMBOLS OF PEACE

Many would see the flood as the most violent event on the face of the earth. "Every living substance was destroyed which was upon the face of the ground, both man, and cattle, and the creeping things, and the fowl of the heaven; and they were destroyed from the earth: and Noah only remained alive, and they that were with him in the ark" (Genesis 7:23). Nevertheless, from this story would arise three great symbols of peace, not of destruction. God had to destroy an evil and corrupt civilization to bring peace back to the world.

The first two symbols are the dove and the olive branch. When Noah could finally see the tops of the mountains, he released a raven and then a dove to see if they could find dry land. "But the dove found no rest for the sole of her foot, and she returned unto him into the ark" (Genesis 8:9). One week later, Noah tried again. This time the dove returned with an olive leaf in her beak, and Noah knew the waters were indeed abating. Consequently, for millennia, the dove and the olive branch have served as symbols of peace and harmony.

The third symbol is the rainbow. As Noah and his wife and children left the ark, their first thought was to build an altar and worship God. They took one "of every clean beast, and every clean fowl, and offered burnt offerings on the altar" (Genesis 8:20). This took great faith on their part. Every living thing on the earth had been destroyed. Their only source of food and supplies were the animals they brought with them onto the ark. It might have been tempting to say, "We will worship God in our hearts, but we don't have enough supplies to risk sacrificing right now. Surely the Lord will understand our circumstances." Many people think this way when it comes to paying tithing and other charitable offerings: "I don't have enough money to pay my bills right now. Surely the Lord will understand if I don't pay tithing until things pick up at work." But this is precisely the time when one cannot afford not to pay offerings to the Lord. Faith is the power by which God works miracles. As we demonstrate great faith, He is able to exercise great power on our behalf. Note that Noah and his family did not offer just one animal as a sacrifice to worship God; they offered one of every edible beast and fowl.

As a result, "the Lord smelled a sweet savour; and the Lord said in his heart, I will not again curse the ground any more for man's sake; for the imagination of man's heart is evil from his youth; neither will I again smite any more every thing living, as I have done" (Genesis 8:21). Here, God acknowledged a sad but simple truth: Just as Hope had remained after Pandora released evil into the world, Sin had remained, even after God cleansed the earth. Nevertheless, "while the earth remaineth," He promised, "seedtime and harvest, and cold and heat, and summer and winter, and day and night shall not cease" (Genesis 8:22). God had encircled them within the safety of the ark as they weathered the storms of the flood, and He continues to encircle us within the safety of His hands as we weather the storms of life and the flood of corruption today. As a symbol of this covenant, God chose the rainbow, saying, "When I bring a cloud over the earth . . . the bow shall be seen in the cloud: and I will remember . . . the everlasting covenant, between God and every living creature . . . upon the earth" (Genesis 9:14–16).

Scientifically, rainbows are easy to explain. They simply occur when sunlight passes through water, splitting the light spectrum into its individual colors. But no one looks at a rainbow as a purely scientific phenomenon. Rainbows are ephemeral and magical, an unexpected gift of nature, just as a testimony is the unexpected gift of the Spirit. When we see a rainbow, we find it hard to take our eyes off it, just as when we feel the Spirit, we find it difficult to take our hearts off it. The rainbow is a perfect symbol of God's love. His love is as natural as light passing through water, yet as unexpected and riveting as the sight of a rainbow.

MOTHER NOAH FORESHADOWS THE TEACHINGS OF JESUS CHRIST

Noah's wife is mentioned only four times in the scriptures: twice as she is entering the ark and twice as she is exiting it. In many respects, that's all we need to know of her. She accepted God's plan and did what she was asked. She may have been an enthusiastic participant, or she may have been full of sorrow, or she may have grumbled all the way (although that is unlikely), but she went.

In the last days of His life, Jesus would teach a parable that could easily describe His ancestor, Noah's wife. On the day after His triumphant entry into Jerusalem, during the last week of His life, Jesus went to the temple to teach. There He told the parable of the two sons: "What do you think of this?" He said. "A certain man had two sons; and he came to the first, and said, 'Son, go work today in my vineyard.' The son answered and said, 'I will not'; but afterward he repented, and went. Then the man came to his second son, and said likewise, 'Go to work in my vineyard.' This son answered, 'I go, Sir,' but he went not" (see Matthew 21:28–30).

Then Jesus asked the Pharisees, "Which of these two did the will of the father?" Of course, they replied that the son who actually did the work was the better son, even though his initial response had been to say no. In the end, it is not what we *say* we will do but what *actually* do that counts. Yes, it would be better if we enthusiastically agreed to do whatever is required of us, without argument or complaint. Yet Jesus Himself paused momentarily as He faced the agony of Gethsemane, pleading, "If thou be willing, remove this cup from me" (Luke 22:42). He never said no, but He did ask humbly if there might be another way.

Few of us will be asked to load an ark full of animals and then embark on a sea journey of six months to begin a whole new life in an unfamiliar land, as Noah's wife did. But we are often asked to do things that require sacrificing our time and talents or entering unfamiliar territories. We might be asked to give up something dear to us, or to do something that is extremely difficult. We might initially say no or ask if there isn't any other way. We learn from Christ's example that looking for another way to accomplish the task is not sinful, as long as we accept the task and the Lord's will when it is shown to us. What matters most is that we do it. Noah's wife entered the ark, and by so doing, she became the grandmother of us all.

SARAH BECOMES A
FRUITFUL BOUGH

*"A fruitful bough, even a fruitful bough by a well;
whose branches run over the wall" (Genesis 49:22).*

ARAI AROSE FROM her prayer with a heavy but determined heart. She knew now what needed to be done. The law provided an alternative for women like her, and God had confirmed to her that this was the right choice. It would require sacrifice and keen disappointment, but she was equal to the task. She smiled with a new hopefulness as she exited the tent to search for her husband. Despite her personal heartache, she would present her plan to Abram with courage and confidence.

Many years earlier, God had promised Abram that he would become the father of many nations. In fact, his posterity was to be "as the dust of the earth: so that if a man can number the dust of the earth, then thy seed also be numbered" (Genesis 13:16). Naturally, Sarai had assumed that the blessing applied to her as well to her husband, and she had waited patiently for the fulfillment of the promise. Yet Sarai had been barren all of her life. Months had slipped into years, and years into decades, and now she was clearly past menopause. What could they do? In Egypt, Sarai had learned of a solution that was provided for women who were barren.[1] Sarai now realized that this was the course they must take. Urging her husband to accept this solution, she said, "Abram, . . . the Lord hath restrained me from [child]bearing; I pray thee, go in unto my maid; it may be that I may obtain children by her" (Genesis 16:2). Together, these women would rear a child for Abram.

Abram reflected as he carefully considered his wife's plan. Sarai was not alone in her concerns; Abram had also started to wonder about God's seeming delay in fulfilling the prophecy. If Abram died without a son, his birthright and all his property would pass to the senior servant in his household, who was an outsider from Damascus named Eliezer. Could this possibly be God's intent, after all that He had promised? Abram, too, had gone to the Lord in prayer and asked, "What wilt thou give me, seeing I go childless, and the steward of my house is this Eliezer of Damascus?" (Genesis 15:2). God had reassured Abram by repeating the promise: "Look now toward the heaven, and tell the stars, if thou be able to number them. . . . So shall thy seed be" (Genesis 15:5). Abram did not doubt God's word; he had always expected that his beautiful wife would eventually present him with the son they so desperately wanted. Now, however, that path seemed irrevocably closed. Sarai was past childbearing. It seemed that something else had to be done if Abram was going to produce a natural heir.

According to the ancient law, a baby born to a bondwoman under a surrogacy arrangement would become the child of the master and mistress. "The children would be considered Sarai's, with the 'second wife' continuing to serve as a handmaiden, or nanny."[2] In fact, in many cases, the bondwoman would be dismissed after the birth and the child reared entirely by his or her adoptive mother.[3] Instead, Sarai proposed to bring Hagar into the family and "gave Hagar to her husband Abram to be his wife" (Genesis 16:3).

Influenced by the confirming Spirit of God, "Abram hearkened to the voice of Sarai" (Genesis 16:2) and soon Hagar conceived. Hagar's pregnancy should have made Sarai happy; after all, it was the whole purpose of the plan. But this was no ordinary slave surrogacy. "By her own design, Sarai [had elevated] Hagar from the status of maidservant to that of wife,"[4] and this woman who had been Sarai's servant now rose above her in social status through the promise of motherhood. Tears stung Sarai's eyes as Hagar preened haughtily in her new role as the wife of her former master, or held her tunic close to her body and turned from side to side, admiring the growing curve of her abdomen. Sarai had endured much hardship, danger, and disappointment throughout her nearly eighty years, but this seemed the hardest of all to bear.

Sarai recalled the luxurious and comfortable life in the busy seaside city of Ur of the Chaldees where she had grown up. Ur was capital city of Sumer and "one of the grandest cities of antiquity."[5] There they had enjoyed fine silks, lovely furnishings, delicate foods, entertaining games, and pastimes.[6] "Ur's lavish marketplace was filled with lemons, mangoes, cinnamon, goats, salted trout, precious oils, dried skins, weavings, yarn, jewels, incense, and pottery. . . . The [city prospered] through trade and bountiful fresh water."[7]

Sarai had faithfully left all that behind to migrate with her husband's family from Ur across hundreds of miles of wilderness to the mountains far away.[8] Their little band included Father Terah; Abram; Abram's brother, Nahor; Nahor's wife, Milcah; Terah's grandson, Lot; and their unnamed servants and cattle. Skirting the Arabian desert along the foothills of the Zagros mountains, they settled in a land named Haran, the same name as Lot's father, who had died in Ur. When Terah passed away, Nahor and Milcah and their household stayed in the bustling crossroads city of Haran.

But a remarkable thing happened to Abram in Haran; "God—unexpected and unannounced—suddenly [started] speaking to him."[9] And Abram recognized His voice. He knew that this was the *one* God, speaking to him, right there in the desert: "Get thee out of thy country, and from thy kindred, and from thy father's house, unto a land that I will shew thee: And I will make of thee a great nation, and I will bless thee, and make thy name great; . . . and in thee shall all families of the earth be blessed" (Genesis 12:1–3). God said "go forth," and they did. Once again, Abram and Sarai took "all their substance that they had gathered, and the souls that they had gotten in Haran; and they went forth to go into the land of Canaan" (Genesis 12:5). Lot and his family went with them. Along the way, they built altars and worshipped God.

When famine had driven them to Egypt for relief (Genesis 12:10), Sarai had again gathered their tents and household goods and journeyed on. Even when Abram had instructed her to tell the Pharaoh that she was his sister instead of his wife, Sarai had complied and was brought to the inner court of the Pharaoh, who was attracted to her exotic beauty (Genesis 12:11–15). She trusted Abram's judgment and believed that his plot would protect his life, and indeed it had. In fact, they had left Egypt not only with their lives but also with "sheep, and oxen, and he asses, and menservants, and maidservants, and she asses, and camels" (Genesis 12:16). One of those maidservants had been Hagar.

After arriving in the land of Canaan, Sarai had watched as Abram said to his nephew Lot, "You decide how we will divide the land, and then you choose which section you will take. I'll take what's left." It surprised Sarai at first. Any mother knows that the best way to divide a special treat is to let one person divide it and the other one choose first. But Abram cared more about family than about riches. He had said to Lot, "Let there be no strife between us, or between our servants, for we are brothers. Take whichever land you want, and I will take the other" (see Genesis 13:8–9). Lot chose the best land, the lush garden plains of Jordan, while she and Abram were left with the bitter, arid land to the west. Lot "pitched his tent toward Sodom" (Genesis 13:12) and eventually moved his family into the town, while Sarai and Abram had lived the nomadic life of shepherds. But the bitter soon became sweet. The Lord made their dry land productive. He blessed them with flocks and servants and silver and gold. They had enough and to spare. They had everything they would need. And now they had a baby on the way. Sarai should have been happy.

But even correct paths can become rocky, and righteous decisions can be fraught with sorrow and misgivings. Sarai found it increasingly painful to see the rich glow of new life on the face of her handmaiden Hagar. It was unnerving to endure the haughty curve of Hagar's neck when Sarai gave her an order. They were quite the pair: Hagar, so fertile that she conceived almost immediately, and Sarai, so barren and dried up that she needed to give her husband a second wife to give him a son.

Who among us has not reached a moment when the light of knowledge no longer marks the path before us and faith alone seems too dim? In that moment, we ask the Lord to take our hand and lead the way until the light of faith can be replenished. Finally, Sarai turned to her prophet husband for comfort and reassurance. "My wrong be upon thee: I have given my maid into thy bosom; and when she saw that she had conceived, I was despised in her eyes: the Lord judge between me and thee" (Genesis 16:5).

Abram and his men had just returned from several long months at war. When Abram's nephew Lot had been caught in the crossfires of a local tribal war, Lot was kidnapped from his home in Sodom (Genesis 14), and Abram immediately set off to rescue him. During those months, 318 men had accompanied Abram (Genesis 14:14), leaving Sarai to oversee the daily activities of their camp with just the wives of those men and a few male servants to help them. This had been no simple task. Sarai had to arbitrate internal disputes; plan the migration for grazing and watering the cattle; monitor supplies; and oversee normal chores such as grinding wheat, gathering fuel, tending livestock, and caring for the servants' children.[10]

Having entrusted Sarai with so much responsibility during those months, Abram now chose not to get involved in this domestic dispute between women. Moreover, Abram understood that, with Hagar's pregnancy, the balance of power between the two women had tipped. Sarai "wanted something from Abram: the restoration of her authority over Hagar. Abram understood . . . that power was the issue, and he restored it to Sarai by giving control of Hagar back to her."[11] "Thy maid is in thy hand," Abram told Sarai. "Do to her as it pleaseth thee" (Genesis 16:6). And so, to her temporary discredit, Sarai "'afflicted,' or 'humbled,' Hagar"[12] and "dealt hardly" with her. Sarai was so harsh, in fact, that Hagar ran away (Genesis 16:6).

Hagar Speaks with an Angel

Slipping out of her tent under a rising moon, the solitary young Egyptian woman tiptoed out of camp. To set out alone into the desert wilderness was simply unheard of, even for a man, but especially for a pregnant woman. Wild animals, marauding men, and insufficient water posed constant dangers. There is no place so bleak or so profound as the desert near Shur.[13] Before long, Hagar was weary, frightened, and hungry. But she was not utterly alone. Here, on Mount Sinai, God would speak to Moses and reveal His law.

Here, Elijah would encounter God in a wilderness cave. And here, Hagar would have the profound experience of discovering that God knows each of us intimately and sees us personally.

As Hagar rested beside a fountain on the way to Shur, God sent an angel to comfort this Egyptian servant. In the angel's voice He asked, "Hagar, Sarai's maid, whence camest thou? and whither wilt thou go?" (Genesis 16:8). This was no ordinary "What are you doing, and where are you going?" Several significant concepts are implied in the question. First, God had sent an angel to watch over Hagar. He was concerned about her. The angel also called Hagar by name, just as Christ would call Mary Magdalene by her name near His Garden Tomb. The angel who spoke God's words knew Hagar, individually, personally. This Egyptian servant woman mattered to Him.

Next, in calling her "Sarai's maid," the angel reminded Hagar of her subordinate position as Sarai's handmaiden and Abram's second wife. God Himself acknowledged it. However, as we have seen, "subordinate" does not mean "inferior." Hers was not a demeaning place of servitude, but rather a specific role essential to God's plan. He was about to make Hagar's descendants part of the vast lineage of Abraham, "that it shall not be numbered for multitude" (Genesis 16:10). This was a plan God had known from beginning to end. Surely this was the reason Abram and Sarai had been guided to Egypt. Hagar, too, was an *ezer kenegdo,* a savior to her descendants and equal to the task before her.

The angel also asked Hagar the metaphysical questions that all humans want to know: "Where did I come from? Where am I going?" Hagar responded quite simply and literally: "I have run away from my mistress" (see Genesis 16:8). She said nothing about where she was going, however. Perhaps her energy was spent and her courage gone, and she was ready to give up. "Perhaps for the first time she consider[ed] just what might await her in Egypt, should she actually survive the journey alone."[14] But the angel was thinking of a grander home and a grander destination. He was sent to remind Hagar that she had a heavenly home, one that takes precedence over any temporary earthly bonds.

He also reminded her that, despite being a bondwoman, she was endowed with her own will. He asked, "whither *wilt* thou go," not "whither *shalt* thou go." The word *shall* implies commandment, while the word *will* implies choice. Hagar would choose her path. Finally, he prophesied concerning her unborn child, telling her that he would be a boy and she should call him Ishmael, "because the Lord hath heard thy affliction" (Genesis 16:11). God was aware of her predicament. He cared about her, Hagar, an Egyptian bondwoman in a foreign land. Hagar learned "that God does indeed hear the cries of the suffering, the downcast, and the abandoned; that every human soul has dignity and worth." This new knowledge empowered Hagar. With God watching over her, she could endure anything.[15]

HAGAR GIVES GOD A NAME

Hagar also recognized that something amazing had just happened. She had spoken directly to God, and God had spoken directly with her, just as He would speak with Moses generations later on Mount Sinai, near this spot. What she did next was almost shocking in its audacity: she dared to name God. "And she called the name of the Lord that spake unto her, Thou God seest me; for she said, Have I also here looked after him that seeth me? Wherefore the well was called Beer-lahai-roi," which means "the well of him who liveth and seeth me" (Genesis 16:13–14). "In the future, other people in Scripture would refer to God by the names He would teach them to use—Adonai or Yahweh—but no one had [yet] invented their own."[16] She chose a name that communicated her relationship with Him: He saw her, He knew her, and He had spoken to her—a woman in a man's world, an Egyptian in a Semite camp, and a slave in the master's tent. Hagar was "not peripheral to God's plan for Abraham or for Sarah—[her story provides] a strong hint that God intended all along to encompass the Gentiles among his people."[17]

And then, as quickly as He had elevated her to see that glimpse of her heavenly status, He plummeted her back to earth. "Return to thy mistress," the angel told her, "and submit thyself under her hands" (Genesis 16:9). Hagar would have to go back, and she would have to resume her status as a bondwoman to Sarai and a second wife to Abram. This hierarchical relationship was the only way the two women would be able to live together in peace. And it was important for them to find peace, because the innocent babe Hagar carried in her womb deserved to grow up under the guidance of both his father and mother. It would not be appropriate to send him away from his father, the prophet Abram, nor would it be appropriate to send Hagar away so that the boy would be reared without her. This was no ordinary surrogacy. Ishmael was now part of the family and covenant of Abram. As his mother, Hagar would participate in the blessings as well.

Moreover, Hagar had a testimony to share with them all: God sees us. He knows us. He cares intimately about us—even those who are seemingly disenfranchised. The blessings that had been promised to Abram were finally coming to fruition in this child who would be called Ishmael. This was no ordinary return of a slave to her masters. In doing so, she asserted her right to choose. "After years of slavery, Hagar's return to Sarah was possibly the first truly free act of her life."[18] Jesus Himself would teach this same principle of self-empowerment when He said, "If any man will . . . take away thy coat, let him have thy cloak also. And whosoever shall compel thee to go a mile, go with him twain" (Matthew 5:40–41). The first would be a mandated act; the second would be a freely chosen gift.

Sarai may have felt glad at first when she discovered that Hagar had run away. Hagar's fruitfulness had been a painful reminder of her own barrenness. But a baby was coming into the world, and that baby deserved to be reared under the influence of his father. Hagar would go back, and Sarai would accept her.

SARAH'S GIFT IS ACCEPTABLE TO GOD

Some have suggested that Sarai acted hastily and with poor judgment when she gave her handmaiden to Abram as his wife, in light of the miracle that would occur in her own womb thirteen years later. But this plan was not a mistake; it was a test and a sacrifice for Sarai and part of God's plan for bringing Abram's posterity into the world. It was a hard thing to do, but she did it. In fact, Paul told the Hebrew Saints in his great sermon on faith, "Through faith also Sara herself received strength to conceive seed, and was delivered of a child when she was past age, because she judged him faithful who had promised" (Hebrews 11:11). The marvelous events that took place shortly after the birth of Ishmael, the son of Abram and Hagar, proved this point. Only then, after they had proven themselves faithful and obedient, did God endow Abram and Sarai with the fulness of the Abrahamic covenant.

Beneath the stars that would number Abram's posterity, Abram and Sarai heard again the voice of God. First, He gave them new names. "Thy name shall be Abraham," He said, "for a father of many nations have I made thee. . . . As for Sarai thy wife, thou shalt not call her name Sarai, but Sarah shall her name be. And I will bless her, and give thee a son also of her . . . and she shall be a mother of nations; kings of people shall be of her" (Genesis 17:5, 15–16). These name changes seem small—almost insignificant, in fact. God simply added a breathy syllable with the letter "H." But it was a most significant syllable indeed. In Hebrew, the name we know as "Jehovah" is "Yahweh" and is spelled without its vowels: *YHWH*. It is pronounced like a sigh, like the very breath of life. In changing their names to Abraham and Sarah, God endowed them with both His Spirit and the breathy sound of His name.

This was not the first time Sarah had been given a different name. According to Jewish tradition, Sarah is Iscah, mentioned in Genesis as the daughter of Haran and sister of Milcah. The verse itself confirms this connection through a lovely little chiasmus: "The name of Abram's wife was Sarai; and the name of Nahor's wife, Milcah, the daughter of Haran, the father of Milcah, and the father of Iscah" (Genesis 11:29). In a chiasmic poem, the first and last words or phrases are equivalent to each other, the second and penultimate lines are equivalent, and so on until the center of the poem or passage is reached. In this verse, Haran, the father, is at the center; Milcah is mentioned second and penultimately; and the names Sarai and Iscah are at its beginning and end. Thus, poetically as well as logically, Sarai and Iscah are one and the same.

Significantly, the name Iscah (Yiscah in the Torah) contains the letters that mean "to see" or "to view," suggesting that Sarah was a prophetess, whose special gift was foreseen even in her youth. She is one of only seven prophetesses mentioned in the Old Testament. Clearly Sarah was a valued daughter of God. Though she momentarily faltered in grief as she saw another woman carrying the child she had hoped to carry for Abram herself, she nevertheless was a noble woman, a seer who was privileged to receive guidance and revelation from God. God did not condemn her for faltering, and neither should we. Nor should we condemn ourselves in moments when we feel weak or disheartened. It is not a sin to grieve for the path not taken.

Abraham's marvelous blessing was threefold. It included posterity, priesthood, and property. First, God repeated the promise that Abraham would be "a father of many nations" (Genesis 17:4). Then He established "an everlasting covenant, to be a God unto thee, and to thy seed after thee" (Genesis 17:7), demonstrating the responsibility and blessing of priesthood in Abraham's posterity. He also gave them "all the land of Canaan," where they currently lived as "stranger[s]," for "an everlasting possession" (Genesis 17:8). As a token of this great covenant and blessing, He gave them the symbol of circumcision, which is like a circle, having no beginning and no end. Though this physical token of the priesthood covenant was manifest only in the men, it included the women as well. "God chose circumcision, not as a symbol of manhood, but of intimacy, vulnerability, and fruitfulness. Circumcision spoke of a man's intimate relationship with his wife and of their union in reproducing children, both physically and spiritually."[19] It was a perfect and permanent reminder of a covenant that would finally be fulfilled after nearly a century of waiting to become parents.

All of this was established *after* the birth of Ishmael, and Ishmael was included in the blessings. "As for Ishmael," the Lord said, "I have blessed him, and will make him fruitful, and will multiply him exceedingly; twelve princes shall he beget, and I will make him a great nation" (Genesis 17:20). The "twelve princes" of Ishmael would become the Arab nations of the Middle East. Through Ishmael, the prophet Mohammed would be born and the Islamic religion would be founded. Three great religious groups would revere Abraham as their patriarch—Jews, Muslims, and Christians. Moreover, as we learn from the experiences of both Hagar and Sarah, God is watching over all. Someday, every knee shall humbly bow and every tongue shall boldly confess that Jesus is the Messiah and Savior of all humankind (see Philippians 2:9–11). Then will true peace be restored, through the atoning sacrifice of Jesus Christ, and the family of Abraham will be reunited in harmony and love.

That God loved, trusted, and approved of Sarah's actions is seen in the fact that, after faithfully and patiently waiting nearly a century for the Lord to give her a child, Sarah would have her baby only after Hagar's son was born. Abraham had waited, as had Adam, for the Lord to give him the promised posterity. And Sarah had stepped forward decisively, as had Eve, to help make things happen, even though the consequences of that step were painful. Hagar's pregnancy caused Sarah to feel the kind of personal sorrow in childbearing that had been foretold to Eve. Nevertheless, she welcomed Hagar back to their home and accepted all that was required of her. The ceremony of circumcision extended to Abraham's entire household, including Ishmael. Receiving the Abrahamic covenant was the most momentous occasion of Abraham's life—until the miraculous birth of Isaac.

A Princess in the Making

Me—a princess! Sarah thought happily as she pronounced her new name, which literally means "princess." *We truly have been blessed,* she admitted as she again reflected on her life. Over the years, she had come to accept and even enjoy Hagar's wild and rambunctious son (Genesis 16:12). She still felt the pang of sorrow at her own barrenness, but she trusted God. As do most women in her childless condition, she had come to terms with her situation and had found other ways to express her womanhood. Wonderful ways, in fact.

She was experiencing one of those expressions of womanhood now. Abraham had visitors, and Sarah was acting in her role as hostess. The men were emissaries representing the Lord Himself, warning of a great calamity that was about to befall Sodom, where Abraham's nephew Lot was still living, and its neighboring town of Gomorrah. Lot had selected the rich and fertile plains of Jordan and had pitched his tent in the direction of the lively crossroads city of Sodom, eventually moving into the city proper. Even after he was kidnapped and Abram rescued him, Lot had returned to the town that had become his home. But Sodom was full of villainy and moral depravity. Abraham had worried for some time about Lot's children and whether they could grow up righteously in that environment. Now these angelic messengers confirmed his worst fears: it was nearly impossible to live virtuously and safely there. The cities themselves ached for relief, and "the cry of Sodom and Gomorrah [was] great . . . because their sin [was] very grievous" (Genesis 18:20). The cities were about to be destroyed, and Lot's family needed to be rescued.

Sarah worried about Lot and his family too. As she finished serving the food, she listened at the tent where the messengers were talking to Abraham. Suddenly, however, she realized they weren't talking about Sodom any more. The messengers of the Lord had spoken her own name. She listened more intently as they asked Abraham where she was. When Abraham told them that she was in the tent, they continued speaking. Sarah knew that she should turn away. She was eavesdropping, after all. But she continued to listen. One of them said, in the name of the Lord, "I will certainly return unto thee according to the time of life; and lo, Sarah thy wife shall have a son."

As Sarah heard these words, her hand flew to her mouth to keep from laughing out loud. She was eighty-nine years old—well beyond the time of childbearing. Was she really going to have a baby at last? She shook with suppressed laughter that wanted to burst forth.

Then she heard the voice of the Lord ask Abraham, "Wherefore did Sarah laugh? . . . Is anything too hard for the Lord? At the time appointed I will return unto thee, according to the time of life, and Sarah shall have a son" (Genesis 18:13–14).

Sarah blushed crimson. "I laughed not," she blurted shyly. The scripture says that "she was afraid," suggesting that the messenger might have spoken sternly or reprimanded her. His response, "Nay but thou didst laugh" (Genesis 18:15), might seem like a rebuke, suggesting an accusatory tone from the visitor. But the word *fear* originally meant "awe and reverence," not "terror," especially in the sixteenth century, when the King James Version of the Bible was translated. Sarah reacted to the miraculous pronouncement in the same way that the shepherds would react "with wondering awe" on the night that angels would announce the Savior's birth. They, too, would be "sore afraid," but they would not be frightened.

It is unlikely that these messengers would have been angry or stern with Sarah on this night of all nights. She and Abraham had waited more than sixty years for this day to come, and these messengers had been given the privilege of delivering the wonderful news. Abraham, too, had "[fallen] upon his face, and laughed" in wonder and hope at the possibility: "Shall a child be born unto him that is an hundred years old? and shall Sarah, that is ninety years old, bear?" (Genesis 17:17). It was a joyful moment for them all. Surely the messenger smiled and wagged his finger at Sarah playfully. "Nay, but thou didst laugh," he must have teased her good-naturedly. And then they all laughed out loud—a glorious, joyful noise unto the Lord, until Sarah wiped the tears from her eyes and returned to the tent to fetch the dates for their guests. The day had finally come. Sadly for Lot and his family, the rich fertile plains of Jordan would soon be covered by the arid dust of Sodom, but the barren womb of Sarah was about to become rich and fertile. God was indeed good to his word. And Sarah laughed again within herself.

SARAH ENJOYS THE RICH BLESSINGS OF MOTHERHOOD

Less than a year later, the hoped-for day finally came. Their baby—Sarah's baby—was born. Fittingly, they named him Isaac, which means "to laugh and rejoice." Surely she thought, *Isaac is the perfect name for this perfect son, and we will strive to be perfect parents, raising him to walk in the perfect paths of the Lord.* God had already said of Abraham, "I know him, that he will command his children and his household after him, and they shall keep the way of the Lord" (Genesis 18:19). God trusted Abraham as the father of nations, and He trusted Sarah, too, as the mother of all nations. "Neither is the man without the woman, neither the woman without the man, in the Lord" (1 Corinthians 11:11). They were a single unit, a partnership of equal but opposite worth. Abraham was overjoyed. On the day that Isaac was weaned, he gave a great feast. He was over a hundred years old, yet life was just beginning.

With the birth of Isaac to Abraham's first and favored wife, the tentative peace between Sarah and Hagar weakened. As Sarah rejoiced in this great blessing of motherhood, the enmity between Hagar and Sarah returned. Ishmael began mocking little Isaac and treating him with disdain, right on Isaac's feast day (Genesis 21:8–9). Sarah could see trouble brewing. By now Ishmael was entering his teens. Once again, Sarah went to Abraham with her concerns. "Cast out this bondwoman and her son," she advised him (Genesis 21:10). "We cannot let our son grow up with Hagar's wild boy." Sarah was determined that Isaac would grow up in the right environment, without hostility from his older sibling.

Where Abraham had been indifferent to Sarah's earlier complaints about Hagar and had indicated that he didn't care what Sarah did with her handmaiden, he now grieved at the thought of sending Hagar and their son away. How could he give up Ishmael, his firstborn? (see Genesis 21:11). This time, however, there was no question that Sarah was right. Abraham had also observed the character of his "wild" son and had petitioned the Lord in his behalf, "O that Ishmael might live before thee!" (Genesis 17:18). The problem would only worsen with time. God Himself confirmed this to Abraham and comforted him. "Let it not be grievous in thy sight because of the lad, and because of thy bondwoman; in all that Sarah hath said unto thee, hearken unto her voice; for in Isaac shall thy seed be called" (Genesis 21:12). With these words, the Lord confirmed to Abraham two important truths: that Isaac was to be the birthright son, and that his wife, Sarah, was a worthy partner and counselor to him. Through Ishmael and his mother, the blessings of Abraham would be extended to the Egyptians (Genesis 21:21), and Ishmael would become the founder of the great Arab nations. But through Sarah's son, Isaac, would the chosen Messiah come.

Abraham had learned obedience through a century of experience. The next morning, he woke up early. With a heavy heart he personally prepared food and water for Hagar and Ishmael to take on their journey (Genesis 21:14). In sorrow, he watched them go, shielding his eyes against the rising sun until they were out of sight. This time, there would be no angel to turn Hagar back. Ishmael was now over thirteen years old. He had reached the age to become a man and was old enough to care for his mother and move on into adulthood. He had enjoyed the tutelage of his father, the prophet. Now it was Isaac's turn.

Hagar, too, had received a great blessing: her child, born under the law of surrogacy, did not belong to her mistress after all. He was leaving with her. "In a world in which slavery was accepted, Hagar and Ishmael were not sold; they were freed. Hagar and Ishmael left Abraham's household as emancipated slaves."[20] Literally and symbolically, they were freed by the word of God. Hagar was endowed with the great blessing foretold for all the daughters of Eve: she was an *ezer kenegdo,* a woman equal to the task of helping her son and his descendants become that great nation. And Ishmael would not be far away. When Abraham died, Ishmael and Isaac would mourn together as they buried their father in the cave of Machpelah (Genesis 25:9). One of Ishmael's daughters would marry Isaac's son Esau and help to soften his heart toward his brother Jacob. The history of the Middle East is a history of two brothers, Isaac and Ishmael, and both belong to the covenant of Abraham.

Sarah did not smile triumphantly as Hagar left their camp. There was wisdom in her decision this time, not anger or jealousy. She knew that this was a necessary parting, but she felt deep compassion for her husband. She had learned through experience both the sorrow and the joy of her decisions.

Sarah Foreshadows the Teachings of Jesus Christ

Sarah had endured much sorrow on her way to motherhood. The Lord had tested her thoroughly. She left a luxurious home in Ur to establish a nomadic home in the wilderness, suffered nearly a century of barrenness, helped rear the son of her husband's second wife, and managed a large community of servants while her husband was away at war. She had even entered the court and harem of the Pharaoh in Egypt, pretending to be Abraham's sister instead of his wife to protect the life of her husband (Genesis 12). Such willing sacrifice was enough; God would not require her to endure the final test with which He would now prove Abraham.

Sarah would not accompany the father and son as they traveled three days to Moriah, part of the mountain chain that would later become the site of the great city of Jerusalem and the hill outside the city walls that would be called Golgotha.

She would not be with them as Abraham told his servants to wait while he and Isaac finished the journey alone, just as Jesus would tell His Apostles to wait as He faced Gethsemane alone.

She would not see Abraham lay the wood of the sacrifice upon Isaac's shoulder, just as Jesus would be made to carry His wooden cross to Golgotha.

She would not watch as Isaac looked trustingly into his father's eyes and asked, "Where is the lamb for a burnt offering?"

She would not share Abraham's supreme grief as he choked out the words, "My son, God will provide himself a lamb for a burnt offering."

She would not see the light of recognition in her son's eyes as he humbly, trustingly, agonizingly accepted what his father was about to require of him while Abraham bound his birthright son to the altar and raised the knife to sacrifice him.

Neither would Sarah share in Abraham's supreme, exquisite joy as the angel arrived just in time to stay his hand and say, in the voice of the Lord, "It is enough. Lay not thine hand upon the lad, for now I know that thou fearest God, seeing thou hast not withheld thy son, thine only son from me."

Surely Sarah would have broken down into tears of joy and cathartic laughter if she had seen the ram in the thicket and realized that it had been provided as the "burnt offering in the stead of [their] son" (see Genesis 22:1–13).

Abraham had learned the principle of obedience. He had been willing to sacrifice that which he valued most—his son—to honor God and gain eternity. But Sarah had demonstrated her own faith and obedience with a sacrifice just as precious. Not once, but twice, she willingly risked that which a woman values most—her virtue— by entering the Pharaoh's court and again by entering Abimelech's harem to protect her husband's life (Genesis 12; 20). The scriptural record remains discreetly silent regarding the details of her ordeals there, and so shall the pages of this book. It is hoped that the angel protected her from the ultimate sacrifice in the same way that He stayed the hand of Abraham just in time. But her willingness was no less profound than Abraham's. She was an *ezer kenegdo*—a savior and equal to her husband in every way. Sarah proved that she could do hard things. She knew, as surely as Jesus would know in Gethsemane, that "all things are possible" unto God (Mark 14:36).

From Dry Desert to Fruitful Bough

Sarah smiled as she watched Isaac return from the journey with his father. She could see something new in the way Isaac walked and moved, a new maturity she hadn't noticed before. He had become a man, it seemed, almost overnight. Soon, it would be time for the next step in Isaac's life—time to find him a wife. They would search carefully for the woman who, through her posterity, would inherit the blessings of Abraham. Sarah knew that it could not be a local girl, raised in the pagan religions of the neighboring tribes. She shuddered as she remembered the devastation of Sodom and Gomorrah, resulting from a moral desolation so severe that it required the refiner's fire of destruction at the hand of the Lord.

She remembered Lot's sons, who had been so caught up in the culture that they refused to escape with their parents and sisters and perished in the destruction. Lot had chosen what seemed to be the easier path when he selected the bountiful plains of Jordan all those years ago, but the dry, hard plains of the desert had proved to be a rich blessing to Abraham and Sarah. Struggle, sacrifice, and sorrow had strengthened and enriched them. Sarah had indeed become a fruitful bough. They would take the time to find the right wife for Isaac. In the meantime, Sarah would enjoy every minute of her time as a mother. *This is the day the Lord has made for me,* she thought. *I will rejoice and be glad in it!* (see Psalm 118:24).

Notes

1. The Code of Hammurabi, the Nuzi tablets, and early Egyptian texts all contain examples of surrogate motherhood through the use of a bondwoman (Bellis, 1994, 68).

2.   Charlotte Gordon, *The Woman Who Named God: Abraham's Dilemma and the Birth of Three Faiths* (New York: Hachette Book Group, 2009), 100.

3.   In an era before test tubes and microscopes, this was essentially a form of surrogate motherhood, and the bondwoman had no voice in the matter. "To contemporary readers, . . . consent seems necessary for the arrangement to be moral. But none of the ancient texts sees any ethical problem with this arrangement. Ancient societies accepted slavery as a regular part of social life. Using another person's body as a surrogate for one's own is part of the fabric of slavery. Just as a slave's muscles can be utilized for the good of the master, so can a slave woman's womb" (Frymer-Kensky, 2002, 227).

4.   Virginia Stem Owens, *Daughters of Eve: Seeing Ourselves in Women of the Bible* (Colorado Springs, CO: NavPress, 2007), 80.

5.   Bruce Feiler, *Walking the Bible: A Journey by Land through the Five Books of Moses* (New York: HarperCollins Books, 2001), 27.

6.   Lawrence Richards and Sue Richards, *Women of the Bible: The Life and Times of Every Woman in the Bible* (Nashville, TN: Thomas Nelson, 2003), 216.

7.   Gordon, *The Woman Who Named God*, 4.

8.   "According to Jewish lore, on the night Abraham was born, a great star passed through the sky, devouring four smaller stars. Advisers told King Nimrod [of Ur] that the sign meant the newly born son of Terah would one day conquer Nimrod's kingdom and change its religion. . . . Even as a boy, Abraham was able to divine from the stars that there was only one God" (Feiler, *Walking the Bible*, 29).

9.   Ibid., 33.

10. Gordon, *The Woman Who Named God*, 76–78.

11. Frymer-Kensky, *Reading the Women of the Bible*, 228 (tense adjusted).

12. Owens, *Daughters of Eve*, 80.

13. Gordon, *The Woman Who Named God*, 119.

14. Owens, *Daughters of Eve*, 81.

15. Diana Webb, *Forgotten Women of God* (Springville, UT: Cedar Fort, Inc., 2010), 142.

16. Gordon, *The Woman Who Named God*, 138.

17. Carolyn Custis James, *Lost Women of the Bible: Finding Strength and Significance through Their Stories* (Grand Rapids, MI: Zondervan, 2005), 94.

18. Ibid., 95.

19. Ibid., 75.

20. Frymer-Kensky, *Reading the Women of the Bible*, 235 (tense adjusted).

REBEKAH GOES THE
EXTRA MILE

*"If any man . . . take away thy coat, let him have
thy cloak also. And whosoever shall compel thee to
go a mile, go with him twain. Give to him that
asketh thee, and from him that would borrow of
thee turn not thou away" (Matthew 5:40–42).*

EBEKAH HOISTED THE heavy earthen pitcher onto her shoulder and shielded the sun from her eyes. The coolness of evening was coming on as she walked cheerfully toward the well outside the city wall, where it was her chore to draw water every day. Some of her friends objected to this job, saying that it wasn't fair; the pitchers were heavy, and the animals could be demanding as they returned from a day of grazing. The girls would have to pour several pitchers into the troughs before the animals were satisfied. Besides, their brothers didn't have to draw water. But Rebekah didn't mind. "We all have our jobs to do," Rebekah reminded them. "I'm glad I don't have to shear the sheep or tan the hides into leather."

Rebekah had learned long before that her own attitude made all the difference in how she felt throughout the day. If her mother asked her to mend a tunic or clean the wool for spinning, she would usually mend a scarf as well and sweep the floor without being asked. It felt good to claim her time as her own in this way and share it willingly with others. The first task was her duty, but the second was her choice. It gave her a sense of freedom to do more than was asked. It made her a cheerful giver.

As Rebekah passed through the city gate and began to fill her pitcher at the well, she noticed an older man standing nearby. He was dressed in clothing of a different stripe than she was accustomed to seeing, and he was dusty, as though he had been traveling for quite some time. His camels looked dusty too. The man seemed to recognize her. He ran toward her and began to speak.

"Let down your pitcher, I pray thee, so I may drink," he said to her in a voice that was strangely excited.

Rebekah smiled. A man was not permitted to speak to a woman in their culture, with the one exception that a stranger could ask for water. She liked this funny old man in his unusual tunic, and she liked giving service. He looked thirsty from his journey. "Drink, my lord," she said kindly, and hurried to turn the mouth of her pitcher down so the water would pour out. When he was satisfied, she said, "I will draw water for your camels also, until they have done drinking" (see Genesis 24:15–19). Custom demanded that a woman dip water for a stranger at the well, but not for his animals too. "Ancient Near Eastern wells were not vertical shafts through which buckets are lowered by rope. They were inclined slopes that the girl went down and came up. To water ten camels after a long journey, [Rebekah] had to go down and come up many times."[1] Nevertheless, she wanted to offer this man more than he asked of her. It filled her heart with gladness.

The man watched her intently as she worked, but he said not a word until she had finished. She wondered what he was thinking, but she shrugged it off. She would show him kindness, whether he said anything or not. It felt good to be outside in the gathering twilight, with the water splashing against her skin and the camels nuzzling her shoulder. Camels were much thirstier than sheep. It took many trips to the well before they were satisfied. Her shoulders began to ache, but she did not complain. When the camels had finished drinking, she nodded graciously to the stranger and turned to leave. Suddenly, the man reached into his pouch and then opened his hand toward her. The waning sun glinted on something shiny. There in his palm she saw a heavy gold earring, at least half a shekel in weight, and two beautiful gold bracelets. *What could this mean?* she wondered.

"Whose daughter are you?" the man asked her with a hint of excitement in his voice. "Tell me, I pray: Is there room in your father's house for us to lodge in?"

Strangely, she felt no fear as she talked with this man. Something whispered to her that she was safe. Calmly, she answered his question. "I am the daughter of Bethuel, the son of Milcah and Nahor."[2] Then she continued impulsively, "We have both straw and provender enough, and room to lodge in" (see Genesis 24:23–25).

The man reacted in a way that sent chills up Rebekah's spine. He knelt humbly on the ground and said, "Blessed be the Lord God of my master Abraham, who hath not left destitute my master of his mercy and his truth: I being in the way, the Lord led me to the house of my master's brethren" (Genesis 24:27). For this was Eliezer, Abraham's most trusted servant and the steward of his household. He was an *ezer* by name and by duty. The enormity of this miracle had not been lost on Eliezer. He knew how slim the odds were of his ever finding this particular girl in this particular town, the daughter of this particular family—a daughter who would have the goodness to offer an old stranger not only a drink for himself, but troughs full of water for his ten camels. He had traveled four hundred miles to find her, and the Lord God of Abraham had directed their paths to each other as surely as if He had been holding their hands. This was a day that the old servant would remember forever and a story that he would repeat again and again.

Rebekah felt it too. Dropping her pitcher, she turned and ran toward her mother's house, calling out with excitement. She told everyone in the house the things that had just happened. A miracle had occurred, right here in her town, right here in her heart, while she had merely been watering the camels.

The Servant of Abraham Tells His Story

Eliezer waited anxiously beside the well. What if Rebekah's family did not believe his story? A young woman as fair and virtuous as she—perhaps they would not trust this old man's word. It was highly unusual for a man to negotiate for a bride; matchmaking was the purview of mothers and aunts in this society. He hoped they would recognize the significance of his asking Rebekah for water, because matchmaking generally began with the women of the groom's family symbolically asking for water at the home of the potential bride's parents.[3]

Eliezer did not have to wait long, however, before Laban, Rebekah's older brother, came hurrying to the well. Laban had seen the gold earring and bracelets, and he wanted to know more about this man with his strange tale. Wedding gifts, called dowries, often had this effect upon the family of a potential bride, and this jewelry was especially beautiful and rich. "Come!" he said when he reached the man. "Why are you waiting here? We have prepared the house, and space for the camels. The women are preparing a feast. Come!"

Laban provided water for the men to wash the dust of the trail from their feet. Then he set food before the traveler. Before Eliezer would eat, however, he insisted on telling his story. Eating a meal together had special significance in their culture. It was "a way to ratify pacts or treaties. By consuming meals together, they symbolically became members of the same family. . . . Even strangers became *companions,* a word whose literal meaning is 'one with whom bread is broken.'"[4] Eliezer was fairly bursting with excitement about this miraculous event that had happened to him, but he would not break bread until an agreement had been reached. Rebekah hovered in the background, shyly listening again to the story of how God Himself had found a match for her.

After telling them what had befallen Abraham after the two families had separated so many years before on the road from Ur to Canaan, the servant explained his mission. "My master is old and cannot travel, so he sent me to find a wife for his son. But I was worried. How would I know the right woman? As I traveled, I pondered this question, but no answer came. Then today I came to the well that stands outside your city gates. I still didn't know what to do. Finally, I prayed to the God of my master Abraham and presented him with a plan. I said, 'When the right maiden comes to draw water from the well, I will say to her, "Give me, I pray thee, a little water to drink," and she will say to me, "While you drink I will also draw water for your camels." Let this same woman be the one you have appointed for my master's son,' I said in my prayer."

The servant felt a sudden thrill as he remembered how specifically the words had come into his mind as he prayed. Then he continued. "Before I had even finished speaking the prayer in my heart, Rebekah came out with her pitcher on her shoulder. I watched her go down to the well and draw water. There was something so special about her; I knew at once that this was the girl. So I said to her, 'Let me drink, I pray thee,' and she quickly brought her pitcher down from her shoulder to quench my thirst. Then, before I had even finished, she said, 'Drink, and I will give thy camels water also.'

"I was so astonished that I simply watched as she cared for my camels. Then I asked her who she was, and lo, she is a cousin of my master—his own brother's granddaughter. Is this not a mighty miracle? It has been done exactly as I rehearsed it to the Lord. So tell me now: Will you deal kindly and truly with my master? Or must I return without the damsel who has been chosen by the Lord to be the wife of my master's son?"

Laban and Bethuel looked at each other. Recognizing the Lord's hand in this story, they said of one accord, "Rebekah is standing right here. Take her and go, and let her be your master's son's wife, as the Lord has spoken" (see Genesis 24:34–51). The servant of Abraham rejoiced. Rebekah had "proved herself the choice of Providence for Abraham's son in three ways: she treated the steward with gracious benevolence; she belonged to the right family; and her family was God-fearing."[5]

Eliezer of Damascus repeated his story to all who would listen for the rest of his life. It was the first time he had experienced so intimate and personal an answer to prayer. He would never forget the feeling.

Rebekah Prepares to Become a Wife

Eliezer reached into his camel bags and pulled out the dowry he had been instructed to give in the marriage negotiations. These negotiations were a significant part of the wedding ceremony, for the groom was in essence paying her family for having prepared his wife for marriage. Eliezer gave jewelry of the finest silver and gold to Rebekah, as well as beautiful clothing befitting a princess. He gave jewels and precious things to her brother and her mother as well. The bargaining went without dispute, for the outcome was known from the beginning. The servant gave the entire dowry to Rebekah and her family, and the family gave Rebekah into Eliezer's care and safekeeping. The betrothal was set. Then the feasting began, and it continued long into the night.

Early the next morning the servant arose and said to her family, "Send me away to my master." He was anxious to begin the month-long journey back to Abraham.

But it had all happened so quickly. In the cold light of morning, with the betrothal accepted, the dowry settled and the excitement of the moment dying down, Laban suggested that they wait. Betrothals usually lasted a year, and weddings were often elaborate affairs lasting several days with extravagant feasting and formal processions. Rebekah's mother, in particular, urged a delay. "Let her stay with us a few days. At least ten," she pleaded (see Genesis 24:55).

Understandably, she was in no hurry to lose this dear daughter who had been such a delight and helper in their home. She was determined to keep Rebekah with her as long as possible. But the servant was just as determined to go quickly. Now that he had found the bride of Isaac, he would take no risks that her family might change their minds. Finally, they decided to let Rebekah herself decide the matter. Perhaps her mother expected that Rebekah would want to delay her departure; perhaps they were simply a family that listened to its women. Whatever the reason, Rebekah was given the opportunity to choose for herself how soon she would begin her new life. Without a moment's hesitation, she nodded her head. "I will go," she said (Genesis 24:58).

In a flurry of preparation, all was made ready. Rebekah and her family gave up the elaborate wedding celebration and sent her to marry her older cousin far away in Lahai-roi. The camels were packed with all of Rebekah's things, including her precious new jewels and clothing. Rebekah would have her bridal procession after all, but not in the usual way. It would not include the customary maids and groomsmen lighting lamps to guide the groom, but she would ride the customary camel, and her maids and her nurse would attend her—all the way to Canaan, four hundred miles away. Her family wished her well, calling out, "Thou art our sister, be thou the mother of thousands of millions" (Genesis 24:60). The blessings of the Abrahamic covenant were starting to fall upon Rebekah. As she bade farewell to her family, her heart was already set upon the future. A great adventure was about to begin, and she was just the girl to enjoy it.

ISAAC GREETS HIS BRIDE

Isaac waited impatiently beside the well of Lahai-roi for his father's servant to return. What if Eliezer couldn't find the woman the Lord wanted for him? What if he found her, but she refused to come? What if thieves fell upon the servant and stole the gifts before he was able to find her? Worries beset him, and he paced the ground as he waited. Finally, he went into the fields beside the well to meditate and calm his nerves. As he prayed, he opened his eyes and looked into the distance. Was it his imagination, or did he see something afar off? Was it simply the wind stirring the dust? Or could it be—he thought it was—yes! It was indeed a caravan of camels moving slowly in the direction of his home. Isaac stood and hurried toward the camels.

Rebekah also scanned the horizon. Spying Isaac across the field, she jumped impetuously from her camel and began to run toward him. Then she stopped and turned back to the servant. "Who is that walking in the field to meet us?" she asked, knowing the answer before it came.

When Eliezer confirmed, "It is my master, Isaac," Rebekah's excitement intensified. She looked at her maids and laughed bashfully. Then she modestly reached for her veil and prepared to meet her husband properly, as a daughter of God is taught to do.

"May I take your hand?" Isaac asked shyly as he approached.

Rebekah grinned behind her veil, her eyes lighting up her response. "Oh, yes," she said joyously. "Take my hand. And take my heart too." It had long been her custom to give more than was asked.

REBEKAH COMMUNES WITH THE LORD

Sadly, Sarah had not lived to see the day that her only son was married. But she left for him a dowry of her own—her tent. This would be their honeymoon suite. Weddings were generally elaborate events in the ancient East, full of ceremonial gifting, feasting, and processions. But "betrothals were legally binding,"[6] so the act of crossing the threshold into the wedding tent could be considered a marriage ceremony, once the negotiations had been settled and the agreement between families solemnized. Isaac immediately took Rebekah into his mother's tent and into his heart, "and he loved her" (Genesis 24:67).

As their marriage continued, their love grew. But they were not without sorrow. Like her mother-in-law before her, and many who would follow, Rebekah suffered the grief of childlessness. For twenty long years, she lived with Isaac, working with him and loving him. But they were not blessed with the children that were promised through the Abrahamic covenant. Father Abraham passed away, an old man, without seeing the grandchildren who would fulfill his promise.

With the tender love of a husband who knew the desire of his wife's heart, Isaac petitioned the Lord on his wife's behalf. The record does not say that he asked for a son for himself; it says he "entreated the Lord for his wife" (Genesis 25:21). Finally, Rebekah did conceive and brought Isaac the joyful news, "I am with child."

Of course, Rebekah never did things halfway. She anticipated the dictum that her illustrious descendant, the living Christ, would teach as part of his favorite sermon: If a man "compel thee to go a mile, go with him twain" (Matthew 5:41). Rebekah was not carrying one child; she was carrying two. After twenty years of waiting, Rebekah and Isaac were expecting twins. From their conception, they were active babies; they "struggled together within her" until she "went to inquire of the Lord" (Genesis 25:22) for understanding. The confident and straightforward Rebekah did not hold back or wait for her prophet husband to do all the praying for their family. She set the standard for all women as she prayed directly to God, and she received direct answers to her prayers. In this case, God entrusted her with a revelation, a warning, and a directive: "Two nations are in thy womb, and two manner of people shall be separated from thy bowels; and the one people shall be stronger than the other people; and the elder shall serve the younger" (Genesis 25:23). This second son would be named Jacob, which means "the supplanter."

In a culture where obedience to tradition was tantamount to obedience to God, any suggestion that the elder child should not be the heir to his father's wealth and office was unusual. These two children were therefore destined for conflict. Wouldn't it have been easier and less disruptive for God simply to orchestrate the order of birth so that Jacob would come out first? There was plenty of time; Rebekah would not go into labor for several weeks. But "one of the underlying themes of the Old Testament is that inheritance of the birthright was based more upon the son's worthiness than just birth order,"[7] "for man looketh on the outward appearance, but the Lord looketh on the heart" (1 Samuel 16:7). The Lord treats each person as an individual, regardless of birth order or gender.

Rebekah never questioned the words God spoke to her. As Mary would do many centuries later, Rebekah pondered this message and kept it close to her heart. She used it to guide her, both as a mother to her sons and as a counselor to her husband.

Twins Are Born to Isaac and Rebekah

The midwives might have shouted their joyful surprise when Rebekah delivered a second son that day, but it did not surprise Rebekah. God Himself had told her that she was expecting twins. The first was born with downy red hair covering his body, almost like a coat of fur. Esau was his name, and he would be hirsute throughout his life. Jacob, with his mother's exuberance for life, grabbed onto his brother's heel and rushed out right behind his twin.

The boys were as different in personality as they were in appearance. "Esau was a cunning hunter, a man of the field; and Jacob was a plain man, dwelling in tents. And Isaac loved Esau, because he did eat of his venison, but Rebekah loved Jacob" (Genesis 25:27–28). Rebekah smiled as she watched Isaac and Esau together. Isaac had been reared without siblings or cousins, and he had waited so long to have a son. It warmed her heart to see them bonding as they hunted and played together.

But Rebekah also felt apprehensive about their closeness. The birth of her twin sons ended Rebekah's long years of barrenness, and she was blessed with many more children (Genesis 27:29). But Jacob and Esau, as the two sons of the birthright, were the two Rebekah watched most closely. Esau was the oldest, as well as Isaac's favorite. When the time came, would Isaac's own preference for his eldest son, coupled with cultural tradition, influence his judgment? Would he be able to discern that Jacob was the birthright son? Rebekah watched and waited. She would not interfere unless it became necessary.

Meanwhile, Jacob was a simple young man of different strengths. He enjoyed staying nearer to home. Rebekah surely loved both her sons, but Jacob, who spent so much time near her, became her favorite. Knowing the prophecy that was foretold before his birth, she taught Jacob carefully to understand the responsibilities connected to the covenant of Abraham. She explained to him the importance of choosing his wife carefully from among their kinsmen. She trusted God to protect her son and to guide her as a mother.

One day, Jacob was in the field cooking a "sod pottage," which is a thick stew of vegetables and beans. Across the field, he spied his brother Esau, who had been out hunting for quite some time and was nearly fainting from hunger. The aroma of the stew must have been dizzyingly delicious. As Esau approached, he called out to Jacob, "Feed me with that same red pottage, for I am faint."

Instead of sharing the stew with his hungry brother, Jacob saw the opportunity to test Esau's commitment to the covenant. "First, sell me your birthright," Jacob told Esau. The birthright entailed much more than physical property; it "involved the spiritual leadership of the family and an obligation to act in harmony with the conditions of the covenant" bestowed upon Father Abraham.[8] Would Esau value the birthright enough to protect it when he felt a little hunger?

Esau thought for only a moment. "I am about to die from hunger," he said. "What good is my birthright if I'm dead?"

Jacob took no chance that Esau might later say he had been joking. "Swear to me this day," he said solemnly.

"I swear," Esau replied, and Jacob handed his brother a bowl of stew and a chunk of bread (see Genesis 25:29–34). And as simply as that, Esau had sold his birthright for a mess of pottage. This moment of Esau's weakness demonstrated his own lack of respect for spiritual leadership and provided Jacob the opportunity to establish his superiority. Inheriting the birthright did not mean that Jacob would inherit an easy life, however. With great blessings come great responsibility—and often great sorrow as well. Jacob had set in motion the journey that God had in store for him, but it would not be an easy path to tread.

When Esau had eaten his fill, he rose up and went his way. Perhaps Esau thought Jacob had been teasing. Perhaps Esau truly thought he would have died without a morsel of food. Either way, his willingness to bargain something so precious as his birthright indicates his misplaced values. His next step reinforced it: without consulting his parents, Esau married Judith and Bashemath, two heathen Hittite women from neighboring tribes. His choice would bring grief to Isaac and would nearly break Rebekah's heart. How would these pagan women be able to rear children who would honor the priesthood and practices of the Abrahamic covenant?

REBEKAH LEADS THE WAY

Jacob and Esau continued to live near their parents, working the land and overseeing the flocks, until Isaac had grown old and his eyes had grown dim. He did not want to die before bestowing his blessing upon his oldest son (Genesis 27:2–4), so he called Esau into his tent. "My son, . . . take . . . thy quiver and thy bow, and go out to the field, and take me some venison; and make me savoury meat, such as I love, and bring it to me, that I may eat; that my soul may bless thee before I die," he said (Genesis 27:1, 3–4). Food is often associated with times of celebration and covenant-making; Isaac saw this as a time to commune and celebrate with his son as he bestowed the covenant upon him.

Overhearing this conversation, Rebekah realized that Isaac had not called Jacob to the meeting. Esau alone was to receive a "bless[ing] . . . before the Lord" (Genesis 27:7). Now she knew why she had been given the revelation before her sons' birth. Rebekah loved and respected her husband. Isaac was a man of great faith and obedience. When the Lord had commanded Abraham to sacrifice him as an offering, Isaac had meekly and calmly accepted the near certainty of death by his own father's hand. But time and old age had clouded Isaac's eyes, and now Rebekah feared that it would cloud his mind as well. Rebekah would not instruct her husband in priesthood matters; she could not put words into his mouth. But Rebekah was an *ezer kenegdo,* a woman equal to the task of protecting her husband and rescuing both her sons from paths they were not intended to tread. Perhaps there was a way that she could guide Isaac to speak the words that had been foretold in the revelation she had received regarding her sons.

Rebekah thought carefully. Then she acted with courage and determination. Quickly she called Jacob to her and told him what to do.

"Obey me, Jacob, and do as I say," she urged him. "Bring me two kids from the flock, and I will make a savory dish for your father, the kind that he loves. Then you must take it to your father and say, 'Bless me, father.'"

Jacob was just as obedient to his mother as Isaac had been to Abraham a generation earlier. He did not understand, but he did not argue with her. He did, however, have a concern of his own. "Esau is a hairy man, and I am smooth skinned. If Father touches me, he will know I am not Esau, and he might give me a curse instead of a blessing."

Worried that Esau might return before she had completed her preparations but certain that she was right, Rebekah urged her son to hurry. She felt confident there would be no "cursing" this day. She knew Isaac. He would recognize the correctness of the blessing in the end. "Let the curse be upon me in that case," she said to calm Jacob's fears. "Just go, and fetch the kid from the flocks, and be quick about it!"

That a grown man in ancient Palestine would obey his mother's words says much about the personality of Rebekah. She was a woman of courage and wisdom who commanded respect. Jacob trusted his mother and did as he was told. When he returned with the goat,

Rebekah set the meat to cook while she prepared the rest of her plan. She brought out a set of Esau's clothing for Jacob to wear. The clothing still bore the musky smell of her more active son. Then she made gloves from the skins of the freshly killed goats and put them on Jacob's forearms and neck. Now all was ready. Placing the meat and bread in his hands, she sent Jacob into his father's tent.

At first, Jacob tried to get by without actually lying. "Here I am, Father," he said to the dim-sighted Isaac without using his name. But it would not be that easy.

"Who are you, my son?" Isaac asked.

This was Jacob's moment of no return. He would have to tell the truth or tell a lie. As had so many of his ancestors, he would have to break one commandment to keep another. He chose the latter. "I am Esau, your firstborn," he said. "I did what you asked. Now eat my venison, and then bless me."

Isaac pressed the issue. "How is it that you are back so soon?" he asked.

Now Jacob brought the Lord into the discussion. In this there was a shred of truth, because he could refer implicitly to the revelation that had guided his mother and the food that ultimately the Lord had provided. "The Lord thy God brought it to me," he declared.

But Isaac was still not persuaded. He pressed further. "Come closer so I can feel you and know whether you are truly my son Esau."

So Jacob stepped closer, and Isaac felt the goatskins on his hands and his neck.

Isaac was now perplexed. "It is Jacob's voice, but the hands are the hands of Esau," he said. Isaac started to pronounce the blessing, but then he halted and asked again, "Are you my very son Esau?"

Jacob replied, "I am." It must have been very uncomfortable for this son who had been carefully taught to respect his father to tell this lie. Only the strength of his mother's assurance that this was God's intent could have kept him moving forward with this deception.

Isaac decided to eat the meal first. He thought as he ate. Finally he said, "Come near and kiss me" (as many a good parent in modern times has done who has suspected a beloved teen of drinking).

Jacob came near and kissed his father. Esau's odor clung to his clothing and entered the nostrils of their father. This seems to have convinced Isaac, and, in fact, it was the catalyst for the blessing itself. "The smell of my son is as the smell of a field which the Lord hath blessed," he said, as he began the blessing. "Therefore God give thee of the dew of heaven, and the fatness of the earth, and plenty of corn and wine. Let people serve thee, and nations bow down to thee: be lord over thy brethren, and let thy mother's sons bow down to thee: cursed be every one that curseth thee, and blessed be he that blesseth thee" (Genesis 27:27–29).

ESAU RETURNS FOR HIS BLESSING

Rebekah, surely standing in a corner where she could hear the proceedings, must have breathed a sigh of relief when she heard the blessing pronounced. For scarcely had Isaac closed the blessing than Esau arrived straight from his hunting with a dish of venison for their father. "Come, let's eat," he said cheerfully to his father, "and then you will give me your blessing."

Confused and unable to see clearly, Isaac asked, "Who are you?"

"It is I, Esau, your firstborn son," Esau replied.

When he heard these words, Isaac began to tremble. "Who? Where is the one who brought me venison? I have eaten all, and I have blessed him!"

Isaac knew the power of the priesthood, and he knew the power of words. He also knew he had felt the promptings of the Spirit guiding him to say what the Lord wanted him to say. Decades of experience as a prophet and seer had taught him how that felt. But Isaac had come to the blessing with certain expectations. Like many worthy, righteous fathers, he had planned for a lifetime to give Esau this blessing, and he must have thought often about the words he might say. He naturally expected this particular blessing would go to his firstborn son—who only incidentally was his favorite. When he pronounced the blessing on Jacob's head, Isaac surely listened to the Spirit and said the words that were placed in his mind. But because he *thought* he was blessing Esau, they were not only the words he heard from the Spirit; they were also the words he expected to hear.

Intellect and inspiration combined to convince him that the words were correct. Everything had felt right to him.

But if it hadn't been Esau, what had just happened? Had he given Esau's blessing to Jacob? Or perhaps to someone else? Had a stranger come into his tent? Then a remarkable thing happened. As he trembled with the thought that he might have just made a mistake with eternal consequences, the Spirit confirmed to Isaac with a jolt almost like electricity that the blessing he had given to Jacob had been right. "Yea, and he shall be blessed" (Genesis 27:33), Isaac declared solemnly, surprised by how forcefully he knew this to be true. His physical eyes had weakened, but his spiritual eyes had seen clearly after all. In that moment, the Spirit confirmed to him that he had *not* made a mistake. Rebekah's quick thinking had helped him give the right blessing to the right son after all.

The correctness of the blessing upon Jacob and the mantle of the prophet that went with it are confirmed in the words of two other blessings. Isaac's own pronouncements echoed the words that had been given to Rebekah all those years before: "Two nations are in thy womb, and two manner of people shall be separated from thy bowels; and the one people shall be stronger than the other people; and the elder shall serve the younger" (Genesis 25:23).

Those words would be reiterated to Jacob himself in a profound way just a few weeks later, in the wilderness outside the city of Haran. There, Jacob would receive the dream of a ladder reaching to heaven with angels ascending and descending it. The Lord would appear in this dream and confirm the blessings of Abraham upon Jacob and his posterity:

"I am the Lord God of Abraham thy father, and the God of Isaac: the land whereon thou liest, to thee will I give it, and to thy seed; and thy seed shall be as the dust of the earth, . . . and in thy seed shall all the families of the earth be blessed. . . . Behold, I am with thee, and will keep thee in all places whither thou goest, and will bring thee again into this land; for I will not leave thee, until I have done that which I have spoken to thee of" (Genesis 28:13–15).

Was Rebekah's intricate plot necessary? Bible readers through the centuries have pondered this question. Isaac was a prophet of God who had demonstrated profound faith and obedience when his father, Abraham, was instructed to offer him as a human sacrifice. Isaac himself carried the wood and patiently waited as his father lifted the sacrificial knife. Wouldn't a man of his spiritual stature have been able to discern the voice of the Spirit and pronounce the proper blessing upon his sons? We can never know with certainty the answer to that question. But Rebekah knew Isaac better than anyone else, and she felt the urgency to intervene. Isaac had grown old and his eyes had dimmed. Perhaps he had developed senility by this time, and Rebekah felt impressed to help and protect him. She was an *ezer* by birth, after all. Certainly the words of the blessing and its similarity to the revelations given to Rebekah and to Jacob confirm that the word of the Lord had been spoken in the tent that day.

Tikva Frymer-Kensky offers this important insight:

"The biblical world valued cunning in the underdog. Only the powerful value honesty at all costs. The powerless know that trickery may save their lives. Early interpreters, both Jewish and Christian, praised Rivka [Rebekah], as did medieval and reformation writers. The censure did not begin until the end of the nineteenth century, when male biblical scholars began to condemn her as a Lady Macbeth. The pendulum is beginning to swing again as we learn more about how the disadvantaged make their way in the world and how women negotiate through the patriarchy. To some contemporary eyes, the ingenuity and cunning of Rivka's plan is itself a mark of divine guidance and her role as divine helper."[9]

Two Sons Rescued by Jacob's Blessing

Significantly, Esau would also experience a beneficial change as a result of this blessing that went to his younger brother instead of to himself. As Rebekah turned her attention to her older son, she would work to soften his heart. Using her feminine influence, she would gently nurture and guide him to make better choices. Eventually Esau would acknowledge that he had been a disappointment to both his parents, especially in the choices he had made in marrying the Hittite women. Isaac loved Esau, but he was not always pleased with him. Before long, Esau would go to his father's brother, Ishmael, and ask for a wife. His uncle Ishmael had been reared by a prophet, the patriarch Abraham himself, and he seems to have taught his daughters to honor the covenant. Through this wise choice, Esau would find his own intended path and become the man God wanted him to be.

Rebekah's long-ago penchant for going the second mile was present this day in that her sons were doubly blessed. Jacob would become the next prophet, but Esau became a better man because of what occurred in his father's tent that day. This would be made abundantly clear in the way that Esau would welcome Jacob and his families with tears of joy when they returned to Canaan decades later.

Rebekah's story stands as a testament to the power of prayer and its availability to all people, not only to prophets and patriarchs. Eliezer, a Damascan, prayed to the God of his master Abraham, and Rebekah fulfilled the words of his prayer in precisely the way it was uttered. Rebekah prayed for wisdom regarding her children and received the spiritual guidance and reassurance promised to all mothers. Isaac prayed as a prophet and a patriarch and uttered the same ideas that were spoken to Rebekah all those years before. The true power of prayer resides in listening to the Spirit and accepting the words God puts into one's mind and one's mouth. Prayer is more about listening and feeling than it is about speaking and asking.

ESAU REACTS TO HIS BROTHER'S BLESSING

If we could see down the vista of time to our journey's end, life and its choices would be much simpler. But Isaac and Esau could not see into this future, and for now, Esau was devastated. So was Isaac. His father's heart was broken. Esau was his favorite and eldest son. His plan had always been for Esau to succeed him, despite Esau's weakness of spirit and his poor choice in wives. As Esau realized what had happened, he cried out bitterly, "Bless me also, my father!" And Isaac cried with him.

Then Isaac told Esau what had happened. "Thy brother came with subtilty, and hath taken away thy blessing," he said (Genesis 27:35). Apparently Isaac was not ready to share with Esau the spiritual confirmation he had just received. Perhaps he feared that Esau would have reacted with scorn to such spiritual revelation.

Now, in his anger, Esau confessed what had happened in the field so long ago. "His name is Jacob indeed, for he has supplanted me twice—first when he took away my birthright, and now he has taken away my blessing as well."

Then the enormity of it all fell upon Esau, and he pleaded with his father. "Have you only one blessing? Oh, bless me too, my father—bless me too!" he begged and wept bitterly.

Isaac reached his hands gently toward his favorite son's head. He bowed his own head humbly and asked the Spirit for permission. Then he uttered the words that came into his mind and prophesied, "Behold, thy dwelling shall be the fatness of the earth, and of the dew of heaven from above; [but] by thy sword shalt thou live, and shalt serve thy brother; and it shall come to pass when thou shalt have the dominion, that thou shalt break his yoke from off thy neck" (Genesis 27:39–40).

This would be a bitter blessing in the short run for Esau, but later generations would reap the fatness of the earth. The land of his inheritance sat atop the world's largest reserves of oil, the future "black gold." Meanwhile, Jacob's descendants, the Israelites, would wander forty years in the wilderness and end up in the only part of the Middle East that does not have oil. For now, however, Esau seethed with bitterness. He hated his brother Jacob (see Genesis 27:41). He made a plan of his own: as soon as Isaac was buried, Esau would murder his brother.

Rebekah Gives Up Her Son to Protect Him

Rebekah soon heard of Esau's vow to kill his brother. Mother Eve had not been able to protect her two sons, Cain and Abel, from such a dark deed, but Rebekah would. Desperate to protect them both from such a catastrophe, she urged Jacob to flee to her hometown to live with her brother Laban until Esau calmed down. It had been decades since the impetuous young Rebekah had watered the camels and fulfilled a prophecy in answer to Eliezer's humble prayer. Now she felt the weight of a family divided. Her two sons were at war with each other, largely because she had initiated a plot that seemed to defraud one in favor of the other. She knew that God's will had been done, in the end. She knew that Jacob was the intended leader of their family. But it was a truth that brought her little gladness.

Just as she had left home all those years ago, never to return, now her son Jacob would have to travel the same distance away from her. They promised each other the separation would be temporary, just until Esau's fury abated. But in her heart, she knew that she might never see her Jacob again. To protect both her sons, she must give one up. And she must do it in a way that would restore the balance between herself and her aging husband, Isaac. She loved and respected this good man. She would not usurp his position in the family, and now she acted gently to restore it. Going to her husband's tent, she asked for his counsel and advice. "I am worried to death because of the daughters of Heth. We can't let Jacob take one of them for a wife. What shall we do?" (see Genesis 27:46).

Isaac thought for a moment, and then sent for Jacob. "You must not take a wife from among the daughters of Canaan," he said. "Go to the home of Bethuel, your mother's father, and find a wife from among the daughters of your mother's brother, Laban." Any anger that had arisen from the deception Jacob and Rebekah had employed seemed to have dissolved. He continued, "May God Almighty bless you and make you fruitful, and multiply you, that you will become a multitude of people. May He give the blessing of Abraham to you and your children, so that you may inherit the land in which you are a stranger" (see Genesis 28:3–4). In this blessing Isaac confirmed the blessing bestowed the day before, but it also confirmed what Rebekah had dreaded: This would not be a separation of a few months until Esau calmed down. Jacob was leaving to start a new life in the land of Rebekah's birth.

Rebekah turned away with a heart full of sorrow. She knew what could restore her cheerful spirit; she had to do more than was asked of her. She needed to give more than her son, of her own will and choice. A sudden, powerful thought came into her mind, reinforcing the attitude that had guided her footsteps all of her life: "If a man will . . . take away thy coat, let him have thy cloak also." Rebekah had more than a cloak. Hurrying to her tent, she gathered her best jewels and scarves. She would send those with Jacob to give to their cousins back home. Being a cheerful giver had always gladdened her heart.

But at this moment, when her mother's heart was breaking, Rebekah could find little to comfort her, even in that.

REBEKAH'S STORY FORESHADOWS THE MISSION OF JESUS CHRIST

James Neil, author of *Everyday Life in the Holy Land*, suggests a "glorious allegory" to be learned from the marriage of Isaac to Rebekah. He writes:

"Surely the courting and wedding of 'the heir of promise' is a glorious allegory. Eliezer, the trustee and dispenser of Abraham's wealth and his trusted messenger, type of the Holy Spirit, is sent forth by the father to find and bring home a bride for his once slain and now risen son; for such virtually was Isaac, whom it is said Abraham 'offered up.' . . . The rejoicing of Isaac over his fair young bride, resplendent in the 'jewels of gold and raiment' that he had provided for her through Eliezer's gifts, is but a faint image of the rejoicing of the Heavenly Bridegroom over His mystic bride, 'the Church of the Firstborn,' endowed with immortal youth and beauty, for this adopted daughter of the King Eternal is 'all glorious within,' that is, 'beneath her veil,' for 'her clothing is gold embroidery'—even the glorious mantle He has given her, the robe of His own perfect righteousness"[10] (Hebrews 11:17–19; Psalm 45:14).

The Bible abounds with allegories that point toward the mission of the Messiah. For example, in the preceding chapter about Sarah we saw a "type," or symbol, of the Crucifixion within the story of Abraham's willingness to sacrifice his beloved son Isaac. In that allegory, Abraham represents God, Isaac represents Christ, and the angel who arrives to stop the raised hand of Abraham is the Holy Ghost (see Genesis 22).

John W. Welch discovered a similar allegory of the Savior's mission in the parable of the good Samaritan. In this story a man "went down from Jerusalem to Jericho, and fell among thieves" (Luke 10:30). A priest and a Levite passed by the wounded man "on the other side," indicating allegorically that the man could not be saved by the church or the law. Only the Samaritan "had compassion on him, and went to him, and bound up his wounds, pouring in oil and wine, and . . . brought him to an inn, and took care of him" (Luke 10:32–34). Before leaving, the Samaritan gave the innkeeper "two pence" and said, "Whatsoever thou spendest more, when I come again, I will repay thee" (Luke 10:35). It is a powerful story inspiring readers to develop compassion and offer service to strangers. But it is also a powerful allegory. As Welch explains, Jerusalem represents heaven, Jericho represents the world, the thieves represent worldly corruption, and the man represents each of us. The oil used to soothe the wounds is a symbol of Christ's priesthood, and the purifying wine is a symbol of His atoning blood. A penny was the price of a day's labor at that time, so the "two pence" represent Christ's time in the tomb, while the Samaritan's promise to repay "whatsoever thou spendest more" represents His infinite Atonement (see Luke 10:32–35). Nestled within these eight verses about the selfless Samaritan we find the entire plan of salvation.[11]

I have found a similar allegory of Christ's mission in the short letter Paul wrote to Philemon from his prison cell in Rome. In it, Paul beseeches Philemon to "receive . . . for ever" the runaway servant Onesimus, using the unexpected phrase, "for love's sake." Onesimus had gone to Rome (like Jericho, a symbol of the world), where he met Paul and was converted from a man "in times past . . . unprofitable, but now profitable" to Philemon. Paul asks Philemon to receive Onesimus not as a slave but as "a brother beloved" and promises, "If he hath wronged thee, put that on mine account; . . . I will repay it." In this surprising allegory, Onesimus represents each of us "departed for a season" from the love of God but redeemed by the infinite Atonement of the Savior. Philemon, whose name means "love," represents God in this story, for all of us are His servants, "in times past unprofitable," but made profitable through the saving grace of Jesus Christ. And, like the Samaritan, Paul is the Christ figure in this story, pleading the case of a sinner and offering to pay his debts in full. Once again, we find the entire plan of salvation hidden within a small Epistle that is often overlooked or misunderstood.

Similarly, as James Neil points out so eloquently, the story of Rebekah is an allegory of the day when the Messiah will return in all His glory to redeem the world. Eliezer, whose name suggests that he was not an ordinary servant but an *ezer,* or "godly helper," is also more than a messenger sent to Haran by Abraham to find a righteous bride for Isaac; he represents the Holy Ghost sent to the earth by God the Father to seek out the righteous "bride of Christ"—the members of His Church. Isaac represents the resurrected Messiah, and Rebekah represents each of us—clothed, as we can be, in "the glorious mantle He has given her, the robe of His own perfect righteousness."[12]

Scattered throughout the scriptures, these allegories resonate deeply within us, subtly reminding us of the mission of the Messiah "to bring [His] ransomed people home."[13]

NOTES

1. Tikva Frymer-Kensky, *Reading the Women of the Bible* (New York: Schocken, 2002), 9.

2. Milcah, too, was a grandmother of Jesus, but almost nothing is known of her. Abram, Nahor, and Haran were the sons of Terah, who came from Ur of the Chaldees, in what is now Iraq. Lot, Milcah, and Sarai were siblings, the son and daughters of Haran (Genesis 11:29). Milcah married Haran's brother Nahor. As they traveled toward Canaan, they stopped in a land called Haran, where Terah lived to a grand old age. Abram, Sarai, and Lot continued onward, eventually settling in the plain of Jordan. But Nahor and Milcah stayed behind with Terah, in this town where Abraham's servant would eventually be guided to search for an appropriate wife for Isaac. Milcah, an unsung and virtually unknown grandmother of Jesus, had quietly and righteously raised a son who would raise a daughter destined to marry the future prophet Isaac. The servant of Abraham could hardly contain his joy.

3. James Neil, *Everyday Life in the Holy Land* (London: Cassel and Co., 1913), 225.

4. Donna B. Nielsen, *Beloved Bridegroom* (Salt Lake City: Onyx Press, 1999), 20.

5. Frymer-Kensky, *Reading the Women of the Bible*, 243.

6. Carolyn Custis James, *Lost Women of the Bible: Finding Strength and Significance through Their Stories* (Grand Rapids, MI: Zondervan, 2005), 165.

7. Brent L. Top, *A Peculiar Treasure: Old Testament Messages for Our Day* (Salt Lake City: Deseret Book, 1997), 14.

8. Ibid.

9. Frymer-Kensky, *Reading the Women of the Bible*, 19.

10. Neil, *Everyday Life in the Holy Land*, 259–60.

11. John W. Welch, "The Good Samaritan: Forgotten Symbols," *Ensign,* February 2007.

12. Neil, *Everyday Life in the Holy Land*, 260.

13. Parley P. Pratt, "The Morning Breaks," in *Hymns of the Church of Jesus Christ of Latter-day Saints* (Salt Lake City: Church of Jesus Christ of Latter-day Saints, 1985), no. 1.

LEAH GATHERS HER CHICKS

"O Jerusalem, Jerusalem, . . . how often would
I have gathered thy children together, even as
a hen gathereth her chickens under her wings,
and ye would not!" (Matthew 23:37).

*L*EAH ADJUSTED HER clothing once more as she waited anxiously for the groom to enter her tent. Covered head to toe in the veils of a bride, and silent throughout the wedding festivities as a bride was expected to be, she had managed so far to keep her secret. In the dim lamplight, he would not see the truth. For one precious night, she would hear the words of love and affection from a man besotted by his bride. For one magical night, she would know how it felt to be caressed and adored. She would be able to keep her secret only until morning. And by that time, it would be too late for Jacob to back out. Having crossed the threshold into her tent and spent the night with her, Jacob would indeed be married to Leah.

JACOB CHOOSES HIS BRIDE

Jacob paused before entering the tent of his new bride and reflected on how he had arrived at this point. After fleeing for his life from his brother Esau's murderous threats, he had slowed his pace as he neared the city of Haran. This was his mother Rebekah's homeland. He wondered if the residents would remember her, the impetuous young girl who had left all those years ago with Eliezer, the servant of his grandfather Abraham. He wondered whether his mother's relatives still lived in this town, or whether they were even living at all. All his life, he had heard his parents tell the story of Eliezer praying for a sign to help him find the appropriate bride for Isaac, and of Rebekah, the girl who had watered his camels. As he approached the city, Jacob saw a well with three flocks of sheep grazing nearby. Could this be the well where his mother had met her destiny? It was early in the day for watering, but a crowd of men had gathered around the well. Jacob asked if any of them knew the family of Laban, the son of Nahor. As if on cue, a beautiful young girl suddenly came into sight. "Here comes his daughter now," the men told him.

Jacob could scarcely believe his eyes. He had not yet entered the city, and here was a member of his family. And not just any member, but a beautiful maiden. Jacob did something as impetuous as his mother had done all those years ago when she slipped from the camel and ran to Isaac's arms. Though it was a woman's work to draw water, Jacob rolled the stone from off the well and watered the flock for Rachel. Then, with his heart brimming with emotion, he kissed her cheek and stammered, "I am your father's brother. Well, not exactly his brother. I am his sister Rebekah's son. We are cousins, you and I. First cousins. Hurry—go and tell your father I have come!" (see Genesis 29:10–12).

Rachel turned and ran to her father's house. The years had been kind to Laban, and he was still strong of mind and body. Jacob caught his uncle in an embrace. They clung to each other, wept, and kissed each other on the cheek. Clasping their forearms, Laban held his nephew so that he could gaze upon his face. He could see a hint of Rebekah in Jacob's eyes. "You are my flesh and my bone," he said happily to Jacob, and he welcomed Jacob into his household as he had welcomed the servant Eliezer all those years before.

As the days grew into weeks, Jacob could not keep his eyes off of Rachel. She was so beautiful and desirable, even for a girl so young. Her older sister, Leah, was cow-faced and weak-eyed, but Rachel was everything Jacob desired in a wife. He loved her.

Laban was a shrewd businessman. He saw how Jacob looked at Rachel. It was highly unusual for a man in this culture to choose his own bride, or even to see her face before the wedding night.[1] But many things about this marriage would be unusual. Matchmaking was usually initiated by the women in a groom's family asking for a drink at the door of the bride's home, but Jacob himself had begun the negotiations when he offered the symbolic drink of water to Rachel at the well. Laban continued the negotiations by seeming to offer Jacob a job. "What should be your wages?" he asked, knowing that Jacob wanted his daughter.

Jacob had no money with him for a bride price, having left his home in haste and fearing for his life, so he had only his own labor to offer as a dowry. Without hesitation, Jacob declared, "I will work seven years for Rachel." Seven years' labor was a steep dowry, but Rachel was a rare jewel. Jacob wanted everyone to know how he valued her. Rachel blushed with pleasure. She loved Jacob too.

If the tale of Isaac and Rebekah is the most romantic love story in the Bible, the story of Jacob and Rachel comes a close second. Jacob seems to have fallen for Rachel the same way his father fell for Rebekah—at first sight. In both cases, the record says simply and unequivocally, "he loved her" (see Genesis 24:67; 29:18). And yet, as with Isaac and Rebekah, Jacob and Rachel would know tremendous heartache, including the sorrows of separation, barrenness, and early death. Finding true love does not necessarily lead to living happily ever after.

None of those future woes were on Jacob's mind as his wedding day approached, however. For seven long years, he had worked and waited. Finally, the day arrived. Full of joy and laughter, he anticipated the moment when he would greet his bride and take her into the tent where they would begin their life together. In a formal wedding ceremony, friends and family formed a procession and lighted the way of the bridegroom. In future centuries, the groom would ride a white horse in the procession to the bride's tent, led by a "mock bridegroom" played by "a very little boy, dressed as a counterpart of the bridegroom, who follow[ed] him about like his shadow, . . . imitating his every movement."[2] Little did Jacob know that a "mock bride" awaited him inside the tent of his beloved Rachel.

LEAH'S STORY

But this is not Jacob's story. Nor is it Rachel's. This is the story of Leah, whose son Judah would become the ancestor of Jesus Christ. For it is Leah, not Rachel, who was destined to become a matriarch of the Messiah. Leah was the oldest daughter. The oldest and the *unmarried* daughter. It had been hard for her to see how much more favored Rachel was. Rachel, with her almond eyes, her perfect nose and teeth, her lips like a ripe fig, her slender waist, and shapely hips. Rachel was the beautiful one, and now she was betrothed—before Leah. It was so unfair to be the ugly one, the one whose very name meant "wild cow."

For seven long years, Leah had watched. So had her father. No matchmakers had come to ask for water at Leah's door. It was humiliating to them both to think that the younger sister would be married before the eldest (Genesis 29:26). As the day approached for Rachel's marriage, Laban devised a plan that would simultaneously rescue Leah's reputation, line Laban's purse, and, in a twist of poetic justice, repay Jacob for the trick he had played on his older brother Esau to receive the birthright blessing from Father Isaac.

We will never know Rachel's part in the plot. Did her father and sister convince her that this was the right thing to do? Or was she locked away in another room, Cinderella-like, while Leah tried on the slipper intended for Rachel? Did God Himself comfort Rachel as her beloved Jacob went into the tent with Leah? The record is silent. And what might Leah have been thinking? Did she love Jacob? Did she think that she could make him love her? Was she spiteful toward her pretty, younger sister? Or was she simply obedient to her father? We do not know. What we do know is that Jacob felt betrayed. In anger he went to his father-in-law. "What have you done to me?" he demanded. "Didn't I serve you seven years for Rachel? And now you have tricked me" (see Genesis 29:25). One can't help but wonder whether these words pricked Jacob's conscience for how he had deceived his own father. In a turn of poetic justice, he had been defrauded in the same way—with false clothing and a celebratory feast. Jesus Himself might have reminded Jacob gently, "With what measure you mete, it shall be measured to you again" (Matthew 7:2).

Laban acknowledged his duplicity and expressed tenderness for his oldest daughter. "Give her the honeymoon week that is her due," he requested of Jacob. "Then you may marry Rachel. But you must agree to work for her another seven years" (Genesis 29:27). Jacob paid seven years' labor for Leah, and then another seven years' labor for Rachel. In this way, Laban established that both his daughters were of equal value; he wasn't just getting a liability off his hands. Laban also secured a productive and hardworking overseer for his cattle. He was indeed a shrewd businessman, as well as a concerned father.

Leah enjoyed just seven days of being the only wife. Rachel and Jacob were married the following week, and Jacob went back to serving seven years for his beloved bride. Marriage was far from blissful for either wife, however. Sibling rivalry would run deep between these two sisters. Whether it existed before their marriages is not known, but it certainly intensified in their adulthood. Jacob loved Rachel best, and he did not hide his resentment toward Leah. In fact, the scripture states that Jacob "loved also Rachel more than Leah, and . . . the Lord saw that Leah was hated" (Genesis 29:30–31). What sad words to read about a sister and a wife.

Jacob loved Leah in the physical sense—that is, he had sexual relations with her—but he did not love her emotionally. He felt understandably betrayed. It's not hard to imagine Leah's sadness and her shame as she saw the relationship between her husband and her younger sister blossom in a rose of love while her own relationship withered to a night bloom. She had made Jacob marry her, but she could not make him love her. God Himself felt "sympathy for Leah because of her humiliating position as the unloved wife"[3] (see Genesis 29:31), so He blessed her in the one way that gave a Hebrew woman status: He gave her children—not just children, but sons. Rachel would continue to be the favorite wife, but Leah would balance that favoritism with the status of motherhood. In short order, she produced Reuben, Simeon, Levi, and Judah.

Meanwhile, frustrated and envious of her sister's fruitfulness, Rachel complained to Jacob. "Give me children, or else I die," she cried (Genesis 30:1). Unlike his father Isaac, however, Jacob did not entreat the Lord on his wife's behalf. Instead, he responded to her tears with "anger," asking, "Am I in God's stead, who hath withheld from thee the fruit of the womb?" (Genesis 30:2). Finally, Rachel devised a plan similar to Sarah's: she would invoke the practice of surrogacy by using her handmaiden to bear children on her behalf. "Behold my maid Bilhah," she said to Jacob. "Go in unto her; and she shall bear upon my knees, that I may also have children by her" (Genesis 30:3). The plan worked. Jacob took Bilhah as his wife, and they produced two sons, Dan and Naphtali. When delivery time arrived, Bilhah leaned against Rachel so that the baby symbolically issued from Rachel as well as from Bilhah, and the two women were united in motherhood of the boys. The name Rachel selected for Bilhah's second son, Naphtali ("good fortune"), indicates the continuing rivalry between Rachel and Leah because, she said, "with great wrestlings have I wrestled with my sister, and I have prevailed" (Genesis 30:8).

This episode of wrestling and prevailing foreshadowed the experience Jacob would have a few years later, when he "wrestled a man [angel] with him until the breaking of the day. . . . And [the angel] said, Let me go, for the day breaketh. And [Jacob] said, I will not let thee go, except thou bless me" (Genesis 32:24, 26). There God would change Jacob's name to Israel, "for as a prince hast thou power with God and with men, and hast prevailed. . . . And Jacob called the name of the place Peniel: for I have seen God face to face, and my life is preserved" (Genesis 32:28, 30). A life with God requires some wrestlings! For now, the struggle was with Jacob's wives.

By this time, Leah had ceased childbearing, either because of menopause or perhaps because Jacob had simply stopped coming into her tent. Nevertheless, her competitiveness with Rachel had only just begun. "Take my maid Zilpah too," she told Jacob, when she saw that the plan had worked for Rachel. So Jacob took Zilpah as his fourth wife, and she bore Gad and Asher as a surrogate for Leah.

The rivalry between Rachel and Leah intensified and soon "degenerat[ed] into a kind of fertility competition."[4] Leah wanted more children of her own. One day, when her son Reuben was out in the field, he found some mandrakes, an herb that was thought to have powers as a fertility aid. But as he was bringing them to his mother, Leah, Rachel intervened, begging, "Please, let me have some of your son's mandrakes, so that I can have children of my own."

Leah was disheartened by the request. She was the first wife, but Jacob had not come to her tent for a long time. "You've already taken my husband," she said, "and now you want my son's mandrakes as well—the mandrakes he picked for me?" (see Genesis 30:14–15).

Believing that Leah was now barren, Rachel negotiated with her sister, just as her husband had once negotiated his brother Esau's birthright in exchange for a bowl of lentil stew. "I will send Jacob to your tent tonight if you will give me the mandrakes," she suggested, thinking there was no chance of Leah becoming pregnant again.

But as Sarah had discovered long before, nothing is too hard for the Lord, especially opening a womb. The deal was struck, and a happy Leah met Jacob as he was coming in from the fields to divert him into her tent. That night, the Lord heard Leah's pleas, and he granted her another son, Issachar, who was followed by Zebulun and then by the only named daughter, Dinah. Leah was happy. "Now will my husband dwell with me," she exulted in naming Zebulun, "because I have born him six sons" (Genesis 30:20). But she was wrong. Jacob still loved Rachel best.

Meanwhile, Rachel endured heartaches of her own. All these years, Rachel had been the favorite wife, but not the favored wife. Like so many of the ancestors of Jesus Christ, she had been barren through the early years of her marriage. Then finally, after ten sons and untold daughters had been born to Jacob through his other wives, God heeded the desire of Rachel's heart as well, and she bore a son whom she named Joseph, which means "Jehovah increases." Surely she was ecstatic, and Jacob was too. They coddled this much-wanted baby and showered him with affection. With the birth of Joseph, the balance between Leah and Rachel tipped even further as the son of his most beloved wife soon became Jacob's favorite. It may have been an unconscious favoritism on his part; perhaps Leah's betrayal clouded his feelings toward her children. But he would pay the price for that favoritism in the unwise actions of his less-favored children.

Jacob was a great prophet and leader, but he was not always an attentive father and husband. The gift of agency is not denied to prophets; they too have the opportunity to learn and grow through experience. In fact, Jacob's own childhood had been marred by envy and competitiveness. His father, the prophet Isaac, had favored the older son Esau (see Genesis 25:28), who then threatened to kill his brother after the birthright blessing was given to Jacob. Some scholars suggest that Jacob may have had "little interest in having children and little knowledge about how to rear them."[5] Even when his beloved Rachel was distraught over her inability to have children, Jacob responded with little compassion, saying, "Am I in God's stead, who hath withheld from thee the fruit of the womb?" (Genesis 30:2).

Despite siring a numerous posterity in short order, Jacob seems to be "a man who stands apart from family life, involved with himself and preoccupied with his own destiny."[6] As is true of many men, Jacob was so busy providing for his growing family and functioning in his role as a tribal leader that he might not have noticed the day-to-day needs of his children. But Jacob did not bear this responsibility alone. In those days, mothers were largely responsible for the early training and care of their children. The age of twelve was "a pivotal year in the life of a young Jewish boy as he transitioned into manhood, moving from the care of his mother to the tutelage of his father."[7]

The sisters' own rivalry must have contributed significantly to the intense rivalry among their children as well. Eventually, the sons of Leah, Bilhah, and Zilpah would conspire to sell Rachel's son Joseph into slavery, because they envied the beautiful multi-colored coat their father would give to Joseph and resented Joseph's prophetic dreams about ruling over them (Genesis 37). Parenting is the most important work we do, but it is also the most difficult, even for prophets and their wives.

JACOB CALLS A FAMILY COUNCIL AND RESTORES PEACE BETWEEN HIS WIVES

More than twenty years had passed since Jacob ran away from home, fearing for his life. He had worked fourteen years for his two wives, and his family had grown to include two more wives and at least eleven sons and one daughter. His skills in animal husbandry also grew. Through Jacob's wise management, the flocks of his father-in-law had expanded, and, through a cunning breeding strategy, Jacob's own share of the flocks had grown even more. Laban began to feel suspicious and resentful toward his son-in-law, and Jacob noticed that "the countenance of Laban . . . was not toward him as before" (Genesis 31:2). Over the years, Laban had become greedier and less righteous. He had dealt underhandedly with Jacob, changing his wages ten times in an attempt to keep more of the income for himself (see Genesis 31:7). Moreover, Laban had lost interest in the God of his fathers. In speaking to Jacob, he made a distinction between "the God of your fathers" and his own household "gods" (Genesis 31:29–30). Laban had been seduced by the pagan religions of the area and had started keeping idols in his home. Even Rachel was tempted by the local gods and customs (Genesis 31:19–35), possibly as a bid for continued fertility. Jacob was concerned by how all this would affect his family. It was time to take his wives, his children, his flocks, and his wealth back to the land of Canaan and his father, Isaac.

But what about Laban? Would he allow them to go peacefully? After praying to the Lord about the decision, Jacob wisely brought his wives together in a family council to discuss it. He told them, "Your father is no longer on my side. I've seen a change in him. He has deceived me and shortchanged me on numerous occasions. Nevertheless, I have prospered as God has strengthened my herds and weakened your father's herds. This makes him even more antagonistic toward me. God spoke to me in a dream and told me we should return to the land of my family" (see Genesis 31:4–13).

Significantly, Jacob did not simply make the decision as the head of the household and tell his wives what they were going to do. Even though God Himself had spoken to Jacob in a dream and told him to go home to Canaan, Jacob still counseled with his wives and asked for their confirming assent. This was an important step. Family members are more inclined to accept difficult paths when they have been included in the decision-making. Choice is an essential part of God's plan, and it should have an essential place in every home.

Moreover, the incident seems to have had a healing effect on the two sisters. After listening to their husband, Rachel and Leah discussed the issue, and both of them agreed. "Whatever God has told you to do, that is what we will do," they said (see Genesis 31:4–16). Though they had experienced intense rivalry and competition throughout the years of their marriages to Jacob, they became united in sisterly harmony as they prepared to leave the only home they had ever known.

Leah in particular experienced a change of heart. Rather than allow bitterness to canker her soul, she focused on nurturing her relationship with God. This subtle change in her character can be seen in the naming of her children. Leah's sorrow was revealed in the words she spoke after her firstborn, Reuben, was born, when she said with sad hope, "Surely the Lord hath looked upon my affliction; now therefore my husband will love me." After Simeon's birth she said, "Because the Lord hath heard that I was hated, he hath therefore given me this son also," pitifully hoping that bearing him sons would cause Jacob to love her. Again, after Levi was born, she said hopefully, "Now this time will my husband be joined unto me, because I have born him three sons."

Finally, Leah seems to have turned to God for comfort and strength, and she found both. After Judah's birth, she said, "Now will I praise the Lord" (Genesis 29:32–34), and her attitude began to change. When her handmaiden's sons, Gad and Asher, were born, she said, "Happy am I, for the daughters will call me blessed" (Genesis 30:13). When her final sons, Issachar and Zebulon were born, she acknowledged the goodness of her blessings. "God hath given me my hire," she said. "God hath endued me with a good dowry" (Genesis 30:18, 20). The name of her daughter Dinah, which means "justice," indicates that Leah felt that God had dealt justly with her after all. As Leah drew closer to the Lord, she felt Him drawing closer to her, and she gained comfort and strength from the relationship.

Now, as Leah and Rachel prepared to leave their childhood home, they began to feel the bond of sisterhood again. They would "remain together, members of the same household, competing but also bargaining, negotiating, cajoling, and ultimately cooperating with each other"[8] as they moved forward in the journey. Their ultimate legacy would be a reputation for unity and forgiveness, not vengeance and rivalry. In fact, the well-wishers at Ruth's wedding to Boaz would call out, "The Lord make the woman that is come into thine house like Rachel and like Leah, which two did build the house of Israel" (Ruth 4:11). In time, these once rivalrous sisters would become united through motherhood, and their sons, too, would find the healing balm of compassion and understanding for each other (see Genesis 42–45).

Leah Suffers the Ultimate Humiliation

At this point, Jacob was still conflicted, however. He was anxious to see his father again, and he knew that God had instructed him to return. Still, he was nervous. How would his brother Esau react? Did Esau still harbor murder in his heart for the way Jacob had taken his birthright? As they neared Canaan, Jacob did what he could to soften his brother's reception. First, he sent messengers to Esau, asking for grace and calling himself "your servant." When he heard that Esau was heading their way with four hundred men, however, Jacob was afraid. He divided his herds and property into two parts and sent his servants in different directions with them, planning that if Esau went after one, Jacob would still have the other. He prayed earnestly for protection. "You promised that my posterity would be as the sands of the sea," he reminded the Lord, referring to the Abrahamic covenant. That promise could not be fulfilled if Jacob's posterity was massacred, he reasoned. Next, he prepared gifts for Esau that included hundreds of goats, sheep, camels, cows, and donkeys. Surely Esau's heart would be softened by so much unexpected wealth (see Genesis 32:1–18). Still there was no response from Esau.

Finally, the moment came when Jacob would have to face Esau and his men. There was no more buffering wealth between them. This was to become the moment of Leah's most humiliating shame, the moment when her rivalry with Rachel rose to its zenith—or more accurately, fell to its nadir. For despite the growing closeness of the two sisters, Jacob still favored his beloved Rachel and would put her safety above all others. As Jacob saw the dust of his brother's four hundred men in the distance, he feared for the lives of those he loved most. He put his concubines, Zilpah and Bilhah, in front with their children. Next, he pushed Leah and her children—her six fine sons and her daughters—into the line of expected slaughter. Rachel and Joseph, Jacob's most beloved wife and son, were kept in the rear where he could protect them until the end (Genesis 33:2).

So that was where Leah found herself in Jacob's eyes: still second place to the wife and child whom he loved more than he loved her. It must have been a moment of intense sorrow as they prepared for the onset of the battle. Leah gathered her little ones toward her to protect them from the onslaught. Even Jacob bowed himself to the ground in one last expression of humility and servitude as he approached his brother. Then he steeled himself for battle (Genesis 33:3).

But the battle never came. Just as it is considered polite in our day to stand in one's doorway until one's visitors are out of sight, it was considered good manners in Canaan to create a procession to greet honored guests. Esau's four hundred men were not warriors after all, but rather a welcoming procession. In one of the most tender moments in all of scripture, "Esau ran to meet [Jacob], and embraced him, and fell on his neck, and kissed him: and they wept" (Genesis 33:4). Esau had truly changed during Jacob's absence. The bitterness was gone. He had married a daughter of Ishmael who had been born and taught under the covenant of Abraham. Ishmael, the "wild" son whose future had filled Abraham with concern and caused him to plead with God, "O that Ishmael might live before thee" (Genesis 17:18), had indeed lived up to his mission of becoming a prince among nations. Moreover, he reared a daughter who married Esau and surely influenced him to overcome his jealousy and anger. Though she is unnamed and unheralded, she too was an *ezer* who rescued her husband from bitterness.

Esau almost assuredly maintained a close relationship with his mother, Rebekah, during the more than twenty years that Jacob was away, even until her death. With her, Esau may have reflected tenderly on the good times he had spent with his brother in their youth. Time and distance had enriched both brothers and healed their rivalry. Time and tenderness would heal the rift between Jacob and Leah as well. If there is comfort to be gained by heartbroken parents who worry for their children who have lost their way, it is this: we must look to the long term with our children, as the Lord does with us.

Leah, too, needed to look to the long term to find peace in her soul. The reconciliation with her husband and her sister would occur years in the future. For now, her journey to Canaan was more bitter than sweet.

LEAH GATHERS HER CHICKS

Leah knew great sorrow both as a wife and as a mother. King David, who also suffered the problem of sibling rivalry among his numerous children, wrote in Psalm 133, "Behold, how good and how pleasant it is for brethren to dwell together in unity! It is like the precious ointment upon the head." But there was no such unifying ointment upon the heads of Leah's children, who were often head-strong and competitive. As they strayed in different directions, she must have chased after them as a hen gathers her scattering chicks. Jacob's favoritism toward Rachel may have contributed to their mis-deeds. It has been said that the most important thing a father can do for his children is to love their mother, and the most important thing a mother can do for her children is to love their father. Jacob did not love Leah the way he loved Rachel, and it showed. Jacob provided for all of his children, but he did indeed show favoritism toward his Rachel and the children she bore.[9] Jacob's favoritism led to pain and hardship for those who were not as favored, and "their antagonism to [Joseph] had removed their father's affection for them."[10] All of his families seem to have suffered for it. Leah's children in particular went astray.

Of course, many factors influence a child's behavior, including parenting, birth order, peer pressure, and the child's innate person-ality. Trouble within a marriage often causes children to rebel or act out as well. It began with Dinah. Leah had surely taught her daughter correct principles of proper behavior, but observing Leah's own insecurity with Jacob and her rivalry with Rachel may have influenced Dinah when she "went out to see the daughters of the land" (Genesis 34:1) as they traveled through Canaan. She may have been looking for affection and approval that she did not feel at home. She may simply have wanted to have some fun. Whatever the reason, "when a woman in the patriarchal world goes out, she leaves her family vulnerable. If something bad happens to her, it not only causes her kin sorrow and loss, it also reflects poorly on the patriarch's ability to protect his family. If she does something of which her family or society might not approve, it is a sign that the father [or] husband cannot control his relatives. The family is dishonored and loses political and economic influence."[11]

Unchaperoned and inexperienced, Dinah was not prepared for the weaker morals of the pagan culture through which they were traveling. Perhaps the local girls she met influenced Dinah. Or she may have been beguiled by the idea that a handsome celebrity—the prince of the land—was interested in her. However it came about, "when Shechem the . . . prince of the country, saw her, he took her, and lay with her, and defiled her" (Genesis 34:2). Shechem seduced Dinah, and she succumbed. To his credit, Shechem's "soul clave unto Dinah the daughter of Jacob, and he loved the damsel" and wanted to marry her (Genesis 34:3). It does not appear that Dinah was raped. But in Middle Eastern culture, motive did not matter. Dinah had been "defiled" and violated. Her virginity, and with it her virtue, was gone. Leah must have been devastated by what had happened to her daughter.

The story also reveals "a profound tension of viewpoints between Jacob and his two sons, Simeon and Levi."[12] As many fathers do who discover that their daughters are in trouble, Jacob tried to make the best of the situation. Waiting for Shechem's family to negotiate a bride price, he "held his peace until they were come. And Hamor the father of Shechem went out unto Jacob to commune with them" (Genesis 34:5–6). Jacob was willing to listen to Hamor's offer of marriage and conciliation. He even agreed to the marriage and uniting of their families. His reaction was "far removed from the impassioned and angry condemnation of her brothers,"[13] who "came out of the field when they heard it; and the men were grieved, and they were very wroth" (Genesis 34:7).

In truth, Jacob's sons were wise to be cautious. Hamor's men revealed their greedy motivation when they noted to each other, outside of Jacob's hearing, "shall not their cattle and their substance and every beast of theirs be ours?" (Genesis 34:23). Still, there was no excuse for what Simeon and Levi did next. Setting a trap, they first insisted that Hamor, Shechem, and all of their citizens acknowledge the Abrahamic covenant by being circumcised. Then, in an act of criminal revenge, they attacked the city of Hamor while its men were recuperating from the procedure. They murdered the men, plundered their wealth, and kidnapped their wives and children.

Jacob bewailed the consequences of their actions. "Ye have troubled me to make me to stink among the inhabitants of the land, among the Canaanites and Perizzites: and I being few in number, they shall gather themselves together against me, and slay me; and I shall be destroyed, I and my house" (Genesis 34:30). The sons showed no remorse, however. "Should he deal with our sister as with an harlot?" they asked defiantly (Genesis 34:31).

Leah must have grieved terribly to see blood on the hands of her sons. First, a pagan prince defiled her daughter, and then her sons defiled themselves through revenge. Judah, too, would go "out to see the daughters of the land" and would impulsively marry a Canaanite woman without the approval or knowledge of his parents (Genesis 38). He "became involved in a Canaanite marriage and, by implication, Canaanite ways."[14] The sons of that marriage, Er and Onan, would become so wicked that God Himself would smite them (Genesis 38). Simeon and Levi instigated the slaughter in Shechem. Later, Reuben would prevent his brothers from killing Joseph, but he would "defile" his father's bed by sleeping with Bilhah, Rachel's handmaiden and his father's third wife (Genesis 49:3–4). Such sorrow for a mother's heart to endure! (See Genesis 3:16.)

It is impossible to know how much these sons and daughters were influenced by nature and how much by nurture; every person is given agency, and ultimately each person is responsible for his or her own choices and actions. Certainly Jacob was a visionary man who communed regularly with the Lord and was guided by revelation. His name was changed to Israel, which means "one who prevails with God," suggesting that he struggled mightily throughout his life and eventually succeeded in cementing his relationship with the Lord.

In the end, Jacob's sons united in harmony and love as they rallied to comfort their aging father (Genesis 42–45), just as their mothers united in harmony after the family moved to Canaan. "If we look closely enough, we will find the battling brothers or sisters are far more connected . . . than they seem at first blush."[15] Nevertheless, again and again Leah's children made foolish, violent, and immoral mistakes. Foreshadowing the sorrowful words of her most illustrious descendant, Jesus Christ, Leah must have lamented, "How often would I have gathered [my] children together, even as a hen gathereth her chickens under her wings, and [they] would not" (Matthew 23:37). Sadly, many of Leah's children refused to be sheltered under the wings of home.

LEAH EARNS HER REWARD

Leah suffered much sorrow during her lifetime, but God had a great plan for her. He knew that through this struggle, Leah would gain strength and that if she persevered, her spirituality would deepen and her character would grow. As time passed, something wonderful began to happen inside her. As the trials of motherhood intensified, she turned to the Lord for strength. In *Women of the Bible,* Sue and Lawrence Richards suggest that Leah "kept looking for love, approval, and acceptance from Jacob, and she was continually disappointed until she reoriented her life toward God."[16] But reorient it she did, successfully strengthening her testimony and her relationship with God.

Leah became a noble woman, beloved in the eyes of God and of her descendants. This growing spirituality seems to have affected Jacob too. When Rachel died giving birth to Benjamin, Leah did not rejoice that her rival was dead; she had learned to genuinely love her sister. Jacob grieved mightily, and her husband's grief also softened Leah's heart. Leah tenderly comforted Jacob when Rachel died, just as Sarah comforted Abraham when Hagar and Ishmael left their home. Women have a great capacity for forgiveness when it is sought. As time went on and Leah grew closer to the Lord, Jacob grew closer to her. Eventually, Leah took her rightful place beside him as the first wife.

The improved relationship between husband and wife might also have contributed to the softening effect on their sons. Years later, Jacob's intense grief over the prospect of losing Rachel's son Benjamin would soften the hearts of Leah's sons. Their jealousy toward Joseph and Benjamin would turn to understanding and empathy toward their father (see Genesis 44:27–34). His tears of sorrow would wash away their bitterness; in fact, Leah's son Judah would offer himself as a ransom for Rachel's son Benjamin. The story of Jacob and Leah should give encouragement to parents everywhere. Though children stray, even for many years, they can return to the fold if the gate remains open to them.

Marriage relationships can be healed as well, as long as that same gate remains open. Jacob's final request suggests that he grew to love Leah, despite their difficult beginning. Many years later, after the family had moved to Egypt because of famine, Jacob gave his sons their father's blessings. Then he made one final request. "Bury me with my fathers in the cave that is in the field of Ephron the Hittite," he instructed his sons (Genesis 49:29). This was where Abraham and Sarah, as well as Isaac and Rebekah, had been buried. Moreover, Jacob had buried Leah there too, before the sojourn into Egypt (see Genesis 49:31). It was there that Jacob wanted his bones to be taken. He would greet the resurrection alongside Leah, not Rachel, who was buried near Bethlehem. Leah's final resting place confirms her position as the first wife and the intended bride for Jacob. Hers is the lineage of Jesus Christ.

Rachel would find honor through her sons as well. Joseph would be "a fruitful bough by a well; whose branches run over the wall" (Genesis 49:22). According to the Book of Mormon, the descendants of her grandson Manasseh would be guided to the Americas, bringing the blood of Joseph's Egyptian wife, Asenath, with them. Those descendants would write "the stick of Joseph," another testament of Jesus Christ. And through a descendant of Joseph's other son Ephraim, that "stick of Joseph" would be translated and the gospel restored in the latter days.

As the first wife, Leah would receive the honor of watching her son become the prophet in Israel, while Rachel's descendants would build a civilization dedicated to God in another part of His kingdom. It had been God's will all along that Leah be the first wife of Jacob.

Moreover, the honor of being a direct ancestor of Jesus Christ was reserved for the tender-eyed Leah. Because of her adversity, Leah had turned to the Lord and gained enough strength to support her through the eternities. Although all of Jacob's descendants would be Israelites, only Judah's descendants would be Jews. Leah's son Judah would head the tribe through whom the Messiah would be born. Jacob prophesied of this son, "The sceptre shall not depart from Judah, nor a lawgiver from between his feet, until Shiloh come; and unto him shall the gathering of the people be" (Genesis 49:10).

LEAH'S LESSONS FOR TODAY

Modern mothers know many of the same heartaches and face many of the same trials as Leah did. Peer pressure, unsupervised Internet relationships, and early dating can lead to the same consequences that Dinah experienced. Violence, gangs, revenge, and vigilante justice abound in underprivileged, under-served communities, just as Leah's sons experienced. Poor education, squandered opportunities, and lack of initiative lead to unachieved potential in modern society, just as Reuben, Simeon, and Levi threw away their opportunities for leadership in a misdirected bid for honor and reputation. Favoritism and poor parenting today create sibling rivalry that can tear families apart. "Studies have consistently indicated an association between maladaptive parenting and borderline personality disorder" in their children;[17] studies also reveal that "fathers' diminished parenting [is] associated with children's insecurity in the family [and] increases in children's externalizing behaviors over time."[18] In short, much can be learned today from the story of Leah and Jacob. Losing a child who has gone astray can be just as painful as losing a child to death.

Lesson One: Restoring Courtship to Marriage

The story of Rachel and Leah can be read as a metaphor for marriage itself. Many a new spouse, in a sense, "goes to bed with Rachel and wakes up with Leah." Brides and grooms may seem to change overnight after the marriage vows are spoken. Suddenly, the mystery and anticipation are gone, and the eyes that were once half closed are now wide open. Weaknesses that could be hidden during courtship now appear as major flaws. Thoughtful little gifts, kind words, and expressions of affection that were a central component of courtship also tend to wane after couples say, "I do." Both spouses may begin to wonder what happened to the person they courted.

Of course, Jacob had not courted Leah; he had courted Rachel. But metaphorically, the principle is the same: many "Leahs" dress up as "Rachel" while they are dating, while just as many "Leos" hide behind the successful, generous mask of a "Richard." Later, in the cold light of housekeeping and bill paying, disguises are removed, and true personalities begin to emerge, along with differences in how to manage money, spend free time, discipline children, and accomplish goals. Romance is pushed to the distant past. How did it happen? Can it be fixed?

Leah thought that all she had to do was marry Jacob and everything would turn out right. But a good marriage requires continued care and effort. Richard Paul Evans writes, "Marriage is *hard*. But so is parenthood and keeping fit and writing books and everything else important and worthwhile in . . . life. To have a partner in life is a remarkable gift. . . . The institution of marriage can help heal us of our most unlovable parts."[19]

When an acquaintance complained that he had married the wrong woman, relationship author Zig Ziglar responded, "It is far more important to *be* the right *kind* of person than it is to marry the right person. . . . Whether you married the right or wrong person is primarily up to you."[20] He offers many suggestions for rekindling the fire in a relationship, including offering praise instead of complaints. "Give your mate something to live *up* to, not *down* to, and you will end up with a 'better' mate, which is the key to a better marriage."[21]

Richard Paul Evans agrees. "Real love is not to desire a person, but to truly desire their happiness—sometimes, even, at the expense of our own happiness." Evans describes a low point in his marriage when divorce seemed the only solution. Then he decided to begin every day by asking his wife, "What can I do to make your day better?" At first, it felt awkward—for both of them. But within two weeks, the walls of resentment fell like tears and honest communication began.[22]

Finding our own happiness instead of expecting the other person to make us happy is another key. As Leah nurtured her relationship with the Lord and turned inward to find her own source of happiness, her outward happiness grew. She became a better wife, and Jacob became a better husband. Jacob learned to love Leah, and in the end, it was at her side that he asked to be buried.

LESSON TWO: SIBLING RIVALRY CAN BE HEALED

Another contemporary problem we see in the story of Leah is the trauma of sibling rivalry. Jacob favored the sons of his favorite wife, Rachel, and this led to bitter resentment among his sons. One of the main causes of sibling rivalry is competition for the parents' attention and approval. Todd Cartmell, author of *Keep the Siblings, Lose the Rivalry,* advises, "The more connected you are with each of your children individually, the easier it is for them to develop healthy sibling relationships . . . [and] venture out and develop other meaningful relationships. When your children are fully connected with you, they can begin to see their siblings as friends and partners, rather than as competitors for parental affection."[23] Jacob caused tension when he gave Joseph special gifts and again when he demonstrated that he would rather give up all of his sons than risk losing Rachel's son Benjamin (Genesis 42–43). *Every* child needs to feel noticed and important. So put down your phone, turn away from your screens, set aside your distractions, and *pay attention.*

Good parents watch for opportunities to reinforce positive sibling behavior. One way to accomplish this is through weekly family meetings that include spiritual lessons, meaningful discussions, expressions of gratitude for service, praise for accomplishments, fun activities, and hugs good night. The rivalry between Rachel and Leah began to heal when Jacob held a family council and included them in family decisions. Having children work together on projects, praising all of them for their contributions, and instilling in them a sense of shared pride in each other's accomplishments will also help. Joseph's brothers finally overcame their resentment when they all worked together to provide food during the famine and protect their father from sorrow. Bitterness faded and love was restored (see Genesis 44–45).

Many years ago, advice columnist Ann Landers received a letter in which a reader described a conversation she had had with her quarreling children. The reader wrote,

"You must become better friends, . . . because, God willing, you will both live a long time. I will be gone, and your father will be gone, and all your teachers and many of your friends will be gone. There may be only the two of you left, and you will remember what you were like as children.

"Nobody else will remember the Christmases you had, the tree house you built, the day you learned to ride a bike, the fun you had trick-or-treating, the teacher you loved in the third grade, and the kittens born in the laundry. There will be only the two of you, and you had better love each other now, because sixty years from now, only you will remember all the wonderful experiences you shared, and those memories will be golden. . . . Sibling rivalry is natural but brothers and sisters who are not good to each other lose something precious."[24]

LEAH'S STORY FORESHADOWS THE TEACHINGS OF JESUS CHRIST

Jesus, too, would observe the difficulties of sibling rivalry and family discord. His own Apostles would vie for His attention, especially Peter and John. Jesus would preach sermons designed to soften the bitterness and resentment that often arise within a family. His parable of the prodigal son is a masterpiece of the need for family forgiveness.

His two close friends, Mary and Martha, also struggled with sibling rivalry. Like Rachel, Mary was beautiful and headstrong. Also like Rachel, who spoke openly to Jacob before they were married and expressed her affection unabashedly, Mary ignored the customs that dictated a woman's domestic role and abandoned her kitchen duties to listen to the spiritual discussions of the Savior and His Apostles. Like Leah, Martha complained about her sister's insubordination to cultural rules. She would be just a bit envious of the close intellectual and spiritual relationship that her sister shared with Jesus. In His infinite wisdom, Jesus would love them all. "Martha, Martha, thou art careful . . . about many things," He said gently, validating her generous contributions of service. Food was necessary, and someone had to prepare it. But "Mary hath chosen that good part, which shall not be taken away from her" (Luke 10:38–42).

The story ends there, just as the story of the prodigal son ends with the elder son still deciding whether he will welcome his brother back home. I like to think that Jesus reached out His hand to draw Martha into the room where she, too, would receive that better part. Through His abiding, infinite love, their rivalry would be cured.

Notes

1.   James Neil, *Everyday Life in the Holy Land* (London: Cassel and Co., 1913), 223–35.

2.   Ibid., 249.

3.   Calum M. Carmichael, *Women, Law, and the Genesis Traditions* (Edinburgh, Scotland: Edinburgh University Press, 1979), 31.

4.   Virginia Stem Owens, *Daughters of Eve: Seeing Ourselves in Women of the Bible* (Colorado Springs, CO: NavPress, 2007), 84.

5.   Francine Klagsbrun, "Ruth and Naomi, Rachel and Leah: Sisters under the Skin," *Reading Ruth: Contemporary Women Reclaim a Sacred Story*, edited by Judith A. Kates and Gail Twersky Reimer (New York: Random House, 1994), 270.

6.   Ibid.

7.   Carolyn Custis James, *Lost Women of the Bible: Finding Strength and Significance through Their Stories* (Grand Rapids, MI: Zondervan, 2005), 170–71.

8.   Klagsbrun, "Ruth and Naomi, Rachel and Leah," 264.

9.   "Parental differential treatment has been linked to individual well-being and sibling relationship quality in childhood, adolescence, and middle adulthood" (see Alexander C. Jensen, Shawn D. Whiteman, Karen L. Fingerman, and Kira S. Birditt, "'Life Still Isn't Fair': Parental Differential Treatment of Young Adult Siblings," *Journal of Marriage and Family*, 2013, 438–52).

10. Carmichael, *Women, Law, and the Genesis Traditions*, 58.

11. Tikva Frymer-Kensky, *Reading the Women of the Bible* (New York: Schocken, 2002), 180.

12. Carmichael, *Women, Law, and the Genesis Traditions*, 33.

13. Ibid.

14. Ibid., 58.

15. Klagsbrun, "Ruth and Naomi, Rachel and Leah," 262.

16. Lawrence Richards and Sue Richards, *Women of the Bible: The Life and Times of Every Woman in the Bible* (Nashville, TN: Thomas Nelson, 2003), 174.

17. Catherine Winsper, Mary Zanarini, and Dieter Wolke, "Prospective Study of Family Adversity and Maladaptive Parenting in Childhood and Borderline Personality Disorder Symptoms in a Non-Clinical Population at 11 Years," *Psychological Medicine* 42, no. 11 (2012): 2405–20.

18. Melissa L. Sturge-Apple, Michael A. Skibo, and Patarick T. Davies, "Impact of Parental Conflict and Emotional Abuse on Children and Families," *Partner Abuse* 3, no. 3 (2012): 385.

19. Richard Paul Evans, "How I Saved My Marriage," *Deseret News*, February 9, 2015, http://www.deseretnews.com/article /print/865621517/Richard-Paul-Evans-How-I-saved-my-marriage .html.

20. Zig Ziglar, *Courtship After Marriage: Romance Can Last a Lifetime* (Nashville, TN: Thomas Nelson, 1990), 11–12.

21. Ibid., 48.

22. Evans, "How I Saved My Marriage."

23. Todd Cartmell, *Keep the Siblings, Lose the Rivalry* (Grand Rapids, MI: Zondervan, 2003), 53.

24. Ann Landers, "Message for Siblings: Learn to Get Along Now," *Reading Eagle*, August 21, 1996.

TAMAR IS DESPISED
AND REJECTED

*"He is despised and rejected of men; a man of
sorrows, and acquainted with grief" (Isaiah 53:3).*

HE STORY OF Judah and Tamar presents many challenges
to the casual reader. At first glance, it seems a small, sordid,
and insignificant tale, revealing a moment of inexplicable
sexual weakness in the man who would become Jacob's birthright
son, the father of the Jews, and a direct ancestor of Jesus Christ.
Within the Bible, it appears as a single chapter that interrupts the flow
of a larger narrative about Judah and his brothers selling Rachel's son
Joseph to the Egyptians. This makes it seem as though Judah took a
quick little side trip to Canaan to find a wife while his brothers were
deciding whether to kill Joseph or sell him to slave traders. Yet the
chapter spans at least twenty years, long enough for Judah to marry
a Canaanite and raise three sons to marriageable age.

Because of its juxtaposition with the story in the next chapter
of Joseph escaping from the immoral clutches of Potiphar's wife
(Genesis 39:7–12), the story of Tamar and Judah is often taught as a
cautionary tale about seductive women—if it is taught at all. Many
readers and teachers simply skip over this disturbing story and move
on to his younger brother's example of supreme moral chastity in the
next chapter.

The story can indeed be troubling on the surface. It appears
that Judah, the son of a prophet, has sexual relations with a woman
dressed as a harlot, who turns out to be his daughter-in-law—and she

has arranged the liaison on purpose. Knowing what religion teaches about the importance of virtue and sexual morality, we might well wonder how Tamar can be part of Jesus's mortal lineage. And Judah shouldn't be let off the hook for his part in the story; both were willing participants in the act. Tikva Frymer-Kensky tries to explain the dilemma in *Reading the Women of the Bible* when she states, "Taken by themselves, incest, adultery, and licentious behavior are subversive acts that could destroy the social order. In most contexts, such behavior . . . can destroy the patriarchal system. However, in the context of the faithfulness of these women to their family and to its men, [these actions were] actually a good thing; [they] enabled women to act in ways that served the family structure and enabled it to survive." For example, "The characteristics of family loyalty, wits, determination, unconventionality, and aggressiveness that Tamar and Ruth brought into the family . . . characterize the Judean monarchy to which these women gave birth."[1]

In discussing the half-truths told by women like Sarah, who pretended to be her husband's sister; Tamar, who pretended to be a stranger; Rahab, who lied to the Jericho guards to protect the Israelite spies; and the Egyptian midwives who hid the Israelite babies, Rebecca Lyn McConkie reminds us, "Plato . . . suggests the existence of what he called the noble lie, meaning that some lies are in fact noble because of the means that they accomplish. . . . Life is not so much a set of rules as it is a turn with principles."[2]

A closer reading, however, reveals a far different story, one that is both heroic and redeeming. Despite Frymer-Kensky's interpretative apology for sexual sin, the details of the story of Judah and Tamar reveal that this was not an act of incest or licentious behavior at all. Tamar knew that law and custom were on her side. As we shall see, through her clever plotting, she maneuvered Judah into keeping an important promise while she also prevented him from committing a grave sin. She was an *ezer kenegdo*. Here is her story.

TAMAR IS ABANDONED

Tamar walked slowly into the tent and quietly removed the sackcloth tunic that had been her standard dress for many years. She was a widow twice over, and of the worst kind: she had no children to comfort her or bring her honor. She was alone and bereft, abandoned even by her husbands' family.

Neither of her husbands had been pleasant; in fact, they had been horrid. Er had been a wicked man, and she wasn't even sure how he died. The villagers simply said that God killed him for his wickedness (Genesis 38:7). Her second husband hadn't been any better. After Er died, her father-in-law, Judah, had given her in marriage to Er's younger brother, Onan, to raise posterity for Er. In those days, "widows without children were protected by levirate marriage, which required that a childless widow marry one of her deceased husband's brothers in order to continue the family line of her dead husband and pass on his land inheritance, or *nahala*. This was seen as a widow's right, and perhaps the only chance a woman would have for security after the death of her husband."[3]

This was called the "levirate law." A levir acted "as his brother's surrogate and incest taboos [were] suspended" for this particular situation.[4] Leviracy provided posterity for the deceased brother, as well as the comfort and protection of motherhood for the surviving widow. It would be codified for the Jews in Deuteronomy 25:5–6: "If brethren dwell together, and one of them die, and have no child, the wife of the dead shall not marry without unto a stranger; her husband's brother shall go in unto her, and take her to him to wife, and perform the duty of an husband's brother unto her. And it shall be, that the firstborn which she beareth shall succeed in the name of his brother which is dead, that his name be not put out of Israel."

The thought of having children had indeed comforted Tamar and given her hope. But Onan had dealt treacherously with Tamar as well, because he did not want to share his inheritance with his dead brother's child. If all three sons were alive, "according to ancient laws of inheritance, Judah would divide his estate into four equal parts. Tamar's husband, Er, as the eldest son, would inherit a *double* portion"[5]—one portion for himself, and the other for his own heir.

But after Er's death, Judah's property would be divided into three portions, one for each surviving son plus one more for the eldest son's heir. As the eldest surviving son, Onan was now entitled to two-thirds of his father's estate. But any son born to Tamar would receive

Er's double portion as the son of the eldest son, and Onan's own portion would revert to that of the second son, or one quarter instead of two-thirds. "When Er died childless, the math changed for his two surviving brothers,"[6] but it would change again if Tamar produced a son through their seed. Perhaps motivated by greed, Onan had refused to honor his filial duty and would not fully consummate their marriage. Instead, he satisfied himself sexually but withdrew his seed and let it fall outside of Tamar. For this outrage, God had killed Onan as well—or so it was said of his death (Genesis 38:9).

Tamar did not object to becoming a second wife. She accepted the real possibility that marriage for love might be out of the question for her. But she deeply desired to have children. She expected that motherhood was part of God's plan for her. A son would comfort her, protect her, provide for her, and continue her husband's lineage. Judah had one more son, Shelah. He had been a young boy when Onan died, not yet of marriageable age. Judah had promised to give Tamar to Shelah when he was old enough to be married. Until then, he had sent her back to her father's house to wait in her widow's sackcloth. So she had waited. And waited. But Judah had proven himself unfaithful as well. The time was far past when she should have been given to Shelah, and her window for bearing children was closing.

Apparently Judah had no intention of giving his youngest son to Tamar. There were rumors that he did not trust her, because he had watched her outlive two of his sons (Genesis 38:11). Despite his sons' wickedness and evil actions, "Judah [did] not suspect God's role" in his sons' deaths. "Instead, he [thought] Tamar may be a lethal woman."[7] But how could Judah blame Tamar for their deaths? Er had been wicked, and Onan had broken one of God's most sacred commandments.

If anyone had killed them, it was God, not she. Moreover, Judah had acted unfairly toward Tamar. "Legally Tamar was a member of Judah's household and under his authority. Yet Judah ignored his obligations to Tamar";[8] "by leaving her to be a 'widow in her father's house,' Judah [bound] her perpetually to his family without intending to provide her a secure future."[9]

One solution was still available to Tamar—a solution that modern readers may find appalling, but one that was acceptable at the time. "Although biblical regulations [would] later prohibit this, . . . in Judah's day the father-in-law was responsible if his son failed to fulfill his duty. . . . Conception by a father-in-law was a legitimate means of saving a family member from being cut off."[10] Tamar had taken this knowledge into her heart and pondered what she should do.

For too many years, Tamar had been "the silent object of male action. Judah took her for his son, gave her to another son, and sent her away to her father's house."[11] Now it was time for Tamar to take action "for her own benefit and the benefit of Judah's house."[12] Her mother-in-law, Judah's wife and the mother of both her husbands, had recently died. Judah had completed his time of mourning and was now heading for the sheep shearing in Timnath. He would be passing by. Perhaps he was lonely. Perhaps he needed a woman. Tamar set aside her widow's weeds and reached for the pretty woolen tunic. It was time to put her plan into action.

As she dressed, she thought about her father-in-law, a prominent Israelite who had chosen to live among the Canaanites instead of with his father and brothers. Judah's father, the prophet Jacob, had endured trouble at home. He openly favored two of his sons, Joseph and Benjamin, who had been born to his favorite wife, Rachel.

This favoritism caused his other sons to become so envious of Joseph that they devised a plan to get rid of him. Several conspired to slay Joseph and convince their father Joseph had been killed by a wild animal, but Judah convinced them merely to sell Joseph into slavery to the Egyptians instead (see Genesis 37:19–27). Immediately after this act of extreme sibling rivalry, Judah left his brothers and went to visit his friend Hirah the Adullamite. "Driven by rejection and jealous anger over his father's preference for . . . Rachel's sons . . . [then] hurt and fed up, Judah left his brothers and migrated into Canaanite territory."[13]

Though the custom of the time was for parents to send matchmakers to arrange a marriage, Judah arranged his own marriage to the daughter of Shuah the Canaanite. Then he "took her, and went in unto her. And she conceived, and bare a son" (Genesis 38:2–3). Judah lived at least twenty years in Canaan, where he "forged alliances with Canaanites, married a Canaanite, and ultimately started behaving like one."[14] He did his best to forget that he was an Israelite. His Canaanite wife bore him three sons, and Tamar had married two of them in succession. Both of those sons had died, and now their mother, Judah's wife, had died too. Judah was a lonely widower as he headed to Timnath for the sheep shearing, and far from the guiding influence of his father, the prophet Jacob. He had become steeped in the culture and morals of the community he had adopted.

TAMAR DISCOVERS A SOLUTION

Tamar pulled the soft woolen tunic over her head and wrapped the girdle around her waist. It felt so good to wear normal clothing against her skin after the rough and scratchy sackcloth of widowhood. She donned the traditional veil that covered all but her beautiful eyes (Genesis 38:14). Those eyes would have to do their trick if her plan was going to work. "Middle Assyrian laws [allowed] only married women to veil themselves, specifically prohibiting prostitutes from doing so";[15] if this custom was true in Palestine as well, then Judah overlooked an important signal when he assumed that Tamar was a prostitute: Tamar may have been dressed to look like a harlot, but in her mind, she was wearing the veil of a bride.

Then she took her seat along the road to Timnath and waited. She was the only woman on this road today, but it was a common practice for women who had fallen into despair—women without husband or family to support them—to accept the harlot's way of earning bread. Tamar would be mistaken for one of them this day, but she would not actually *be* one of them. Nevertheless, she put herself in danger by being alone on the roadside. Carefully, she averted her eyes, waiting for the one man who could resolve her dilemma and help her achieve God's purpose for her and her intended posterity.

When Judah saw Tamar, he was indeed attracted to her. She was different from the actual harlots he had passed before. Mockery and despair were written in their body language, but he detected confidence and self-respect in this woman's demeanor. He felt strangely drawn to her. Though he might never have entered a harlot's tent before, he stopped now and said, "Please, let me come in unto thee."

"What will you give me," she asked, "if I let you come?"

Judah was on his way to visit his flocks at shearing time. He had neither goats nor sheep with him and nothing to give this woman. "Let me come in now," he proposed, "and I will send you a kid from my flock."

This was exactly what Tamar had hoped he would say. Now she would elicit the words she needed to hear. "Give me your pledge," she told him, "until your servant returns with the kid. If you will give me your signet ring, your bracelets, and the staff that is in your hand, I will let you come in unto me now."

Judah, overcome with desire, gave her all these precious personal belongings before crossing the threshold into Tamar's tent. Afterward, Judah went on his way. Tamar took off the veil and put on her widow's garments. She was satisfied. She knew that if it was God's will, she would conceive. She would no longer be alone (Genesis 38:15–18).

As soon as Judah arrived at the shearing, he sent his friend Hirah the Adullamite back to the roadside to give the woman the kid he had promised her and to retrieve his signet, bracelets, and staff. But Hirah could not find the woman. He asked everyone, but they all said the same thing: there were no harlots in this place, so he must be mistaken. Judah, surely embarrassed by the whole affair, decided to let it drop rather than stir up publicity by searching further for the woman. After all, it wouldn't do to have others know that he had entered the tent of an unknown woman. He gave up on ever regaining his property and vowed not to get himself into this predicament again.

Three months later, it became apparent to all that Tamar had indeed received the promised "kid" from Judah—but it was not the four-legged kind. She was pregnant, and the nosy neighbors could not wait to bring this salacious news to Judah. "Tamar . . . hath played the harlot; . . . she is with child by whoredom," they told him (Genesis 38:24). This is where the word *harlot* enters the story—not from the narrator, but from the gossipy neighbors.

Judah had virtually abandoned his sons' wife by sending the twice-widowed Tamar back to live with her own father. Nevertheless, as her father-in-law, he was responsible for her behavior and had authority for disciplining her. When he heard that she was pregnant, he was outraged. Despite his own guilty experience—or maybe because of it—he meted out the fullest punishment available to him. "Bring her forth," he exclaimed, "and let her be burnt" (see Genesis 38:24).

The Old Testament relies heavily on justice, and its laws are often accompanied by heavy consequences. Children who disobeyed their parents could be stoned to death, for example. Even breaking the Sabbath by gathering sticks to build a fire carried a death penalty. But these capital sentences were rarely enforced. They were maximum penalties, not mandatory ones, designed to deter crime by threatening severe punishment.

Moreover, the concept of "burning" could have several connotations. The first is a literal burning to death and is still carried out in some Middle Eastern cultures today. A more natural consequence for the crime of harlotry might be the painful burning that results from sexually transmitted diseases incurred from having multiple sexual partners. Depending on the circumstances, women in this situation might be shunned or even banished, suffering the burning shame of scorn and rejection. It appears that Judah intended the harshest of punishments for Tamar: the literal burning of fire.

Most women would have run away upon hearing this sentence. But Tamar acted with the courage of a woman who knew she was right. Setting aside her fear, she faced her father-in-law. "By the man, whose these are, am I with child: . . . Discern, I pray thee, whose are these" (Genesis 38:25). Dramatically, she opened her hand to reveal the signet ring, the bracelets, and the staff.

Judah's heart fell as he heard these words. Perhaps the weight of twenty years in Canaan, away from his father's spiritual influence, also fell onto Judah's shoulders in that moment. "She has been more righteous than I," he admitted, "because I promised to give her to my son Shelah, and I did not. She has made me keep my promise."

Keep his promise indeed; it was a promise that carried eternal consequences for an entire nation. Tamar had been promised a levirate husband from the fledgling tribe of Judah—a tribe that then included only two men: Shelah and Judah himself. In securing Judah's pledge with a ring, she had, in essence, secured Judah's hand in marriage. In ancient times, a man's word was his bond, and marriages were often sealed with a promise.

In fact, when Rebekah and Isaac met in the field two generations earlier, there is no mention of a wedding ceremony. The scripture simply says, "Isaac brought her into his . . . tent, and took Rebekah, and she became his wife; and he loved her" (Genesis 24:67). The marriage negotiations between Rebekah's representatives and Abraham's representative had already created a legally binding contract, and the act of crossing the threshold into the tent sealed it.

Similarly, under the levirate law, "the marriage becomes valid as soon as it is consummated. This sort of union required no dowry and no new marriage contract because all the arrangements of the first marriage remained in force."[16] Moreover, the taboo against a father-in-law acting as levir would not be established until the law of Moses, several generations later.[17] Nevertheless, Judah did produce a dowry. By securing Judah's pledge with his ring, Tamar had sealed the promise he had made to her long before. With the bracelets, she had received the requisite dowry.

Significantly, it was almost the same dowry that had been presented to Rebekah: a ring and bracelets (see Genesis 24:22). When Judah crossed over the threshold into Tamar's tent, he did so as her levirate husband, whether he intended to or not. He would not suffer the fate of his brother Reuben, who lost his birthright through immorality (Genesis 49:4).

The record says that Judah "knew her again no more" (Genesis 38:26), meaning that they did not have sexual relations again. Perhaps "the years Judah had disregarded Tamar's needs, and her understandably hostile feelings for him, made it impossible for a personal relationship to develop between them."[18] Perhaps she simply did not want to leave her community and accompany Judah to his father's home. Nevertheless, Judah had legitimized their relationship and their children by giving Tamar his signet ring in advance. Crossing the threshold into her tent had sealed the promise. Pharez and Zerah would be listed among the sons of Judah who traveled to Egypt during the famine (Genesis 46:12), and "Tamar's child was considered to be not Er's but Judah's."[19] In a twist of mistaken identities that would have impressed even Shakespeare, Tamar had managed to secure a ring, a dowry, a family crest, and a birthright son.

A Righteous Son of Judah

As it turned out, Tamar was carrying twin boys. And like the twin boys of their grandmother Rebekah, these two would come into this world creating controversy regarding their birthright. Rebekah's Esau had been born first, but Jacob had been chosen by God to be the leader. Similarly, during the birth of Tamar's twins, the baby who would be named Zarah stuck his hand out first, and the midwife tied a scarlet thread around his wrist to show which of the children had first felt the air of earth. Nevertheless, during the trauma and struggle of delivery, the boys shifted, and the one who would be named Pharez emerged from the womb before Zarah. This Pharez was the fourth-great grandfather of Boaz, whose wife Ruth was the great-grandmother of King David, whose wife Bathsheba was fourteen generations removed from Mary, who was the mother of Jesus.

Tamar could have continued to live in her father's home as a barren widow. But she was determined to have a baby who would carry the name and inheritance of her first husband, Er, the eldest son of the house of Judah. But Er and Onan were not the intended ancestors of Jesus Christ. They were not taught by their mother to walk in the paths of righteousness. In fact, Er and Onan were both described as wicked men whom God Himself slew. Tamar would not make that mistake with her sons. We do not know the details of Pharez's life, but we know that he was a man of honor and respect. When Boaz decided to marry Ruth, his relatives would wish him well by saying, "Let thy house be like the house of Pharez" (Ruth 4:12). The courageous widow of Er and Onan had suffered much heartache because of her husbands, but she was a good mother who raised her sons in righteousness. Through Pharez, she would become a matriarch of the Messiah.

Tamar was also an *ezer kenegdo*. She rescued Judah from his apostasy and helped him return to the proper path. Hurt, angry, and suffering from sibling rivalry, Judah had left the proper path for several years to live among the Canaanites. He rashly chose a wife without the help and advice of his father, Jacob, who had traveled hundreds of miles to the land of his cousins to find an appropriate wife for himself. Judah's great-grandfather, Abraham, had sent a trusted servant those same four hundred miles to choose a proper wife for Isaac. God intended that Jesus would be born through Judah's lineage, but the daughter of Shuah the Canaanite was not the intended maternal ancestor; Tamar the Canaanite was.

Carolyn Custis James points to Judah's use of the word *righteous* in vindicating Tamar for her part in the plot. "The Bible doesn't carelessly throw around a word like 'righteous,'" she writes. "Righteousness belongs to God and is the comfort of his people. . . . No Old Testament person, especially someone from Judah's background, would ever thoughtlessly apply 'righteous' to a Canaanite like Tamar. The word simply means too much."[20] And yet he did use this word to describe Tamar, because she had indeed been "more righteous than he."

"Put more bluntly, Judah deliberately engaged in prostitution. Tamar fought for his family. . . . He [was] seeking pleasure for himself. She [was] laying down her life for others."[21] Tamar helped Judah remember what it means to be part of a covenant-making family. She could have exposed him publicly, but instead, as Joseph would do later with Mary, she came to him privately with the symbols of his pledge. "While Tamar had first bypassed Judah's plans, she showed him the ultimate honor by placing her trust in him, hoping that he would prove to be the godly man she believed him to be."[22]

And he did rise up. Through bitterness and rivalry, Judah had lost his way, but Tamar helped him find it again. Tamar reminded him of his responsibility not only to her, but also to his ancestors and to his posterity. Imagine the joy Jacob must have felt when, after Judah had this soul-changing experience with Tamar, he left the Canaanites and returned to live with his father and his brothers. There, he became a strong example and leader.

Later, when famine drove them to Egypt in search of food, Judah would lead the way toward healing their rivalry with Joseph and Benjamin. In fact, Judah would offer himself as a ransom in Benjamin's place to spare their father the sorrow of losing both the sons of his favorite wife, Rachel. This short but significant chapter, sandwiched as it is between the story of Joseph sold into slavery and then redeemed as the governor of Egypt, suggests that Judah's sojourn in Canaan led to a spiritual captivity as dark as his brother's physical captivity.

But it was not a one-way path. Judah too was redeemed. Judah's story gives hope to parents whose children have strayed from faith and family, even for decades. I think of them not as wayward children, but as children who have lost their way. As long as there is life, there is opportunity for repentance and regaining the right path.

Tamar rescued Judah from Canaan and saved him from his own folly. She set him back on the right path, where he regained his position as leader of the Israelites. It was a hard thing to do, but she was equal to the task.

TAMAR FORESHADOWS THE COURAGE OF MARY, THE MOTHER OF JESUS CHRIST

Tamar was a risk-taker and a problem-solver. Acutely aware of the scorn reserved for women who became pregnant outside of marriage, and knowing that her punishment could be banishment or even death by burning if her plan was misunderstood, she courageously chose to move forward with her plot to secure her right to the blessings of motherhood. Having risked so much, she did not squander the opportunity, and her sons blossomed. As Tivka Fryer-Kensky points out, "We should not be scandalized by Tamar's actions, because we know her reasons. Biblical authors rarely do this, but the stories about Lot's daughters, Ruth, and Tamar all tell us why these women act unconventionally."[23] Each of them had been abandoned by the traditional family structure of support, and each was driven by the desire to have children and perpetuate the family line. Alice Ogden Bellis adds, "Like many other biblical women, Tamar must use deception to achieve her ends. [And] like many other biblical women, she must become a mother to have a place in society. . . . In a culture that came to be fearful of women and especially of foreign women, Tamar's story is a ray of hope."[24]

Tamar's risk foreshadows the risk Jesus's own mother would accept in becoming a mother before she was married. Of course, Mary did not devise a plan to become the mother of the mortal Messiah; it was a complete surprise to her. But she humbly accepted that calling and all its implied consequences. Like Tamar, Mary knew the scorn that could come her way from nosy neighbors. Like Tamar, she knew that the punishment for being with child and without husband was banishment or even death. But she moved forward with humility and strength. Like so many of the maternal ancestors of Jesus, including Tamar, Mary would willingly risk honor, reputation, and personal comfort to achieve God's righteous purposes. In the end, Mary became the most respected of all women.

NOTES

1. Tikva Frymer-Kensky, *Reading the Women of the Bible* (New York: Schocken, 2002), 276–77.

2. Rebecca Lyn McConkie, "Rahab the Harlot: Her Place in the Hebrew Bible," *Selections from the Religious Education Student Symposium 2004* (Provo, UT: Religious Studies Center, Brigham Young University, 2004), 79–91.

3. Jennie R. Ebeling, *Women's Lives in Bliblical Times* (New York: T&T Clark International, 2010), 134.

4. Frymer-Kensky, *Reading the Women of the Bible*, 267.

5. Carolyn Custis James, *Lost Women of the Bible: Finding Strength and Significance through Their Stories* (Grand Rapids, MI: Zondervan, 2005), 107.

6. Ibid., 107.

7. Frymer-Kensky, *Reading the Women of the Bible*, 267.

8. Lawrence Richards and Sue Richards, *Women of the Bible: The Life and Times of Every Woman in the Bible* (Nashville, TN: Thomas Nelson, 2003), 235.

9. Frymer-Kensky, *Reading the Women of the Bible*, 268.

10. James, *Lost Women of the Bible*, 111.

11. Frymer-Kensky, *Reading the Women of the Bible*, 280.

12. Ibid., 280.

13. James, *Lost Women of the Bible*, 115.

14. Ibid., 115.

15. Frymer-Kensky, *Reading the Women of the Bible*, 270.

16. Diana Webb, *Forgotten Women of God* (Springville, UT: Cedar Fort, Inc., 2010), 151.

17. James, *Lost Women of the Bible*, 111.

18. Richards and Richards, *Women of the Bible*, 235.

19. Frymer-Kensky, *Reading the Women of the Bible*, 253.

20. James, *Lost Women of the Bible*, 113–14.

21. Ibid., 115.

22. Tamar Frankiel, "Ruth and the Messiah," *Reading Ruth: Contemporary Women Reclaim a Sacred Story*, edited by Judith A. Kates and Gail Twersky Reimer (New York: Random House, 1994), 331.

23. Frymer-Kensky, *Reading the Women of the Bible*, 269.

24. Alice Ogden Bellis, *Helpmates, Harlots, and Heroes: Women's Stories in the Hebrew Bible* (Louisville, KY: Westminster/John Knox Press, 1994), 92.

RAHAB RECEIVES THE LIVING WATERS

"Whosever drinketh of the water that I shall give him shall never thirst" (John 4:14).

RAHAB GLANCED NERVOUSLY behind her as she hurried toward the door of her house. Quickly she grabbed the dishes left by her visitors and stashed them on the shelf. Nothing else seemed out of place. Smoothing her scarf, she took a deep breath and willed her heart to slow to a normal pace. As she reached for the door she spied fibers of fresh flax dangling from the sleeve of her tunic and felt her heart quicken again. Quickly she shoved it out of sight beneath her girdle just as the pounding resumed. "Open the door, harlot," the king's men ordered. "We know you're in there!"

Striking a languid pose and adopting a look of casual disinterest that she did not feel, Rahab complied. She pulled back the door with an air of annoyed defiance. "What do you want?" she asked haughtily. Sometimes being known as a harlot had its advantages. This was one of those times.

"Bring us the strangers who came here last night," the soldiers demanded.

"There are no strangers here," Rahab told them truthfully, for they were no longer strangers to her.

"We saw them enter your house. They are spies from the Israelite camp." The soldier looked past Rahab into her house, but she did not move aside.

"Oh, those two," Rahab responded, forcing her voice to sound casual. "They didn't stay. They wouldn't even talk to a woman like me. I saw them leave the town about the time of the shutting of the gate, when it was dark."

"Where did they go? Which way?" the soldier demanded.

"I don't know. But hurry! If you leave now, you shall surely overtake them."

Rahab moved to close the door, but one soldier leaned in to her and snarled. "You had better not be lying."

"Why would I protect men like that?" Rahab asked with disdain. "Now go! Hurry! And when you catch them, tell them they should not have treated Rahab the innkeeper so disrespectfully!"

Rahab watched the king's men turn and run toward the city gate. She forced herself to stand nonchalantly until they were out of sight. Then she snapped her door shut and ran up the ladder to the roof where she had been "retting" the flax, "a process that loosens the linen fibers from the stalks by drying them in the sun after the dew has wet them."[1] Hurrying toward a large mound of flax, she began to claw big handfuls off the pile.

"It's safe now. They're gone," she whispered. "Only be very quiet, for my neighbors have sharp ears."

Two men sat up from the flax, wiping the dust and straw from their faces and clothes. "The flayed stalks of flax made a thatch-like matting, perfect for concealing two grown men."[2] They were dressed in the rough woolen tunics of nomads, and their sandals were old and worn. "Thank you," they said. "But why have you helped us this way?"

Rahab spoke sincerely. "I know who you are, and I know that the Lord has given you this land. All of us live in terror of your people. We have heard how the Lord dried up the water of the Red Sea for you, when you came out of Egypt. We heard how you utterly destroyed the two kings of the Amorites, on the other side of Jordan. Everyone's heart has melted in fear, and our men have no courage to face you.

"But I am not afraid of you," she continued with fervor. "I know that the Lord your God is God in heaven above, and in earth beneath. I know that He follows you and protects you. Now I ask you this favor: As I have shown you kindness, will you also show kindness to my father's house? Give me now your promise and a true token that you will save my father and my mother, my brothers and my sisters, and all that they have, when you return to destroy our city. Please, deliver us from death!"

The men looked at each other cautiously. Could they trust this woman? She was a stranger and a harlot. They had been commanded to "smite [the Canaanites], and utterly destroy them; [and] . . . make no covenant with them" (Deuteronomy 7:2). Yet there was something special in her voice, a sincerity they had not heard in any other woman. She had courage, and she was a quick thinker. She had hidden them under the flax at the peril of her own life. Then she had turned the king's men away. Yes. They would risk their safety with her one more time.

"You have saved our lives; now we will save yours," they promised, "if you will not utter a word about us and our business. Then, when the Lord has delivered this land into our hands, we will deal kindly and truly with you."

Rahab was satisfied. She quickly devised a fresh plan. "My house is built on the city wall," she told them. "On the other side of this roof is freedom. I will let you down by a cord through the window while it is still dark. Run and hide in the mountains. The king's men who are pursuing you will return after three days. Then it will be safe for you to return to your camp."

The Lord's men looked Rahab squarely in the eyes. "We will keep our promise. Take this scarlet thread, and when we return, let it dangle out of your window so that we know where you are. Bring your father's family and his entire household into this house and wait for us. Make sure they stay here. If anyone leaves your house and goes into the street, we cannot guarantee their safety. But we will be responsible for the blood of all who remain with you." Then, still wondering if it was folly to put their lives into the hands of this admitted harlot, they reminded her sternly, "If you tell anyone about us, we are no longer bound by this promise."

Rahab nodded. "I will do all that you have said. Now go quickly."

Jericho was a crossroads city of the Amorite kingdom known for its violence, depravity, and paganism.[3] Rahab was the only resident among the entire community of Jericho willing to accept the God of Israel and hide these men. Perhaps "a harlot would be more open to outsiders than other citizens of Jericho."[4] Perhaps the shame of her demeaning occupation led to her conversion. Some people are hardened by sin; others are humbled and softened when they recognize and acknowledge it in themselves. This humility makes them open to the influence of the Spirit. Like the woman whom Jesus would meet at the well in Samaria, Rahab had a spirit that was humble and open. Even when the Israelite spies exhibited distrust, she was not offended. She persevered to get what she wanted—safety in this life, and redemption in the next. The scarlet line the men gave her suggests the scarlet blood of Christ and the lifeline He provides. Rahab accepted this scarlet thread. And then she waited.

Joshua Fights the Battle of Jericho

Rahab had been influenced by reports of the miraculous parting of the Red Sea, when the Israelites had passed over on dry land forty years earlier. Unbeknownst to her, a miracle just as spectacular was about to occur not far from her own city walls. With the positive reports brought back by his advance scouts, Joshua was ready to lead his men into battle to reclaim the land that God had promised to Abraham and his descendants. Now Joshua said to the people, "Sanctify yourselves: for tomorrow the Lord will do wonders among you" (Joshua 3:5). Wonders indeed! God was about to part the Jordan River, just as He had parted the Red Sea forty years before.

This was an important moment for the Israelites, and for us all. As they entered the next stage of their lives, it was critical for them to realize that it was not Moses who performed the ten plagues, parted the Red Sea, and provided food and water during the long trek through the wilderness; it was the power of God's priesthood. Joshua had been ordained to that same power. Prophets throughout the centuries have held it as well. Faith and priesthood are powers as invisible as electricity and just as tangible. They are the powers by which miracles are performed. Joshua gathered the people together and proclaimed, "Hereby ye shall know that the living God is among you" (Joshua 3:10). Then, with the ark of the covenant at the forefront and representatives from each of the twelve tribes leading the way, the people took the step of faith directly into the waters of the Jordan River. This was no muddy river bottom with a trickle running through it, as some skeptics have suggested was the case when the Israelites crossed over the Red Sea with Moses. It was harvest time, and the Jordan River was overflowing its banks (Joshua 3:15). The men stepped directly into the flowing water.

And then a miracle happened, as mighty as any miracle performed by Moses. As their feet touched the water, "the waters which came down from above stood and rose up upon an heap . . . and those that came down toward . . . the salt sea, failed, and were cut off: and the people passed over right against Jericho" (Joshua 3:16). What a magnificent and terrifying sight that must have been! It required each and every person to demonstrate individual faith as they stepped into the riverbed and hurried past the roiling waters heaped up to their right. Symbolically they had "passed over" the Red Sea at the beginning of their journey from Egypt, and now they "passed over" the Jordan to enter the promised land. It was another reminder of the God who had guided them along their way and would come in the meridian of time to offer Himself as the Passover Lamb.

Before continuing on their mission, they stopped to acknowledge the hand of God. Hefting twelve large stones from the riverbed as they walked across, they built an altar as "a memorial unto the children of Israel for ever" (Joshua 4:7). Then they renewed their covenant through circumcision, since no one had been circumcised in the wilderness, and they ate the feast of the Passover. They were ready.

Rahab was ready too. The town of Jericho was completely shut. No one was allowed to go out, and no one was allowed to come in. Such was their fear of the Israelites. But Rahab sat at her window in the wall of the town and watched. She had already gathered her family and their belongings to her. The scarlet line was hanging from her window, almost like the blood of the lambs that had been smeared on the doorways of the Israelites as they prepared to leave Egypt. Now, with the tremendous sight of the host of Israel assembling outside, she waited for the onslaught.

But the onslaught did not come. Instead, something peculiar happened. Rahab watched as the Israelites silently and respectfully lifted a beautifully crafted box onto their shoulders, using heavy wooden staves to carry it. Seven men, dressed in ceremonial robes, led the way, carrying trumpets made of rams' horns. Then the rest of the people joined the procession, with the armed men close behind the box and the others taking their places at the rear. They spoke not a word but marched silently until they had completely compassed the city of Jericho. The only sound was the blowing of the *shofars*, or rams' horns. Then they returned to their camp, still without speaking a word. It was eerie. Rahab continued to watch, but nothing else happened that day. She went to bed puzzled and on edge, as did all of the residents of Jericho.

The next morning the same thing happened. Not a word was spoken, and not a sound was heard, except for the blaring of the *shofars*. After circling the city once, the Israelites returned to their camp. This continued for six days. The citizens of Jericho began to scoff. "They can't even find a way into our city," they laughed. "These Israelites are not so ferocious. They blow their horns and give up." But Rahab did not laugh, and she did not give up. She encouraged her family to be strong and have faith. "The very God of heaven and earth guides these strangers," she assured them. "They will not forget their promise. We will wait. And we will be ready." She returned to the window, and checked that the scarlet thread was still in place.

Just as Noah and his family had waited seven days inside the ark for the rains to begin, Rahab and her family waited seven days inside the inn. On the seventh day, the Israelites returned at dawn. Again they circled the city, but this time they did not leave. They continued to circle the city. Seven times they compassed the city walls, moving in complete silence except for the blowing of the *shofars*. At the end of the seventh circuit they stopped. Rahab leaned out her window. She could feel that something remarkable was about to happen. She felt a thrill of dread as she heard their leader cry out, "Shout; for the Lord hath given you the city!" (Joshua 6:16).

What he said next thrilled her even more. "The city shall be accursed, even it, and all that are therein, to the Lord: only Rahab the harlot shall live, she and all that are with her in the house, because she hid the messengers that we sent" (Joshua 6:17). The men had remembered their promise to the insignificant woman waiting at the inn. The God of heaven and earth was watching over her indeed!

Moments later, a great ululating shout was heard, like a wave that strengthened and increased until it reached the very heaven. Rahab felt it in her bones. The stones of the city wall began to vibrate. Rahab ran to her family and gathered them together. Then the walls of the great city Jericho came tumbling down, one upon the other, until the entire city was flattened.

Rahab and her family were safe. But what should she do next? The men had told her to stay inside her house, but her house was no more. Even more worrisome, the people of Jericho had heard her name called out by the leader of the Israelites. She had been revealed as a traitor to her town.

Before she could even think of a plan, she heard her name called out. "Rahab! Rahab, come quickly." With a flood of relief she saw them. The two young spies had returned for her, just as they had promised. In the confusion of battle, as Israelites destroyed the city and all who were in it, the two young spies shepherded Rahab and her family to the Israelite camp and then returned to the battle. Like the city of Sodom so many years before, Jericho had become filled with sin and corruption, so much so that no one could live righteously. Even Rahab, a woman who instinctively recognized the Spirit when she heard it and felt it, had adopted some of the corrupt practices of the city. Like Lot, she and her family were the only ones who could be saved. Surely the Lord wept as He saw what He had to do.

Rahab was welcomed into the Israelite camp as a great hero and dwelled with them until the end of her days. She married Salmon, a member of the tribe of Judah, and was the mother of Boaz, who was the grandfather of King David. She is mentioned in the New Testament's great sermon on faith, for truly her life demonstrates "the substance of things hoped for, the evidence of things not seen" (Hebrews 11:1).

Rahab had not been raised in the faith of the Israelites, but the Light of Christ burned within her. Through the confirmation of the Spirit she recognized the truth when she heard it. She was willing to risk everything—even her own life—to embrace it. Like Noah and

Lot, she survived with the aching sorrow of knowing that her home, her neighbors, and everyone but her immediate family had been destroyed. And also like Noah and Lot, she escaped "the destruction with the knowledge that it was her assistance that made the conquest possible."[5]

The Israelite spies also took a significant risk when they decided not only to trust this woman but also to make a covenant with her. In Deuteronomy the Israelites were given two specific commandments as they prepared to enter the promised land. The first was "thou shalt smite them, and utterly destroy them," and the second was "thou shalt make no covenant with them" (Deuteronomy 7:2). The spies wasted no time in breaking both commandments. They made a covenant with Rahab, and they rescued from destruction both Rahab and her family members who waited with her in her house.[6]

Just a few generations later, Saul would make the same decision to ignore an identical commandment given to him through Samuel the prophet: "Now go and smite Amalek, and utterly destroy all that they have, and spare them not; but slay both man and woman, infant and suckling, ox and sheep, camel and ass" (1 Samuel 15:3). Instead, Saul "took Agag the king of the Amalekites alive . . . and the best of the sheep, and of the oxen, and of the fatlings, and the lambs, and all that was good, and would not utterly destroy them: but every thing that was vile and refuse, that they destroyed utterly" (1 Samuel 15:8–9).

For this disobedience Saul lost his calling and David was anointed king. The Israelites were taking a big risk when they rescued Rahab and her family. But there was a big difference between the two stories: Saul stayed the execution of the enemy king and kept the items of monetary value, while the Israelites rescued a humble woman of great worth whose heart had been converted.

In many ways, Rahab represents fallen humanity, redeemed through faith. The adversary wants us to believe that we are damaged goods—that we can never measure up to the requirements of God. But Rahab learned this simple but glorious truth: although virginity cannot be restored, virtue can. As happens to many people who have been redeemed from a sinful past, Rahab's virtue became exemplary, and she taught her sons virtue as well; Boaz, the future husband of Ruth and grandfather of King David, would be a model of gentlemanly respect for womanhood.

In the words of the New Testament, "By faith the walls of Jericho fell down, after they were compassed about seven days. By faith the harlot Rahab perished not with them that believed not, when she had received the spies with peace" (Hebrews 11:30–31). We know from Peter that "charity shall cover the multitude of sins" (1 Peter 4:8), but this is not to say that Rahab's previous sinful actions could be justified by her good works alone.

Instead, her good works toward the Israelite spies were the kindling of her faith, a faith that was flamed bright when she realized that she truly could be saved—not only in this life, by the dangling of a scarlet thread, but in the life to come, through the scarlet blood of Jesus Christ. She is one of four women mentioned in Matthew's genealogy of Christ. She is remembered not for her past but for her future. Through her courage and her faithfulness, the harlot of Jericho repented and became a grandmother of the Messiah.

RAHAB FORESHADOWS THE TEACHINGS OF JESUS CHRIST

The Atonement of Jesus Christ is infinite. There is only one unforgivable sin: blasphemy against the Holy Ghost (Matthew 12:31–32)—that is, the deliberate decision to reject the Atonement after one knows without doubt that Jesus Christ is the Savior. Ever constant, the Lord will respect our right to choose for ourselves, even if the choice is to turn away from His love and sacrifice. The Savior does not withhold His love and Atonement from the sinner, however; the sinner withholds it from himself by refusing to accept the gift. Christ stands at the door—every door (Revelation 3:20). We must open it of our own free will and invite Him in.

One of the greatest examples of this principle is found in the story of the Samaritan woman at the well. The Apostle John tells us that Jesus was traveling from Judea to Galilee when He came to a well outside the town of Sychar, near the land that Jacob had given to his son Joseph. This was not just any well; it was known as Jacob's well (John 4:1–6).

The Samaritans were a mixed race of people who traced their lineage to the Jews who had been left behind at the time of the Babylonian captivity and the non-Jewish invaders who had remained in Canaan with them. As a result, the Jews looked down on these "half-breed" Samaritans and would go out of their way to avoid them, even walking extra miles to skirt the land of Samaria. In fact, Jesus's disciples "marvelled that he talked with the [Samaritan] woman [saying] . . . why talkest thou with her?" (John 4:27).

Nevertheless, Jesus walked directly through Samaria, directly to Jacob's well, and directly to the woman whose heart was ready for conversion. Like Rahab, this woman had an unchaste past, and Jesus knew it. He said to her, "Thou hast well said, I have no husband for thou hast had five husbands; and he whom thou now hast is not thy husband: in that saidst thou truly" (John 4:17–18).

Many women would have been offended or hurt by such directness, but not this woman. Jesus knew something even more important about this woman than her unchaste past. He knew her heart. She had felt her spirit quicken when Jesus had said, "Whosoever drinketh of this water [at the well] shall thirst again: But whosoever drinketh of the water that I shall give him shall never thirst; but the water that I shall give him shall be in him a well of water springing up into everlasting life" (John 4:13–14). This Samaritan woman would suffer any embarrassment or discomfort to drink of that living water. "Sir," she said simply, "I perceive that thou art a prophet" (John 4:19). After she heard Jesus's wonderful message, she "left her waterpot, and went her way into the city, and saith to the men, Come, see a man, which told me all things that ever I did: is not this the Christ?" She knew Him, because He first knew her.

Rahab seems to have been a lot like the Samaritan woman— dynamic, outgoing, confident, and pragmatic. She may have engaged in sexual activity with several partners, just as the woman at the well did, and as many men and women of today have done. But when she was introduced to the teachings of the Israelites, she felt their power, just as the woman at the well felt the power of the gospel. Rahab loved her family and included them in the promise made by the Israelites, just as the woman at the well rushed to tell her family and friends the wonderful news of the living waters. Rahab was not yet a mother, but she was already an *ezer*. She protected the men of God and helped them to escape death, and then she rescued her own family by sharing with them her faith in these men of God. The story of Rahab is an important example of risk taking, sacrifice, promise, and redemption.

Rahab's rescue of the Israelite spies has been compared to the midwives' rescuing of the babies born in Egypt. Pharaoh commanded the midwives to kill all the baby boys, but the midwives pretended to be slow and inefficient. "The Hebrew women . . . are lively, and are delivered before the midwives come in unto them," they explained disingenuously. Similarly, "Rahab [hid] the Israelite spies just as Moses' mother hid her baby."[7] In both cases the courageous women defied a king and risked their own lives. In fact, Rahab is an integral part of the chiasmic story recorded in Exodus. It begins with Moses hidden in the bulrushes; it ends with "Rahab acting as the 'midwife' of the embryonic Israel"[8] reborn in the land of Palestine. The symbolic blood of the Passover lamb that prevented the slaughter of the firstborn in Egypt at the beginning of the story is mirrored in the scarlet thread that prevents the slaughter of Rahab's family at the end. Moses led the Israelites across the Red Sea on dry ground, just as Joshua would lead them across the Jordan on dry ground. At the center of the Israelites' return to their homeland is Rahab, "the first of the inhabitants of the land to declare her allegiance to God, and . . . the first to join Israel."[9] Alice Ogden Bellis adds, "Rahab is a hero because she protects the Israelite spies. She is also heroic because she is a woman of faith who takes risks based on that faith. In addition, she is clever, like the midwives of Exodus. She outwits the king of Jericho, ignores his death-affirming command, and acts in a way that affirms life—for herself and the Israelite people."[10] Like the other matriarchs of the Messiah, Rahab is an *ezer kenegdo*, a savior who risked her own life to protect a people she did not yet know. She is a warrior in the army of God.

If Jericho represents the world, Rahab's story represents every human's experience of sin and redemption. Significantly, all four of the women listed in Matthew's genealogy of Christ—Tamar,

Rahab, Ruth, and Bathsheba—are non-Israelites. "Such is the inclusive nature of the Abrahamic covenant, a system that refuses to deny admittance to anyone who truly seeks it," writes Rebecca Lyn McConkie of Rahab's conversion. She continues, "Character always trumps lineage. . . . Perhaps the story of Rahab is included to remind readers that God is less concerned about our heritage and our family than He is about our own actions and allegiance to His covenant."[11] The Apostle Paul reminds us, "All have sinned, and come short of the glory of God" (Romans 3:23); therefore, all of us need the Atonement. It is not for us to judge others, but to rejoice and be glad for the saving power of God's grace.

NOTES

1. Virginia Stem Owens, *Daughters of Eve: Seeing Ourselves in Women of the Bible* (Colorado Springs, CO: NavPress, 2007), 203.

2. Ibid.

3. John MacArthur, *Twelve Extraordinary Women: How God Shaped Women of the Bible and What He Wants to Do with You* (Nashville, TN: Thomas Nelson, 2005), 52.

4. Alice Ogden Bellis, *Helpmates, Harlots, and Heroes: Women's Stories in the Hebrew Bible* (Louisville, KY: Westminster/John Knox Press, 1994), 113.

5. Rebecca Lyn McConkie, "Rahab the Harlot: Her Place in the Hebrew Bible," *Selections from the Religious Education Student Symposium 2004* (Provo, UT: Religious Studies Center, Brigham Young University, 2004), 79–91.

6. Ibid.

7. Tikva Frymer-Kensky, *Reading the Women of the Bible* (New York: Schocken, 2002), 36.

8. Ibid.

9. Ibid., 37.

10. Bellis, *Helpmates, Harlots, and Heroes*, 114.

11. McConkie, "Rahab the Harlot."

RUTH GLEANS IN A GOOD FIELD

"Entreat me not to leave thee, or to return from
following after thee: for whither thou goest, I will go;
and where thou lodgest, I will lodge: thy people shall
be my people, and thy God my God" (Ruth 1:16).

RUTH CLUNG TO her mother-in-law's neck and wept. How could she turn away from this good woman who had lost almost everything? Husband, home, sons—Naomi had nothing left. Nothing but her two daughters-in-law, Ruth and Orpah, who were childless widows as well. Now she was sending them back to their parents' homes. What good could she be to them now?

Naomi had lived in Bethlehem with her husband, Elimelech, and their two sons, Mahlon and Chilion, until a famine forced them to find respite in Moab, a land on the eastern side of the Dead Sea. The fact that Elimelech "would take his family to Moab is a measure of the famine's frightening severity. The land of Israel was evidently both spiritually and physically parched, and times were desperate."[1] There Elimelech died, leaving Naomi and her sons alone in a foreign land. Perhaps she should have returned to the land of Judah when Elimelech died, she thought now. But she and her sons had remained in Moab, and her sons had married girls from among the pagan Moabites who were descended from Abraham's nephew, Lot. Finally both her sons followed their father in death, leaving behind two widows who had not been fruitful during their marriages. No, Moab had not been a good move for Naomi, and she did not want to spend the rest of her days reminded of her losses. Naomi decided to go back home to Bethlehem.

Naomi was familiar with the levirate law, which required a man to marry his brother's widow if the brother died without children (Deuteronomy 25:5–10). But Naomi had no more sons to give to Ruth and Orpah. Even if she were married, "would you wait for them until they are grown?" she scoffed bitterly. In fact, she told people to call her Mara, which means "bitter," instead of Naomi, which means "pleasant," because, she said, "the Almighty hath dealt very bitterly with me" (Ruth 1:20). "Providence had handed her a bitter cup to drink."[2]

Naomi felt completely bereft, and she wanted Ruth and Orpah to have more opportunities for happiness. She knew that life would not be easy for Moabite women in the land of Judah, where the residents harbored a particular resentment toward these distant cousins. The original Moab was the son of Lot and his own daughter, an incestuous relationship that was an abhorrent embarrassment to the Israelites (Genesis 19:30–38).

In addition, the Moabites had dealt treacherously with the Israelites as they returned from Egypt, obstinately refusing to sell food and water to the Israelites as they passed through on their way to the promised land (Deuteronomy 2:26–30). In fact, Naomi and Elimelech had violated the Mosaic law when they allowed their sons to marry Moabite women (Deuteronomy 23:3–5). Surely Ruth and Orpah would remain friendless widows if they moved with Naomi to Bethlehem.

Knowing all of this, it was with kindness and resignation that Naomi released her daughters-in-law from their obligations to take care of her. "Return to your mothers' homes," she told them gently. "May the Lord deal as kindly with you, as you have dealt with our dead, and with me. I hope the Lord will grant you new husbands, and children," she said, and she kissed them (see Ruth 1:8–9).

Orpah received the kiss sadly and then wept as she returned to her family. Naomi encouraged Ruth to stay in Moab as well. "Orpah has gone back to her people, and to her gods," she said. "Won't you go back too?"

But Ruth was ready to move forward, not backward. She clung to Naomi, this good woman who had treated her so well, and refused to leave. She understood that Naomi's bitterness was temporary, borne of abject grief and the depression that often accompanies it. Ruth also realized that she stood at a crossroads. She would choose for herself which path she would take, and it was empowering.

With tears in her eyes she proclaimed her love and her testimony. "Entreat me not to leave thee, or to return from following after thee: for whither thou goest, I will go; and where thou lodgest, I will lodge: thy people shall be my people, and thy God my God: Where thou diest, will I die, and there will I be buried: the Lord do so to me, and more also, if ought but death part thee and me" (Ruth 1:16–17). "Her words [were] so full of love, animated by a tender yet powerful passion"[3] not only for Naomi, but also for Naomi's God. Like all members of the human family, Ruth had been endowed with the great gift of agency. She was given a choice as she stood on the road between Moab and Bethlehem—a choice between the pagan gods of her youth and the one true God of eternity—and she chose well.

Ruth Becomes a Gleaner of Grain

Together Ruth and Naomi made the long trek from Moab to Bethlehem, just as Ruth's descendant, Mary, would make the long trek with her betrothed husband, Joseph, from Nazareth to Bethlehem many generations later. As that weary young couple would do, Ruth and Naomi traveled in poverty, not knowing what to expect when they arrived.

And like Mary and Joseph, they arrived during the barley harvest, which is associated with the Feast of the First Fruits and the Passover. Little did these women know that through Naomi's tribulations, Ruth herself would become an ancestor of the First Fruits of the Resurrection, Jesus Christ. Just as Job would lose children, property, health, and friends in a supreme test of his faith, Naomi had suffered devastating losses. And like Job, she would have much more restored to her as a result of her faith. It was part of God's plan to bring this particular Moabite girl back to Bethlehem, where she would meet a particular Jewish man named Boaz who would, with her, become the ancestor of a particular Jewish child named Jesus.

But this great mission was still in Ruth's uncertain future. For now, she and Naomi needed a place to stay, and they needed food to eat. Naomi and Elimelech had left behind a parcel of land when they moved to Moab, but there were rules regarding abandoned land. "Naomi could not suddenly reclaim her dead husband's field from the person who had been working it in her absence. Even if she could ultimately gain the use of the land, the present harvest belonged to the one who planted the barley."[4] Consequently they would need to find food from another source.

Ruth learned that there was a certain rich man, "a mighty man of wealth, of the family of Elimelech," who owned vast fields in the area (Ruth 2:1). Ruth was a willing worker. Could she find work in his field? With a hope in her heart that she might "find grace" in the sight of the field's owner, she left Naomi to rest after their long journey and went into the fields to glean after the reapers.

What was a gleaner? Jesus once said, "The poor you will always have with you" (see Matthew 26:11), and that has certainly been true. How to provide for their needs is a continuing problem. Wisely, the Lord established a system within the Mosaic law that would provide welfare for the poor while still preserving their dignity and self-respect. It would also reduce greediness or selfishness in the wealthy. He said, "When ye reap the harvest of your land, thou shalt not wholly reap the corners of thy field, neither shalt thou gather the gleanings of thy harvest. And thou shalt not glean thy vineyard, neither shalt thou gather every grape of thy vineyard; thou shalt leave for the poor and the stranger: I am the Lord your God" (Leviticus 19:9–10). "Gleanings" were the part of the harvest that fell from the baskets and bags of the hired reapers. A parsimonious steward would return and pick up all the harvest that dropped. But the Lord told them to leave the droppings where they were, so that "the poor and the stranger" would have food.

The Mosaic law did not simply tell landowners to hand over a portion of their goods to the poor; instead, it provided a way that the poor could work and support themselves. This was wise counsel, providing a hand up rather than a hand out. People who were temporarily out of work or just traveling through town could earn what they needed, but it did not allow idleness to become a way of life. The Lord's way of encouraging self-reliance while offering temporary assistance is powerfully effective.

Ruth went early to the field that day and set right to work. She wanted to gather the large plump ears of barley before they had been picked over. In fact, she went boldly to the overseers and asked, "I pray you, let me glean after the reapers among the sheaves" (Ruth 2:7). She wanted to glean right among the servants who belonged to the field, not just in the corners. At noon she noticed the master of the field as he came to check on the harvest. He was a fatherly man named Boaz who spoke kindly to his workers. Boaz noticed Ruth right away too. "Whose damsel is this?" he asked. He was drawn to this exotic young woman with the pretty face and strong work ethic.

Boaz was a good man with a strong sense of propriety, both in the sense of behaving properly and also in being respectful of property belonging to others. He was relieved to learn that this woman was not indentured to another field. When the women who worked for him told him that she was Naomi's daughter-in-law, Boaz was even more impressed. He had already heard of this Moabite woman who had left her homeland to care so tenderly for her widowed mother-in-law. Setting aside whatever prejudices his neighbors might have felt toward a Moabite, he immediately made special provisions for her. But it apparently never occurred to him to think of this lovely young girl in romantic terms. Boaz was older and somewhat set in his ways. Romance eluded him. If anything, he felt a fatherly affection toward Ruth.

"I want you to work only in my fields," he told her kindly. "I have already told the young men to treat you respectfully and leave you alone. When you are thirsty, you may drink from the vessels that my young men have drawn. And when it is lunch time, come and eat with my reapers."

Ruth was pleased by the kindness that was shown to her. Many women in her condition—poor, unmarried, alone, and a stranger in town—had to worry about young men taking advantage of them sexually. Boaz made certain that none of his men would treat her so. Even the offer of water was unusually kind, since it was normally a woman's responsibility to draw water for the men, and not the other way around. Once again, a romantic meeting began with the offer of water, just as it had for Rebekah and for Rachel. But the lunch! Boaz sat beside her and offered her food from his own dish. The food was so plentiful and so delicious that she slipped some into her pocket to bring to Naomi that evening.

Best of all, Boaz told his young men to grant Ruth's request to "glean even among the sheaves," where the best and most plentiful grain fell. A frugal man lives by the dictum "waste not, want not," and it is indeed wise counsel. However, the Lord's law of the gleaning was to "waste a little, so that others will not want." Where Ruth was concerned, however, Boaz told his men to "waste a lot!" He wanted there to be plenty of grain for this generous young stranger with the pretty smile and kind heart.

Naomi was relieved when Ruth returned home that night safe, happy, and bearing a bushel of grain. Ruth had worked diligently from morning until evening. Then she had beaten the stalks on the threshing floor, producing a full *ephah*, or bushel, for her day's labor. Naomi grinned as she munched on the bread and parched corn that Ruth had saved from her lunch for her mother-in-law. When she had heard the full story of the landowner who gave Ruth such privileges, Naomi asked, "Where did you glean today? Blessed be the name of the man who has treated you so well."

"I was in the fields of Boaz," Ruth responded simply.

Naomi was astounded. "Boaz! Blessed be he of the Lord, who has not left off his kindness to the living and to the dead. Boaz is near of kin to us" (see Ruth 2:18–20). Naomi was already beginning to form a plan.

Ruth continued, "He told me to stay close to his young men until the end of the harvest."

Naomi agreed. "Yes, you must work only in his fields. Stay close to his maidens, and his young men will protect you. You are very beautiful, my daughter. Many would take advantage of you. Do not take chances by going into strange fields or associating with people you do not know. You must watch carefully to protect yourself."

All through the spring Ruth stayed close by the maidens of Boaz. She gleaned throughout the barley harvest and the wheat harvest.

She worked hard, and she was happy. Her muscles were strong, and her skin was bronzed with the sun. She made good friends among the young girls who worked for Boaz. It felt good to be alive. Even Naomi had learned to smile again.

Ruth Becomes a Gleaner of Men

As the harvest ended, Ruth began to wonder what they would do next. But Naomi had already set out "to be Providence's helper by devising a strange plot."[5] She had been watching and waiting all through the harvest season, hoping that Boaz himself would think of the levirate law and invoke it on behalf of Ruth. He had known from the first that they were closely related. He had eaten beside Ruth and shared his own meal with her. He had given her special privileges in his field and had offered her the matrimonially symbolic drink of water. Clearly he felt drawn to her. But he could not or would not see her as anything more than an insignificant servant girl. Perhaps it was their age difference that kept him from thinking of her in that way. Perhaps it was her Moabite heritage. Now Naomi would set the plan into motion herself.

Naomi turned to Ruth. "My daughter, you have worked hard all season. Shall I not find rest for you from the fields?" she asked with a twinkle in her eye. Ruth looked puzzled.

"Boaz is our kinsman," Naomi said. "Our *near* kinsman," she added with emphasis. "He is a *go'el*—a redeemer![6] He could marry you and raise up a son in the name of Mahlon. I'm sure he will be with his men on the threshing floor tonight, winnowing the barley. Now let's get you cleaned up. Wash your hair and anoint yourself with sweet-smelling ointment. Put on your best clothes. And then go down to the threshing floor" (see Ruth 3:1–4). Then Naomi told her what to do once she got there. It was time for Boaz to open his eyes and see Ruth in a completely different way.

This is good counsel for anyone who is looking for a mate—male or female. Clean yourself up. Fix your hair. Put on your best clothes. Be friendly and kind. While you are waiting to meet the right someone, get on with your life, just as Ruth did. Work hard, and become self-reliant. Respect your employer, and protect yourself.

Employers too can learn much from Boaz's example. Be honest and generous. Provide good working conditions, and protect your employees. And keep your eyes open. The right person might be standing in front of you all along.

There was more to this liaison than simple matchmaking, however. It was risky and dangerous. "It is clear that Naomi [was] sending Ruth to do something which is totally inappropriate behavior for a woman, and which can lead to scandal and even to abuse."[7] Naomi's plan went much further than simply putting on fresh makeup and a clean dress. It entailed considerable personal risk to Ruth's reputation and her standing with her benefactor in her new town. Just as Esther, a later heroine, would do, Ruth girded herself with courage as well as with her best clothes.

Winnowing was heavy, dusty work. The men would throw the grain up into the wind with great winnowing forks. The heavier grain would fall to the threshing floor, while the lighter chaff and straw would blow away with the wind. The grain would then be piled into huge mounds and stored in granaries to be used as needed throughout the year. The dust and chaff made the men parched and thirsty. Despite the arduous nature of the task, Boaz was not the kind of landowner who stayed at home while others worked. He oversaw the planting, harvesting, and threshing himself. He would be at the threshing floor throughout the night.

Following Naomi's instructions, Ruth waited in the shadows until the men had finished eating and drinking. Boaz was in a merry mood. The harvest was good, and he enjoyed being with his men. They would stay on the open-air threshing floor to protect the grain from foraging animals and plundering thieves until it could be stored safely in the granaries. Finally he lay down at the bottom of a heap of grain, and the room became quiet. The men began to snore softly. This was the moment Ruth had waited for. She tiptoed quietly onto the floor and uncovered his feet. Then she lay down at Boaz's feet as a symbol of her proposal and waited for him to wake up.

Boaz was sleeping deeply. About midnight he awakened and realized a woman was sleeping at his feet. "Who are you?" he asked in fear. Although it was common in some places for women of disrepute to come to the men in the evening after they worked, Boaz had a strict policy against immoral practices. Women were not allowed on his threshing floor, and he did not want to set a bad example for his men by giving even the impression of impropriety. "Let it not be known that a woman came into the floor," he said with concern.

But this was no harlot at his feet. "I am Ruth, thy handmaid," she told him humbly. "Spread your skirt over me, for you are a near kinsman."[8]

This request was not literal but symbolic of Ruth's desire for Boaz to protect her and provide for her through the bonds of marriage. "Asking him to spread his cloak over her [was] an act of betrothal. . . . She had come to offer herself to Boaz, who as the *go'el,* the redeemer, would be able to reacquire Elimelech's field from whoever now had it, and would have first right of purchase if Naomi then sold it."[9] Ruth had had ample opportunity throughout the harvest season to engage in liaisons with the young men in Boaz's field, but she had behaved modestly around them. She had not chased any of them or flirted with them, either for love or for money. It would have been completely out of character for her to trap a man who did not need trapping. Ruth was neither straw nor chaff, to be tossed away lightly into the wind. She was a grain of true wheat on the threshing floor that evening. Clearly, her invitation for Boaz to "cover her with his skirt" was symbolic of a protective relationship, not a euphemism for a sexual one.

Boaz was genuinely moved by Ruth's proposal. (Her sweet-smelling ointment, her clean face, and her best clothes might also have affected him favorably.) He exclaimed, "God bless you, my daughter, for you have shown much kindness. I will do all that you require" (see Ruth 3:10–11). Naomi had told Ruth to do whatever Boaz instructed her to do; now Boaz was promising to do whatever Ruth instructed him to do. Already they were becoming partners, *ezerim kenegdo,* a couple who would support, complement, and complete one another. As a further symbol of his honorable intent, Boaz sent Ruth home with six measures of barley in her veil, "which in context is a form of bride-price or betrothal present."[10] Naomi received the dowry with pleasure.

Boaz Negotiates for His Bride

Boaz was a man of such integrity that he would not claim this lovely young woman under the levirate law until her nearer kinsman had the opportunity first to accept or reject her. This kinsman remains nameless in the story; he is known only by the service he was supposed to render: "redeemer."

This was a serious responsibility. According to the law, "if the man like not to take his brother's wife, then let his brother's wife go up to the gate unto the elders, and say, My husband's brother refuseth to raise up unto his brother a name in Israel. . . . Then the elders of his city shall call him, and speak unto him: and if he stand to it, and say, I like not to take her; then shall his brother's wife come unto him in the presence of the elders, and loose his shoe from off his foot, and spit in his face, and shall answer and say, So shall it be done unto that man that will not build up his brother's house. And his name shall be called in Israel, The house of him that hath his shoe loosed" (Deuteronomy 25:7–10).

The very next morning Boaz left the winnowing and called a council of the city elders to meet with him and the other kinsman on Ruth's behalf. Explaining the situation, he said to the cousin, "Naomi wants to sell a parcel of land that belonged to our kinsman Elimelech. You are the nearest kinsman, so it is your right to decide whether to take it. But if you choose not to exercise your right, I will redeem it myself. It is good land, but of course it will be an inheritance for Elimelech's heirs. If you buy it, Ruth the Moabitess will go with it, and you must raise up an heir to Mahlon, the son of Elimelech" (see Ruth 4:2–5).

The kinsman thought for only a moment. The law stipulated that "the redeemer who acquires the land . . . will have it only in trust for a child who will inherit it, and he will not be able to add the land to his own patrimony. He will use his own money to redeem the land, he will use the produce to support two women, and eventually the land will pass to someone who is not his legal heir."[11] This was too much of a sacrifice for the nearer kinsman. "I cannot redeem it for myself, for I have heirs of my own to consider," he said. He declined the offer. Boaz was delighted. Ruth was relieved. Naomi was satisfied.

Ruth apparently declined her right to spit in the face of the would-be redeemer, but she did use his shoe as a symbol of the new path she would walk. It was the custom in those days to seal a contract by taking off a shoe and handing it to the one with whom the contract had been made. Thus Ruth began the negotiations by uncovering Boaz's feet, and the kinsman concluded the contract by taking off his shoe and handing it to Boaz, in effect granting Boaz the right to stand in his stead as *go'el* for Ruth and Naomi. Proclaiming to the council and all who would hear, Boaz proclaimed, "Ruth the Moabitess, the wife of Mahlon, have I purchased to be my wife, to raise up the name of the dead upon his inheritance, that the name of the dead be not cut off from among his brethren" (Ruth 4:9–10).

Just as the cloak was a symbol of protection, the shoe had become a symbol of unity. Boaz would "step into his dead brother's 'shoes,' and by treading should produce 'first-fruits' for his deceased, childless brother."[12] Boaz became a redeemer for the family of Elimelech, and in so doing he would become a grandfather to the Redeemer of the world, whose own bare feet would bear the emblems of His sacrifice. Boaz's act of levirate redemption also redeemed Father Abraham's nephew Lot and his unnamed wife and daughters, whose lineage to Christ was restored and grafted in through their granddaughter Ruth, the gentle and gentile Moabite.

Boaz beamed as the neighbors congratulated them and wished them well. Calling on the name of Jesus's earlier maternal ancestors, they said, May "the Lord make the woman that is come into thine house like Rachel and like Leah . . . and let thy house be like the house of Pharez, whom Tamar bare unto Judah" (Ruth 4:11–12).

Naomi had lost almost everything in Moab; her husband had died, and then both of her sons had died too. But she had gained a daughter—a wonderful, generous, tender-hearted daughter. When Ruth's first child was born, she placed him into Naomi's arms and allowed Naomi to be his nurse. "There is a son born to Naomi," the neighbors cried in happiness for the good fortune of this woman who had suffered so much loss. Such tender care is to be desired between all women who are brought together by their love for the same man, one as his mother and the other as his wife. Ruth was truly a mother of godliness.

RUTH FORESHADOWS THE
TEACHINGS OF JESUS CHRIST

The relationship between Naomi and Ruth has been a symbol of loyalty and love for centuries. Naomi's friends said of Ruth, "Thy daughter-in-law, who loves you, is better to you than seven sons" (see Ruth 4:15). This is strong praise indeed. "Thy people shall be my people, and thy God my God," Ruth said in her heartfelt determination to forsake her own family and culture to follow her mother-in-law. This sentiment would be echoed in Jesus's instruction to His Apostles through Mary Magdalene at the Garden Tomb when He said to her, "Go to my brethren, and say unto them, I ascend unto my Father, and your Father; and to my God, and your God" (John 20:17). There is but one God, and He is Father of us all. Naomi knew it. Ruth learned it. And Jesus confirmed it.

Similarly, Naomi's sorrow foreshadowed the sorrow of Jesus's own mother. Mary knew from the beginning the mission that her Son faced, and the sorrow that was in her future. Surely she encouraged Him in His mission and gave Him strength to endure. Jesus shared Ruth's loving loyalty in the final moments of His agony on the cross, when He made sure that His mother would be cared for the rest of her days. He entrusted her to His beloved friend and Apostle, John, as a surrogate son who would be as kind and attentive to Mary as Ruth had been to Naomi.

The story of Ruth is a story of redemption—the redemption of an entire people. It begins with the shame of Lot and his family fleeing from the wickedness of Sodom, the city they had called home for several decades. Lot had chosen to "pitch his tent toward Sodom," even though "the men of Sodom were wicked and sinners exceedingly" (Genesis 13:12–13). Even after Lot was captured in a tribal war and had to be rescued by Abraham, Lot chose to return to the sordid excitement of Sodom rather than join the spiritually safer nomadic life of Abraham (Genesis 14). Warned of the coming destruction, Lot ultimately escaped with his wife and daughters and raced for the hills, but his wife turned back for one last lingering look and "became a pillar of salt" as she faced the destruction of the city she had called home (Genesis 19:26).

According to legend, Lot and his daughters found refuge in a cave, where his daughters, thinking that they were the only three people left on earth after the catastrophic destruction they had just witnessed, plied their father with wine and then seduced him in order to become pregnant and perpetuate the race. The child of the firstborn was Moab, father of the Moabites (Genesis 19:30–38). Thus Ruth traced her lineage back to an incestuous relationship. Boaz's lineage, too, seems less than reputable; his mother was Rahab, the harlot of Jericho, and his paternal great-great-great-grandmother was Tamar, who seduced her father-in-law. But as we have demonstrated, both of these women were redeemed through their faith, their actions, their motives, and ultimately through the blood and Atonement of Jesus Christ.

The story continues with the treachery of the Moabites toward the Israelites, when they refused to sell bread and water to the Israelites as they were returning from Egypt. This bolstered the anger and resentment between the two tribes and led to the Deuteronomic injunction against Israelites marrying Moabites (see Deuteronomy 23:4–5). Nevertheless, Ruth embraced Naomi, Boaz embraced Ruth, and the entire village of Bethlehem embraced their union and their baby. The sting of resentment would be soothed by the healing balm of kindness expressed by every character in this story.[13] Naomi prayed that the Lord would "deal kindly" with her daughters-in-law because they had "dealt kindly" with her sons. Ruth sought grace as she went into the fields to glean, and she found that grace in the kindly Boaz, who knew how kindly she had treated Naomi. Boaz continued to extend kindness to Ruth throughout the harvest season, causing Naomi to exclaim, "Blessed be he of the Lord, who hath not left off his kindness to the living and the dead." Boaz equated kindness with virtue when he said to Ruth, "Blessed be thou of the Lord, my daughter: for thou hast shewed more kindness in the latter end than at the beginning, inasmuch as thou followedst not young men, whether poor or rich." In fact, he said, "All the city . . . know that thou art a virtuous woman," because of her reputation for kindness.

Again and again the word was used, wiping away sorrow, wiping away hurt, wiping away sin.

Kindness shares the same root as the word *kindred*, for genuine acts of kindness lead to a familial bond. Through sincere charity, which is the pure love of Jesus Christ, we become part of the family of Christ. When the Creator said, "Let us make man in our own image," He meant much more than physical appearance; He endowed humans with the power to become like Him in every way. To be like Him is to be compassionate, generous, sacrificial, and wise. As Carolyn Custis James suggests, "The call to bear God's image is an invitation to get to know God deeply."[14] This is the most important step in the process of redemption. All have sinned, but all are invited to turn away from sin, take God's hand, and step onto the right path. His promise never falters: "His hand is stretched out still" (Isaiah 9:12). Through kindly acts we grow to love those whom we serve with a cheerful heart. Rebekah learned it. So did Leah. So did the Moabites and the Bethlehemites. So does everyone who bears the image of God.

When the kindly gentleman of Bethlehem redeemed the kindly widow of Moab, an entire nation was redeemed. The Moabites had refused bread and water to the Israelites, but three generations later they would succor the parents of King David of Israel and provide a safe haven for them (1 Samuel 22:3). Generations after that, Jesus Christ would offer Himself as a *go'el*—a "Kinsman-Redeemer"[15] who would give His own life as a ransom for all who have sinned. His body and His blood would become the living bread and water that would not be withheld from the parched and thirsty lips; through them He would redeem all humankind from the Fall.

Truly "the Lord had visited his people in giving them bread" (Ruth 1:6). Through Ruth and Boaz, Moab would be reabsorbed into the larger family of the Israelites. Lot and his family would be redeemed and restored to their family line. Yes, Ruth was right when she said, "Thy God will be my God." "Ruth claims the God of Israel out of her own ontological understanding. She knows—she knows directly, prophetically—that the Creator of the Universe is One."[16] John MacArthur concludes, "Ruth is a fitting symbol of every believer, and even of the church itself—redeemed, brought into a position of great favor, endowed with riches and privilege, exalted to be the Redeemer's own bride, and loved by Him with the profoundest affection. . . . The extraordinary story of her redemption ought to make every true believer's heart resonate with profound gladness and thanksgiving for the One who, likewise, has redeemed us from our sin."[17]

RUTH'S LESSON FOR TODAY: TWO WOMEN, ONE MAN

Ruth's profound example of love and loyalty sets a standard for all in-laws to follow. Yet the relationship between the woman who bears a son and the woman who marries him is often fraught with trials and discord. Seventy percent of women report having rocky relationships with their mothers-in-law or daughters-in-law. What causes this problem, and can it be fixed?

Elisabeth Graham observes, "A mother is naturally territorial when it comes to her family. A wife is just as territorial. Standing in the middle of these two overlapping territories is a man—the son of one and husband of the other. It's in everyone's best interest for the son to step out of the overlapping territory and fully into his wife's territory—and the sooner he does this the better."[18] Of course, that leaves the mother standing alone in her now empty territory. Transitions can be difficult, and the transition from mother to mother-in-law is one of the most difficult to accept. It requires a woman to redefine herself and her relationship with her own child. Is it any wonder that jealousy and competition sometimes flare?

Nevertheless, a comfortable relationship between mother-in-law and daughter-in-law can be established. First, recognize that each will have some difficulty getting used to her new position, so be gentle and kind with one another. Ruth knew that Naomi's bitterness was temporary, so she was patient with her mother-in-law. Similarly, the wise mother will step back graciously and allow her son's new wife to step into her new role. She will encourage and compliment her daughter-in-law and watch for cues that tell her what is working and what is not. A mother who treats her son's wife with love and respect will earn her son's love and appreciation.

At the same time, the sensitive daughter-in-law will make room in their life for her husband's mother. Like Ruth, she will compliment her mother-in-law, ask for advice from time to time, and share happy experiences. A wise man will also participate in establishing boundaries that lead to lifelong harmony. He will love his mother, but he will gently let her know that he must "leave his father and mother, and shall cleave unto his wife" (Genesis 2:24). When a wife feels confident that her place in her husband's heart is secure, she can make room in her own heart for his mother, and a loving relationship can flourish.

Next, establish appropriate boundaries. Observe basic courtesies such as calling before visiting and asking instead of just assuming that grandparents will babysit. Avoid topics of conversation that might be off limits, such as how money is earned or spent or how the children are being raised. Respect family rules about what grandchildren are allowed to do, wear, eat, or see. Recognize that the new family might want to establish its own traditions, even on special occasions like holidays. Boundaries should not become barriers, however; as Robert Frost observed, "Good fences make good neighbors." Treat your child's spouse as you treat your own, and embrace the spouse's extended family as well. Avoid such hurtful comments as, "Now let's have photos with just the real family."

Use words to heal and encourage, not to tear down or malign. Always ask yourself, "Is it kind? Is it necessary? Is it true?" Be quick to forgive and slow to take offense. Occasionally a mother-in-law will hear those most-welcomed words, "What would you do?" When that happens, Annie Chapman suggests "keeping [the] advice brief and sweet. . . . And if they do not ask for help, then a mother-in-law would be wise to pray and ask God to send information and inspiration to them through some other source."[19]

As Ruth and Naomi discovered, a good relationship between in-laws can bring lifelong joy and satisfaction. Adopting the kindness of Ruth can repair even a damaged relationship: Do kindly deeds, harbor kindly thoughts, express sincere appreciation, and seek the other's happiness. You will find it returned to you a hundred-fold.

NOTES

1. John MacArthur, *Twelve Extraordinary Women: How God Shaped Women of the Bible and What He Wants to Do with You* (Nashville, TN: Thomas Nelson, 2005), 71.

2. Ibid., 75.

3. Merle Feld, "At the Crossroads," in *Reading Ruth: Contemporary Women Reclaim a Sacred Story*, by Judith A. Kates and Gail Twersky Reimer (New York: Random House, 1994), 167.

4. Tikva Frymer-Kensky, *Reading the Women of the Bible* (New York: Schocken, 2002), 242 (tense adjusted).

5. Ibid., 247.

6. John MacArthur explains: "The Hebrew word translated 'one of our close relatives' is *goel*. It is a technical term that means much more than 'kinsman,' [just as an *ezer* is much more than a helper]. The *goel* was a relative who came to the rescue. The word *goel* includes the idea of redemption, or deliverance. . . . Old Testament scholars sometimes speak of the *goel* as a 'kinsman-redeemer' . . . and sometimes as 'avenger'" (MacArthur, *Twelve Extraordinary Women*, 79).

7. Frymer-Kensky, *Reading the Women of the Bible*, 248.

8. This interchange has puzzled Bible scholars for centuries. Were Ruth's actions and request merely symbolic, or did she and Boaz engage in sexual activity that night? Was the covering of his skirt a symbol of his agreement to protect her and accept her proposal of marriage? Or did she wait until he was drunk and then seduce him, as her ancestor, the daughter of Lot and mother of Moab, had done many centuries before?

Certainly Ruth had the opportunity and the means to seduce Boaz. But logic and decency cry out against this notion. She proved her virtue and trustworthiness by demonstrating what she *could have* done, while choosing not to do it. Surely Ruth did not transgress the law, nor did she sin against Boaz. In the first place, Ruth did not need to force Boaz into marriage through such degrading means; she had the levirate law on her side. Second, they were in a very public place, surrounded by Boaz's servants and completely open to the wind and air. Moreover, the scripture says that "she lay at his feet until morning, and she rose up before one could know another," which, in the Biblical sense, means before they could have sexual relations. Finally, and most important, Boaz's own words negate the possibility of sexual sin that night, for he says of her, "My daughter, fear not, for all the city of my people know that thou art a virtuous woman" (Ruth 3:11). It seems unlikely that two such virtuous people who had not even kissed one another before would suddenly commit adultery. Moreover, if they had engaged in sexual relations, it is unlikely that Boaz would have offered Ruth in marriage to her nearer kinsman the next day. For all these reasons it is much more likely that Ruth's request that he cover her with his skirt was a symbolic request for protection.

9. Frymer-Kensky, *Reading the Women of the Bible*, 248 (tense adjusted).

10. Ibid., 249.

11. Ibid., 251.

12. Calum M. Carmichael, *Women, Law, and the Genesis Traditions* (Edinburgh, Scotland: Edinburgh University Press, 1979), 75.

13. Tamar Frankiel, "Ruth and the Messiah," in *Reading Ruth: Contemporary Women Reclaim a Sacred Story*, edited by Judith A. Kates and Gail Twersky Reimer (New York: Random House, 1994), 321–35.

14. Carolyn Custis James, *Lost Women of the Bible: Finding Strength and Significance through Their Stories* (Grand Rapids, MI: Zondervan, 2005), 34.

15. MacArthur, *Twelve Extraordinary Women*, 80.

16. Cynthia Ozick, "Ruth," in *Reading Ruth: Contemporary Women Reclaim a Sacred Story*, edited by Judith A. Kates and Gwail Twersky Reimer, (New York: Random House, 1994), 228.

17. MacArthur, *Twelve Extraordinary Women*, 85.

18. Elisabeth Graham, *Mothers-in-Law vs. Daughters-in-Law: Let There Be Peace* (Kansas City, MO: Beacon Hill Press, 2010), 12.

19. Annie Chapman, *The Mother-in-Law Dance* (Eugene, OR: Harvest House, 2004), 39.

BATHSHEBA BECOMES
A TRUSTED QUEEN

*"Though your sins be as scarlet, they shall
be as white as snow" (Isaiah 1:18).*

ATHSHEBA WAITED PATIENTLY as her *shomeret* poured
water from the rooftop cistern into the basin and checked
her body for any stray foreign substances that would symbolically pollute the purifying water. Then she stepped out of her
robe and began to wash in the cool waters of the *mikveh*. She sighed
contentedly. She always looked forward to the ritual bathing that
ended the seven days of purification. Here in the privacy of her rooftop, under the waning heat of the late afternoon sun, the water felt
refreshing and good.

If only her husband, Uriah, were home, she thought again.
Under normal circumstances this would be their night for coming
together after the fourteen days of ritual separation. She missed him.
But the wars with the Philistines had kept him away for months at a
time. How long had it been, she wondered? Is this how "normal circumstances" would always feel for the wife of a high-ranking officer
and member of the palace guard? She closed her eyes and symbolically immersed herself in the cleansing water of the springtime rains
that represented renewal and a new start.

Suddenly Bathsheba shook the droplets of water from her face
and instinctively hid herself. Their home was just outside the palace
walls. Was someone walking on the king's balcony? Surely not. It
was spring, "the time when kings go forth to battle" (2 Samuel 11:1).

King David should be with his soldiers, defending Israel from the encroaching Philistines. He should be with Uriah. Surely her eyes and ears had deceived her. The king would not be in the palace. Not at this time of the year. Nevertheless, she reached for her robe as she heard a commotion at her door.

King David was indeed at home that day. While Joab and "all Israel . . . destroyed the children of Ammon, and besieged Rabbah, . . . David tarried still at Jerusalem" (2 Samuel 11:1). That was his first misstep on the path that would lead to tragedy, yet it seemed a minor one. Like many men who have fallen into temptation, he should have been busily occupied, but he decided to take some time off. This put him in the wrong place at the wrong time: pacing his balcony in the cool of the evening at just the moment when Bathsheba was finishing her rooftop ablutions. David cannot be blamed for that first unintentional glance; he had not come to his balcony intending to look for a woman. But that first glance should have been the end of this story. He should have quickly and modestly averted his eyes. He should not have looked twice.

But Bathsheba was a beautiful woman, and David was a king with a penchant for beautiful women. King David looked again. And again. This was his second misstep, and it was closely followed by a third step toward tragedy. He sent for a servant. "Tell me, who lives in that house over there? Who is that woman?"

The servant looked closely and responded, "Isn't that Bathsheba, the wife of Uriah the Hittite?"

Once again, this should have been the end of the story. David was married, and so was Bathsheba. Adultery in ancient Israel was considered a great sin, second only to murder. It was even punishable by death. Moreover, "Bathsheba [was] not simply any married woman. Both her father, Eliam, and her husband, Uriah, [were] members of David's trusted inner 'circle of thirty.'"[1] To take Bathsheba would violate not only her marriage vows but also David's relationship with a loyal soldier. Nevertheless, lustful desire had overtaken David. He was deeply attracted to this voluptuous woman. He sensed danger— but also passion. "Go get her," he said to his servants. "Tell her King David wants to see her." This was David's fourth misstep.

Bathsheba was brought to the king's palace. Whether she was invited or commanded, the record does not say. Nor do we know whether she came willingly or by force. Generations have painted her as a seductress who deliberately flaunted herself while bathing on her rooftop; others suggest that she was a victim of abusive power and possibly raped.[2] David was the king, after all. His very title commanded obedience. The record says that the messengers "took her," implying that she was not given a choice.

However, the fact that she continued her relationship with David and came back to him when she was in trouble suggests that she might have succumbed as a willing participant that night, as attracted to this handsome and powerful king as he was to her. We only know for certain that David sent for her, the messengers took her, and that David "lay with her" (2 Samuel 11:4) with no mention of love. He looked, he sent, they took, he lay . . . the words are deeply reminiscent of the words used to describe Leah's daughter Dinah's experience: "When Shechem the son of Hamor the Hivite, prince of the country, saw her, he took her, and lay with her, and defiled her" (Genesis 34:2). That was David's most inexorable misstep.

Bathsheba was devastated when she realized she had conceived that night. She hadn't seen her husband in months. Soon everyone would know that she had committed adultery. And Uriah! What would he think? What would he do? Oh, what had she done? And what should she do now?

David and Bathsheba were not the first couple to suppose that they could keep an extramarital affair secret. It is a sin as old as the hills and as new as last night's text message. Few people set out to destroy a marriage or inflict pain on a spouse. It may seem innocent at first: A couple of emails. A shared joke. Just a friendship. Maybe a playful tap on the arm while telling a story, or a look that lingers too long. *Who is that good-looking woman near the water cooler?* he wonders. Nothing serious. An innocent flirtation. And then . . . disaster. In the eloquent words of the prophet Jacob, "Ye have broken the hearts of your tender wives, and lost the confidence of your children, because of your bad examples before them; and the sobbings of their hearts ascend up to God against you. And because of the strictness of the word of God, which comes down against you, many hearts died, pierced with deep wounds" (Jacob 2:35). Infidelity of any kind, including emotional and social infidelity, is as hurtful and damaging as sexual infidelity. In fact, sometimes giving emotional affection to another is even more hurtful to the injured spouse than the physical act of infidelity. There is simply no gray area where fidelity is concerned.

David Attempts to Cover His Sin

Bathsheba sent a message to David containing four simple words: "I am with child." How quickly a short-term passion had produced a long-term consequence. This should have been David's final misstep. He was a king chosen by God and anointed by a holy prophet. He was the ruler—the one called to establish the standard and set the example of righteous living. It was time for him to lead the way, confess their actions, accept the consequences, and plead for mercy. But David wasn't ready for that. This king who had courageously vanquished a giant over nine feet tall, killed a lion and a bear singlehandedly, and faced thousands of enemies in battle did not have the courage or the humility to confess his adultery. Instead, he continued to cover his tracks and proceeded down the tragic path toward murder.

David and Bathsheba had already conceived a child; now David conceived a plot. He believed that the affair would remain hidden if Uriah could be convinced that the child was his. But Uriah had been at the battlefront, far away from his wife, for several months, so David sent a message to his chief officer, Joab, ordering him to send Uriah back to Jerusalem for a meeting. After hearing a quick report on the progress of the war, David told Uriah to go home and "wash his feet" (see 2 Samuel 11:8). He even sent along some special foods for the occasion. But "Uriah slept at the king's door" with the king's guards that night (see 2 Samuel 11:9). Exasperated, David asked him why he didn't go home. Uriah replied, "The ark, and Israel, and Judah, abide in tents; and my lord Joab, and the servants of my lord, are encamped in the open fields; shall I then go into mine house, to eat and to drink, and to lie with my wife? as thou livest, and as thy soul liveth, I will not do this thing" (2 Samuel 11:11). This honorable soldier was too noble to enjoy relations with his wife while his men were sleeping in tents at the battlefront.

Undeterred, David forged ahead with his plan and insisted that Uriah stay in Jerusalem another day. He invited Uriah to eat and drink with him, expecting that alcohol would weaken Uriah's resolve. He hoped that Uriah would become filled with as much lustful desire for Bathsheba as David had been. But once again Uriah refused to take part in the domestic enjoyment that was denied to his men. Even though he was inebriated, he stayed with the palace guards all night.

Time was running out. David was desperate to save Bathsheba's reputation and possibly her life, since the punishment for adultery could be death. He was also concerned for the life and reputation of Bathsheba's baby—*his* baby. Only Uriah could know for sure that he had not slept with his own wife. And now there was the added concern that Uriah was behaving in a subtly defiant manner. If David could get Uriah out of the way for good, Bathsheba and the baby would be safe, and so would David. So David proceeded to the biggest mistake of his life, committing a sin of the greatest magnitude: conspiracy to commit murder. For, of course, these were not merely missteps or mistakes, as we so often fool ourselves into believing. They were deliberate choices. And they were sins.

David wrote what amounted to a letter of execution and sent it to Joab by Uriah's own hand. "Set ye Uriah in the forefront of the hottest battle, and retire ye from him, that he may be smitten, and die" (2 Samuel 11:15) were his clear and explicit instructions. William Shakespeare would be so moved by this story that he would incorporate it in the tragedy of *Hamlet, Prince of Denmark* when Rosencrantz and Guildenstern unwittingly deliver a letter calling for their own execution.

Uriah was the best and most devoted of David's men, and a member of the elite palace guard. He was a Hittite, not even a man of Israel, yet consider his devotion to his king! Nevertheless, David ordered this valiant soldier abandoned at the battlefront to cover his own shameful sin. Not only was Uriah killed, but also many of the soldiers who fought closest to him were killed in this deliberate massacre. But David was unmoved. "Let not this thing displease thee," he wrote to Joab, "for the sword devoureth one as well as another: make thy battle more strong against the city, and overthrow it" (2 Samuel 11:25). David assuaged his own guilt by suggesting that a soldier is a soldier, and if it hadn't been Uriah, it would have been someone else who was killed; "the sword devoureth one as well as another," he defended himself (2 Samuel 11:25). But this was not an act of war. It was premeditated murder.

When she heard the news, Bathsheba "mourned for her husband" (2 Samuel 11:27). How far she had fallen in so little time from that spring evening when she had entered the cleansing waters of the *mikveh*! She had felt flattered by this handsome man who was the king of Israel, the most powerful man in all Canaan. The flame of desire had kindled between them. Now she felt only sorrow and shame. David, too, had acted out of character. He was not one to act rashly or impetuously to take what he thought was his.

Until now, he had been a patient, humble king. The prophet Samuel had anointed him to become the king when he was but a little child, yet he had waited patiently and respectfully for King Saul to live out his life and die by other causes. Even when David had opportunity to kill Saul and take his own place on the throne, he said, "The Lord forbid that I should do this thing unto my master, the Lord's anointed, to stretch forth mine hand against him, seeing he is the anointed of the Lord" (1 Samuel 24:6).

Shakespeare was so impressed by David's patient loyalty that he wrote *Macbeth* as a foil for David, contemplating how a lesser man might have reacted to the prophecy that he was foreordained to become king. Moreover, David should have remembered how he met and married the beautiful Abigail. For Bathsheba was not the first married woman who had caught David's eye.

DAVID MEETS ABIGAIL

Before he met Bathsheba, David had fallen in love with another woman who was married. The story begins during another lull in battle, but instead of being home at the palace, David was leading his troops on a long march. It has long been the custom during wartime for soldiers to commandeer food and other supplies from farmers and other settlers. Since the soldiers are risking their lives to protect the residents and their property, this is considered appropriate payment. However, it was not David's custom to rob or plunder, even in the name of national security.

One day when David and his men were patrolling an area, he sent a message to Nabal, a wealthy landowner whose servants were shearing sheep. He instructed the messenger to remind Nabal that the soldiers came in peace, and had not harmed the shearers or the sheep. In fact, the presence of David and his soldiers had kept other marauders from entering Nabal's fields. Then he asked Nabal to give "whatsoever cometh to thine hand"—that is, whatever Nabal could spare—"unto thy servants, and to thy son David" (1 Samuel 25:8). Nevertheless, Nabal was "churlish, and evil in his doings" (1 Samuel 25:3). He refused David's request, saying contemptuously, "Who is David? and who is the son of Jesse [that I should respect or obey him]?" (1 Samuel 25:10).

David was uncharacteristically furious. They had protected Nabal's flocks, and this was their treatment? He threatened to send his four hundred men into the fields to take what they needed by force, and then destroy everyone in Nabal's household, including his servants and their families. Nabal's men were terrified. Knowing that "a man cannot speak to [Nabal]" with any kind of reason when Nabal was in this mood (1 Samuel 25:17), they immediately sent word to their master's wife, Abigail, "a woman of good understanding, and of a beautiful countenance" (1 Samuel 25:3).

As is true of many couples, Nabal and Abigail were "unequally yoked" (2 Corinthians 6:14). She was accustomed to cleaning up after her husband's outbursts, using diplomacy and tact to calm those who were offended by her husband's arrogant and abusive ways. Without telling Nabal of her plan, Abigail immediately gathered food and wine and piled it onto donkeys to send to David and his men. Then she met David herself and bowed on the ground before him, appealing to his good nature and begging for mercy. Skillfully she reminded David of how his heroic acts had made him a legend in all Israel, and warned him that his reputation would be destroyed if he committed this heinous act of revenge against the innocent servants of the churlish Nabal.

The courage of this beautiful woman charmed David. Relief flooded him as he thought of what he might have done, and how such an act would have affected his standing with the Lord. "Blessed be thy advice, and blessed be thou, which hast kept me this day from coming to shed blood, and from avenging myself with mine own hand," he told her (1 Samuel 25:33). His heart was drawn to her, as it would later be drawn to Bathsheba. But Abigail was a married woman. Appropriately, David thanked her profusely and went on his way.

That could have been the end of this story. But it isn't. That night Nabal held a great feast. He drank until he passed out. The next day Abigail told him all that had happened, and how close they had come to disaster because of his selfish refusal to provide food for David's men. Nabal was so shocked that "his heart died within him." He fell into a coma, and ten days later he died. As soon as David heard of Nabal's death he sent for Abigail and asked her to be his wife. Abigail "hasted" to comply. It is apparent that these two felt a strong affinity toward one another. One could even call it "love at first sight." But they did not act on that feeling. They remained chastely apart from each other until Abigail was released from her marriage through Nabal's death by natural causes (1 Samuel 25:36–42).

David should have remembered this experience when he met Bathsheba. If God truly intended for Bathsheba to marry David, Uriah would have died naturally in battle. David did not need to force the situation and arrange for Uriah's death. Until and unless that happened, he should have stayed away. He would pay for this rash and lustful decision with remorse and penance for the rest of his life.

NATHAN TEACHES DAVID THE PARABLE OF THE EWE LAMB

Shortly after Uriah's death, the Lord sent the prophet Nathan to David with a problem. He said, "There are two men living in one city. One is rich, and the other is poor. The rich man has many flocks and herds, but the poor man had nothing except one little ewe lamb, which he had purchased and nurtured. This little lamb was so special that the man raised it in his own household. It played with his children, ate from his table, and even slept beside him. One day a traveler came to the rich man's home and asked for food. Instead of feeding the traveler from his own large flock, however, he took the poor man's ewe lamb and cooked it for the wayfarer. What should be done?"

David was incensed toward the selfish rich man. He did not realize yet that Nathan was telling a parable aimed directly at the king. "By God," David said, "the man who has done this shall surely die."

Nathan responded boldly, "Thou art the man" (2 Samuel 12:1–7).

For months David had been fooling himself into believing that he could cover his tracks and no one would be the wiser. He never set out to kill Uriah when he looked out across his balcony that day, but way led on to way, and that had made all the difference.[3] This was where the path he chose had led. Now he realized that God saw and knew all. With his own words he had condemned himself.

Significantly, Nathan did not condemn Bathsheba in this parable. She was the "little ewe lamb" in the story. She had not been sunbathing in the nude in hopes of seducing a king; she had been an obedient Israelite woman performing a religious ritual when the king sent for her. We cannot know whether she was a willing seductress or an obedient subject later that night, but it was not her purpose that day to sleep with the king, according to Nathan's parable. David, on the other hand, was represented as the selfish rich man in the story, taking advantage of his poor neighbor. King David could have had any unmarried woman he wanted. The Lord had granted him permission to marry multiple wives and concubines. But like the rich man in the story, David had become greedy. He wanted the other man's lamb.

Nathan continued with a litany of the goodness God had shown toward David. "He gave you the throne. He gave you wives. He gave you riches. He made you the head of the house of Israel and the house of Judah. If you had wanted anything else, he would have given it to you. Why did you do this great evil? Why did you kill this noble officer, and take his only wife?" Then Nathan added the punishment that David himself had decreed: "The sword shall never

depart from your house, and even your wives will be given to others"
(see 2 Samuel 12:11).

David's heart must have throbbed with grief and shame as he
heard these words. He knew all this was true. His pride and sense
of power had clouded his judgment and directed his actions. He
was devastated, and in this moment his arrogance was gone. With
deep humility he bowed his head and acknowledged, "I have sinned
against the Lord."

In that moment the Lord looked into David's heart and accepted
his repentance. "The Lord also hath put away thy sin; thou shalt not
die," Nathan said. This did not mean, however, that David would not
continue to feel the searing pain of remorse and the ongoing process
of repentance. Actions have consequences, and those consequences
would continue to unfold. God gives us our agency to choose what
we will do, but he does not let us choose which consequences we will
accept. We can't pick up just one end of a stick; the other end of the
stick comes with it. David's stick was heavy with guilt and remorse.

Nevertheless, David had been redeemed from spiritual death.
His relationship with God had not been severed. David would nurture that relationship by worshipping and praising God for the rest
of his life. As the Lord's representative, Nathan had immediately
acknowledged David's ultimate destination of repentance, but the
journey would take time. We see his soul-searing regret and soaring
gratitude in the powerful emotion of the Psalms written by David.

DAVID SEEKS FORGIVENESS

The Psalms are religious hymns of praise and supplication.
David wrote most of them. They reveal a king humbled by sin and
made hopeful through repentance. Several stand out as significant
for our story. In Psalm 32 he acknowledges the folly of hiding his sin,
and then expresses the peace that came from hiding it *in* the Lord
instead of *from* the Lord: "When I kept silence, my bones waxed old
through my roaring all the day long. For day and night thy hand
was heavy upon me. . . . I acknowledged my sin unto thee, and mine
iniquity have I not hid. . . . I will confess my transgressions unto the
Lord. . . . Thou art my hiding place; thou shalt preserve me from

trouble. . . . Many sorrows shall be to the wicked: but he that trusteth in the Lord, mercy shall compass him about. . . . Shout for joy, all ye that are upright in heart."

In Psalm 51, "David pleads for forgiveness after he went in unto Bath-sheba" (Psalm 51, supra-script). He writes poignantly, "Have mercy upon me, O God, according to thy loving kindness: according unto the multitude of thy tender mercies blot out my transgressions. Wash me thoroughly from mine iniquity, and cleanse me from my sin. For I acknowledge my transgressions: and my sin is ever before me. . . . Hide thy face from my sins, and blot out all mine iniquities. Create in me a clean heart, O God; and renew a right spirit within me. Cast me not away from thy presence; and take not thy holy spirit from me. . . . Then will I teach transgressors thy ways; and sinners shall be converted unto thee."

Through this eloquent psalm we see the steps of true repentance: first, recognize God's goodness, mercy, and power; second, confess one's sins before the Lord's representative; third, experience a complete change of heart by turning away from sin; fourth, renew one's relationship with God; and finally, desire to share God's goodness with others. David also expresses the importance of being honest with God, who "desirest truth in the inward parts" (Psalm 51:6). This means that before we can truly repent, we must "remove the mask" of trying to hide our sins from others and even from ourselves.

Ralph Waldo Emerson wrote in his journal, "The whole of Virtue consists in substituting *being* for *seeming,* & therefore God properly saith *I AM.*"[4] David thought he could cover his sins, but only when he acknowledged "truth in [his] inward parts"—within his own soul—could he progress. The Psalms provide ample witness that David's remorse was great, and that his pleading for forgiveness and support was genuine. Like Jacob, he "wrestled" with God (Genesis 32:24–32) and like Leah, he worked at nurturing their relationship. He pleaded for the peace and comfort that would come from knowing, as he declared in Psalm 16, "thou wilt not leave my soul in hell."

Centuries of readers have felt the magnitude of David's emotion while reading the Psalms. His words bring comfort and solace, even as he watered his pillow with his tears (Psalm 6). Peace and comfort would not come on this day, however. Nathan added one final consequence in his interview with David: "The child that Bathsheba bore to you will die." David returned to Bathsheba with a heavy heart.

BATHSHEBA BECOMES A TRUSTED QUEEN

Bathsheba, too, needed the sweet balm of repentance in her life. The *mikveh* symbolizes "a new start in the aftermath of pain and trauma," but for Bathsheba, that evening bath on her rooftop had not been the aftermath; it had been just the beginning. The guilt of infidelity, the panic of pregnancy outside of marriage, the fear of execution should Uriah want her put to death, the death of her husband—all of these weighed heavily on her. Nevertheless, it was time to move forward. After her days of mourning were past, David brought her into his house, and she became his wife.

But the worst was yet to come: the baby son born to David and Bathsheba would not survive the year. True to Nathan's prophecy, the child sickened. David fasted and prayed. He prostrated himself on the ground in humble prayer. The elders of the house sought to comfort and strengthen him, but he would not relent in his supplication. Nevertheless, the Lord had spoken. On the seventh day, the baby died. The stick David had chosen to pick up was heavy indeed.

It is not our place to judge who is worthy of the Atonement of Jesus Christ. Jesus Himself befriended "publicans and harlots." He did not condone sin, but He offered to heal people of their vices, saying, "They that are whole have no need of the physician, but they that are sick: I came not to call the righteous, but sinners to repentance" (Mark 2:17). An important element of repentance is restitution, or restoring that which has been taken or damaged. Sins such as murder and adultery are particularly heinous because life and virginity cannot be restored; once they are taken, they are gone. However, as in the case of the Samaritan woman at the well, the woman taken in adultery, Rahab, Bathsheba, and countless others, we know that repentance is available to all. While virginity cannot be restored, through the healing power of the Atonement *virtue* can.

Repentance is sweet to those who humbly yield to the Spirit and accept God's will. It has a uniting power for those who repent together. Lawrence and Sue Richards suggest that David's public confession and repentance contributed to Bathsheba's ability to forgive his monumental treachery in sending for her as a married woman, defiling her, and then murdering her husband by proxy. The only way for a relationship involving abuse or brutality to be salvaged, they write, "is for the man to take full, public responsibility for his actions. Confession and forgiveness then can lead to a healing of a violated relationship, and to the building of a happy, healthy marriage."[5] They note that after Nathan confronted David, he did just that, instructing his chief musician to play Psalm 51, in which he pleads for forgiveness for his sin with Bathsheba, in public worship. David's public acknowledgment of his blame in their affair allowed Bathsheba's wounds to heal, and "laid the foundation on which a strong, loving, and lasting marriage could be built."[6]

Despite the trauma of their beginning, Bathsheba and David did forge a strong marriage together, and Bathsheba became a noble and respected queen. David already had many wives and concubines when he met Bathsheba, but Bathsheba was the wife whose son, Solomon, became the heir to the throne. After their first baby died, "David comforted Bath-sheba his wife" and they drew strength from the sorrow they shared (2 Samuel 12:24).

The death of a child is the most traumatic event any couple can experience. Some couples cannot withstand the pain and their marriage ends in divorce. Others draw closer to each other in grief and the marriage becomes even sweeter to them. David and Bathsheba seem to have fallen within the latter camp. A genuine love was forged. Soon Solomon was born, followed by three other sons and probably daughters. They named one of their sons Nathan, in tribute to the role the prophet played in helping them through their repentance (1 Chronicles 3:5). Their son Nathan's name is listed in the priesthood genealogy of Christ recorded by Luke.[7]

That the Lord accepted their repentance and sanctioned their marriage can be seen in the fact that the Lord Himself selected Solomon as the birthright son, before he was even born. David wanted to build a great temple, but he had been a soldier all his life, and he had directed the death of Uriah. The Lord said, "Thou hast shed much blood upon the earth in my sight. Behold, a son shall be born to thee, who shall be a man of rest; and I will give him rest from all his enemies round about: for his name shall be Solomon, and . . . he shall build an house for my name; and he shall be my son, and I will be his father; and I will establish the throne of his kingdom over Israel for ever" (1 Chronicles 22:8–10).

David had fathered numerous sons by at least half a dozen wives before he married Bathsheba, including a son by the plucky and beautiful Abigail. Nevertheless, it was Bathsheba's son Solomon who was foreordained before his birth to become the king and build the temple. Surely Bathsheba kept this knowledge in her heart and in her mind as she nurtured and taught this special young man.

We catch another glimpse of Bathsheba's relationship with King David in the waning days of his life. Just as Rebekah had needed to step in and prevent her aging husband from giving the birthright blessing to Esau instead of Jacob, Bathsheba was called on to prevent civil war by reminding David that Solomon was the crown prince. Like Isaac, David had become old and enfeebled. Adonijah, the son of David and his wife Haggith, put on the trappings of leadership and began to gather followers while David was yet alive.

The prophet Nathan could foresee that Adonijah would massacre all the supporters of Solomon unless something was done immediately to ward off this impending treachery. Recognizing Bathsheba's influence with her husband, Nathan urged her to go in to the king and remind him of his promise to make Solomon king. Only after Bathsheba had spoken privately and tenderly to David did Nathan enter the bedchamber to confirm what she had said. He warned David that mischief was afoot; Adonijah was already acting as though he were the king.

David honored and respected Nathan, but he loved Bathsheba. He called her back into the room and said, "As the Lord lives, who has redeemed my soul out of all distress, . . . assuredly Solomon your son shall reign after me, and he shall sit upon my throne in my stead" (see 1 Kings 1:29–30). Then he did what wise kings do before they die; he established his successor publicly. David "made Solomon his son king over Israel. And he gathered together all the princes of Israel, with the priests and Levites" to announce it, so that there would be no misunderstanding (1 Chronicles 23:1–2). Solomon, born to a couple whose relationship had begun in sin, became the wisest king in all of Israel's history. Bathsheba had taught him well.

BATHSHEBA FORESHADOWS THE TEACHINGS OF JESUS CHRIST

Jesus demonstrated compassion and forgiveness throughout His ministry. He does not condone sin, but when a person repents He forgives readily, joyfully, and wholeheartedly. To repent does not mean to punish, but to turn away. A person who has repented of an act does a spiritual U-turn and heads in the opposite direction, away from both the sin and the temptation that led to the sin. Thus the Lord can treat the repentant sinner as though the act never happened, because in truth the person is no longer the sinner who committed the act. The person has changed.

This principle is made abundantly clear in the way Jesus treated the woman who was taken in adultery (see John 8:1–11). Jesus was teaching inside the porticos of the temple when several scribes and Pharisees brought a woman to Him for judgment. "This woman was taken in adultery, in the very act," they told Him. "Now the law of Moses commands us that such should be stoned: but what do you say?"

Jesus did not have the civic authority to condemn or acquit this woman. He was simply a teacher exercising the custom of teaching within the temple grounds. But the woman's accusers were not looking for a judge. They wanted Jesus to voice His opinion, so that they could use His own words against Him. The law of Moses was strict, and the prescribed punishments were severe. But these were *maximum* penalties, not mandatory. Stoning was a hypothetical punishment that was seldom, if ever, imposed. Nevertheless, it was the law. If Jesus said, "Don't stone her," which leniency was the common practice, He could be accused of inciting rebellion against the law. But if He said, "Stone her," it would violate the gospel of love and forgiveness that He had been preaching, and His followers would have been appalled and offended. Either way, He would lose. They were clever, these scribes and Pharisees, as they set their trap for Jesus.

But Jesus was not just clever; He was wise, even wiser than Bathsheba's son Solomon. Patiently He drew on the ground for a few minutes and then looked up nonchalantly. "Whoever is without sin among you, let him cast the first stone." Now the scribes and Pharisees were caught in their own trap. No one actually wanted to throw stones at this woman and inflict on her a slow, torturous death there in the public square. But if they did not pick up a stone, it would be an implied admission of guilt. The tables were turned.

These were prideful men motivated by jealousy and revenge, but they seem to have been affected by Jesus's calm spirit and demeanor that day. The scripture says they were "convicted by their own conscience [and] went out one by one, beginning at the eldest, even unto the last" until they had all slunk away (John 8:9), suggesting that each realized his own culpability. Some have even suggested that these were the very men who had had sexual relations with the woman, but that may be reaching beyond the mark. What matters most is what happened next.

When they were completely alone, Jesus stood up and asked, "Woman, where are those thine accusers? Hath no man condemned thee?"

The woman replied hesitantly, "No man, Lord."

And then she heard the words that we all long to hear, in those moments when our "eyes water the pillow" in torment from our sins: "Neither do I condemn thee: go, and sin no more," He said gently (John 8:1–11).

This is the legacy of Bathsheba. Virginity cannot be restored, but virtue can. Though our "sins be as scarlet, they shall be as white as snow" (Isaiah 1:18), through the gracious Atonement and merciful love of our Savior, Jesus Christ.

NOTES

1. Tikva Frymer-Kensky, *Reading the Women of the Bible* (New York: Schocken, 2002), 146.

2. Alice Ogden Bellis, *Helpmates, Harlots, and Heroes: Women's Stories in the Hebrew Bible* (Louisville, KY: Westminster/John Knox Press, 1994), 149–51.

3. Robert Frost, "The Road Not Taken," in *Robert Frost: Collected Poems, Prose, and Plays*, edited by Richard Poirier and Mark Richardson (New York: Penguin Putnam, 1995), 103.

4. Ralph Waldo Emerson, *Emerson in His Journals*, edited by Joel Porte (Cambridge, MA: Harvard University Press, 1982), 140.

5. Lawrence Richards and Sue Richards, *Women of the Bible: The Life and Times of Every Woman in the Bible* (Nashville, TN: Thomas Nelson, 2003), 24.

6. Ibid.

7. Matthew and Luke record two different genealogies of Christ. Both are the same through David, but then Matthew follows the lineage of Solomon, while Luke follows the lineage of his brother Nathan. Some scholars suggest that Matthew's list is the royal line of David through whom the Messiah would inherit his royal throne, while Luke's list is the priesthood lineage of the Jews and appears right after the story of Jesus's baptism. Still others suggest that Matthew provides Joseph's lineage, while Luke provides Mary's lineage. Matthew's gospel is directed mostly to the Jews, while Luke's account is written for a gentile audience. While the later lineage becomes murky, we know that Jesus is "the stem of Jesse" and a descendant of David through his wife Bathsheba.

MARY IS BLESSED
AMONG WOMEN

*"My soul doth magnify the Lord, and my spirit hath
rejoiced in God my Saviour" (Luke 1:46–47).*

MARY SMILED WITHIN herself as she thought of her
approaching marriage. Her parents had made such a
wonderful match for her. Joseph was a bit older, but he
was kind and gentle. His hands were strong, but they were softened
by the olive oil he rubbed into the wood in his workshop. She envi-
sioned herself working beside him in the carpentry shop, perhaps
with a baby at their feet. Perhaps two. Perhaps an army of children!
She smiled at the thought.

Nazareth was a small village of meager homes set high on a hillside nearly one hundred miles north of Jerusalem and populated by
working class farmers and craftspeople. Its reputation was so poor,
in fact, that Nathanael, the Apostle "in whom there was no guile,"
would scoff, "Can there any good thing come out of Nazareth?" when
Philip told him that he had found the Messiah and that He was a
Galilean from Nazareth (John 1:46). Nathanael would discover that
yes, indeed, something wonderful could come out of Nazareth.

Mary's smile suddenly faded. She sensed that she was no longer
alone in the house. She looked, and a strange man was standing
near her. She had never seen him before. He smiled respectfully and
bowed his head slightly. When he spoke, his voice was as gentle as
a breeze, yet strong as thunder. "Hail," he greeted her, "thou that

art highly favoured, the Lord is with thee: blessed art thou among women" (Luke 1:28).

Mary stepped back. What could this mean? What was he talking about? She was just a young village girl, betrothed to a carpenter, living under the rule of the Roman invaders. Why would anyone call her "favored"? Had he been sent by one of the Roman soldiers to take her? She looked around fearfully, wondering how soon her mother would return from the market.

Recognizing her concern, the angel calmed her. "Fear not, Mary: for thou hast found favor with God. And, behold, thou shalt conceive in thy womb, and bring forth a son, and shalt call his name Jesus. He shall be great, and shall be called the Son of the Highest; and the Lord God shall give unto him the throne of his father David. And he shall reign over the house of Jacob for ever; and of his kingdom there shall be no end" (Luke 1:30–32).

Mary felt the immediacy of the messenger's words. This was no generic prophecy about a child she would have sometime in the future. She would indeed have a son. Right away. And His name would be Jesus.[1] He would be the Son of the Highest, who is God. He would be the king of Israel forever. It was very clear: Gabriel was speaking of the promised Messiah.

But this wasn't possible. Mary was a simple village girl—no one special. Yes, the blood of King David flowed in her veins, but it flowed in the veins of most of the villagers. Why would God choose her to be the mother of the Messiah, she wondered humbly. Moreover, Mary was unmarried, and a virgin. She was betrothed, but she and Joseph had not spent intimate time with each other. They would not know each other physically until after they were married. "How is this possible," she asked, "since I have never had relations with a man?"

The angel reassured her. "The Holy Ghost shall come upon thee, and the power of the Highest shall overshadow thee: therefore also that holy thing which shall be born of thee shall be called the Son of God" (Luke 1:35). Then, observing that she was still troubled, the angel added, "Behold, thy cousin Elisabeth hath also conceived a son" (Luke 1:36). Could this be possible? Elisabeth had been barren for many years. Yes, it was true—"in her old age: and this is the sixth month with her," the angel added as he saw the incredulous look on Mary's face. Then the angel smiled and concluded his message, using nearly the same words that Sarah had been told all those centuries before when she, too, had conceived through miraculous means: "With God nothing is impossible."

Mary bowed her head. It was swimming with questions and consequences. She felt no personal pride in this announcement of her mission, but only humble acquiescence. And concern. How would she tell her parents? What would her friends think of her? Would anyone believe this incredible tale? How would she tell Joseph? Dear, kind Joseph. Her heart pounded within her chest as she contemplated the new path before her. She felt exhilarated and terrified at once. But her voice was firm as Rebekah's when her path had suddenly veered toward Isaac's tent, four hundred miles from her home, and she had replied, "I will go." "Behold the handmaid of the Lord; be it unto me according to thy word" (Luke 1:38), Mary said without hesitation. Her Son would follow her example thirty-three years later when He groaned in agony and said, "Not my will, but thine, be done" (Luke 22:42).

And with that, the messenger was gone. The angel had arrived without fanfare, and left in the same way. Mary would follow his example, maintaining a low profile regarding the wondrous news. She sat and pondered his message. What should she do now? She wasn't ready to share the news with anyone in her family yet. Would they believe her? Would they understand? She needed wisdom. Then she realized that the angel had told her what to do. There was one person who would understand everything, one person who would not scoff at news of this miraculous conception. That person was her cousin Elisabeth. Elisabeth was old, and according to the angel, she was expecting a baby. It was easy for Mary to gain permission from her parents to help this dear cousin in the last months of her pregnancy. Mary hurried to the city of Juda and the home of Zacharias and Elisabeth.

If Mary was concerned about how to explain her situation to Elisabeth, those fears were unfounded. As soon as she arrived at their home, Elisabeth's baby "leaped in her womb; and Elisabeth was filled with the Holy Ghost" (Luke 1:41). Before Mary could even tell her,

Elisabeth knew. As surely as if He had been standing right in front of her, as surely as she knew that the child in her own womb was a miracle baby, Elisabeth knew that Mary was carrying the promised Messiah who had been foretold by the prophets for centuries. The Spirit testified to her before Mary even had a chance to tell her the glorious secret.

Elisabeth wrapped her arms around her young cousin and welcomed her into their home. What wonderful conversations they shared during the three months they spent together! As her testimony burst forth, Mary praised the power and glory of God in a psalm that would become known as the Magnificat (Luke 1:46–55). Her words revealed that she had been well trained in the scriptures as they echoed the words of Leah, Hannah, Isaiah, Malachi, and the Psalms.[2] Her psalm began, "My soul magnifies the Lord," just as Hannah had exulted "My heart rejoiceth in the Lord" when she finally became pregnant with Samuel after pleading with the Lord for a child (1 Samuel 2:1).

Mary marveled that God would choose an ordinary young girl to be the earthly mother of His Son. "He has regarded the lowly state of his handmaiden," she sang, again recalling the words of Hannah, "you will indeed look on the affliction of thy maidservant and remember me, and not forget thy maidservant" (see 1 Samuel 1:11). She humbly acknowledged her responsibility to future generations as she sang, "Behold, henceforth all generations will call me blessed," echoing the words of Leah, "Happy am I, for the daughters will call me blessed" (Genesis 30:13), and of Malachi, who prophesied, "All nations shall call you blessed" (Malachi 3:12). "Holy is His name!" she exclaimed, joining her voice with Hannah's "No one is holy like the Lord" (see 1 Samuel 2:2) and with David's "Holy and awesome is His name" (see Psalm 111:9). She sang of His might and His mercy, His strength and His justice.

Mary did not recoil from the path on which she was about to embark, for "His mercy is on them who fear Him from generation to generation." She may have recalled this great truth in part from Psalm 103: "The mercy of the Lord is from everlasting to everlasting upon them that fear Him, and His righteousness unto children's children" (verse 17). "He has shown strength with His arm," she asserted, reflecting the words of Isaiah, "the Lord hath made bare His holy arm in the eyes of all the nations" (Isaiah 52:10). She gained further courage from the psalm of Hannah: "The Lord maketh poor, and maketh rich; He bringeth low, and lifteth up. He raiseth up the poor out of the dust, and lifteth up the beggar from the dunghill, to set them among princes, and to make them inherit the throne of glory" (1 Samuel 2:7–8). Mary expressed Hannah's thought in her own song of praise: "He has put down the mighty from their thrones and exalted the lowly."

Mary concluded her psalm with a reference to the Abrahamic covenant of posterity, property, and priesthood. Her words, "He has helped his servant Israel, in remembrance of His mercy, as he spoke to our fathers, to Abraham and his seed forever," echo Psalm 105: "O seed of Abraham . . . He remembers His covenant forever, the word which He commanded, for a thousand generations, the covenant which He made with Abraham" (see verses 6, 8–9). Mary recognized that this covenant would be fulfilled in the child she was carrying. Clearly she found strength, knowledge, and courage in the scriptures that she had been taught as a child and that were magnified in her visit with her wise and righteous cousins. She was well prepared to raise her Son with the words of the prophets in His ears.

This beautiful hymn revealed Mary's humility regarding her calling. Just as her Son would bear the sins of the world but give the glory to His Father, Mary gave all glory to God and drew no undue attention to her part in the plan. Her Son was the King and Savior, but she would not act the part of a queen. She acknowledged her role as the humble handmaiden of the Lord and praised God for His goodness.

The months she spent with Elisabeth and Zacharias were a happy, peaceful time for Mary. Elisabeth and Zacharias were "both righteous before God, walking in all the commandments and ordinances of the Lord blameless" (Luke 1:6). Zacharias had been serving in the temple just six months earlier when he, too, had been visited by the same angel. It had long been his habit to pray for the desire of his heart, and the desire of his wife's heart—that they might have a son. The time had long passed for Elisabeth to bear children, but "almost out of habit as it were, he continued to make his supplication to the

Lord."[3] As he stood beside the altar an angel appeared to him with a similar glorious message: "Thy prayer is heard; and thy wife Elisabeth shall bear thee a son" (Luke 1:13). The news was so astounding that Zacharias was stricken mute until the baby's birth, when his tongue would be loosed after he wrote the simple words, "His name is John" (Luke 1:63). Zacharias praised God after the birth of his son John with a glorious hymn of his own:

"Blessed be the Lord God of Israel; for he hath visited and redeemed his people . . . that we should be saved from our enemies, and from the hand of all that hate us; to perform the mercy promised to our fathers, and to remember his holy covenant; . . . and thou, child, shalt be called the prophet of the Highest: for thou shalt go before the face of the Lord to prepare his ways; to give knowledge of salvation unto his people by the remission of their sins, through the tender mercy of our God; whereby the dayspring from on high hath visited us, to give light to them that sit in darkness and in the shadow of death, to guide our feet into the way of peace" (Luke 1:68, 71–72, 76–79).

Less than three years later, when King Herod ordered the slaughter of all children under the age of two, Zacharias would give his own life rather than reveal the whereabouts of his wife and his precious miracle son, John.[4] John had a special mission of his own to fulfill: he would baptize the Savior of the world and stand as a witness to Christ's divinity, sending many converts to follow Him. Mary could have found no better people to help her prepare for her calling as the mother of the Lord Jesus Christ than Elisabeth and Zacharias.

MARY TELLS JOSEPH THE NEWS

After spending three months in the peace and tranquility of Elisabeth's companionship (Luke 1:56), Mary was ready. Returning to Nazareth she told her betrothed husband, "Joseph, I am with child." Joseph knew, of course, that the child was not his. Could he believe the story she told him of a miraculous conception? Or would he assume she had been unfaithful during the months that she had been away?

Joseph was indeed shocked and distraught. His beautiful Mary, "most beautiful and fair above all other virgins" (1 Nephi 11:15), was pregnant. Their betrothal was as legally binding as a marriage, so it fell to him to decide Mary's legal consequences. The rules regarding adultery and unwed pregnancy were strict. He could make a public spectacle of her and bring shame upon her and her whole family, or he could divorce her privately and send her to another community, where she would have the baby alone and unsupported. Under extreme circumstances, he could even have her stoned to death.

But Joseph was a kind and merciful man. His heart was saddened, but he loved this young girl to whom he had pledged his life and his honor. However she had become pregnant (and he found it hard to believe her story), he could not shame her publicly, nor had stoning ever entered his mind. Instead he was "minded to [send] her away privily" (Matthew 1:19), which was the softest consequence available to him.

Joseph was not one to make hasty decisions, however. That night as he pondered Mary's amazing story and thought about what he should do, an angel appeared to him in a dream and said, "Joseph, . . . fear not to take unto thee Mary thy wife: for that which is conceived in her is of the Holy Ghost. And she shall bring forth a son, and thou shalt call his name Jesus: for He shall save his people from their sins" (Matthew 1:20–21). Then the angel explained that this was the fulfillment of Isaiah's prophecy of a virgin birth. "The Lord himself shall give you a sign," he reminded Joseph. "Behold, a virgin shall conceive, and bear a son, and shall call his name Immanuel" (Isaiah 7:14), which means "God is with us."

That was all Joseph needed to hear. He couldn't go back to sleep. Rushing to Mary's house, he told her that he, too, had received a vision verifying this wonderful news. "Mary, I know now that this is truly of the Lord. I will do everything in my power to protect you and this baby," he said. Their betrothal had made them legally married. Taking her into his home would constitute the confirmation of their vows. Joseph took Mary into his home and she became his wife, although they did not have marital relations until after Jesus was born (Matthew 1:25). Then they surrounded Jesus with siblings, including James, Joses, Simon, and Judas, as well as unnamed sisters

(Matthew 13:55). Jesus's childhood home would be a happy, bustling, busy place, and Joseph would be a loving, caring stepfather.

Mary Becomes the Mother of the Messiah

As a direct descendant of King David, Mary was a princess who carried the blood of royalty within her veins. But the Jews had lived in subjection for many years. First the Babylonians had invaded their country, then the Greeks, and finally the Romans had thundered into Israel fifty years before Mary was born and created a protectorate. For the most part the lives of the Jews went on as normal. "Unlike the Greeks, the Romans had no desire to impose their pagan religion on conquered countries. Their passion was for peace, order, Roman justice, and the prompt payment of tribute."[5]

The Israelites worked, produced, traded, worshipped, and lived as Israelites. But they were required to obey the Roman soldiers and governors and pay them tribute money for their "protection" from other invading nations. Now Caesar Augustus, who was the emperor of Rome at this time, wanted an accounting of all his subjects, including the Jews in Israel. Consequently, Caesar decreed that every person must return to the city of his ancestry to be counted and taxed. Although Mary was in her ninth month of pregnancy, she would travel with Joseph to the City of David, called Bethlehem, to participate in the census and pay the tax.

When Joseph and Mary entered Bethlehem it was teeming with activity. Not only were people in town for the census, but it was also Passover week, traditionally a time of celebration and family gatherings. Local residents hawked their wares to weary travelers. Weary travelers looked for lodging. Roman soldiers dotted the streets to keep the peace. Joseph looked futilely for a place where they could stay. It had been a long journey of more than one hundred miles from their hilltop home in Nazareth, skirting the despised land of Samaria, passing the capital city of Jerusalem, and finally trudging into Bethlehem. Mary had traveled most of the way on the back of a donkey. Although its even-gaited hips were more comfortable than the loping gait of its cousin, the horse, the ride had been long and exhausting, and Mary was nearing the time of her baby's delivery.

Joseph was anxious to find a place for her to rest, but no innkeepers would open their doors to this poor dusty couple who looked as though they hadn't two pennies between them—not when wealthier travelers with more silver in their pockets were also descending on Bethlehem. Little did they know that they were turning away the King! Finally one innkeeper took pity on them.

"I can offer you a place in the stable," he said. "It is quiet there, and you can spread fresh straw for a bed. If your wife's time for delivery comes, I will send one of our girls to help."

Mary smiled her thanks as the innkeeper directed them to the tiny rock grotto behind the inn. Joseph did his best to clean the area and lay fresh straw for a pallet. He spread a blanket on the straw and gently helped Mary down onto the makeshift bed. It was a smelly, dirty place, but they were grateful for the privacy, because she was already in labor. While crowds of visitors observed the miracle of the Passover in their homes and lodgings with a paschal lamb, the very Lamb of God was born in a humble stable.[6] The moment all of eternity had been waiting for had come. The world would never be the same.

That night Mary wrapped her Son tightly in the swaddling clothes she had brought with her on the journey. The soft bindings made the baby feel cozy and secure. She held Him close and looked into His trusting eyes. Her heart leaped. She had never known such love and peace, such utter joy. Joseph wrapped his strong arms around them both, swaddling them with his comfort and protection. He would be an *ezer kenegdo* as well—a partner equal to the task before him. Joseph would be a pillar of strength and a roof against the storm.

Soon a parade of visitors came to the stable, including humble shepherds who had been watching over their flocks on the hill outside the city.

"An angel came and told us the wonderful news," one of them said.

"A whole host of glorious angels," another added, "singing and praising God, right up there in the sky! We came to see."

"Beautiful songs. Glorious songs!" another added with rapture on his simple face.

Mary turned the babe's cherubic face so the shepherds could see. They smiled and pointed and nudged one another. Several wiped tears from the corners of their eyes. They were simple peasants, but they had seen the King. They hurried to tell all their friends. The Messiah had been born.

Mary leaned back against the straw and cradled the baby in her arms. She pondered all the things she had seen and heard over the past nine months and kept them close to her heart. This baby belonged to the entire world, she knew. But tonight He belonged only to her.

A Gift Unites Mary and Jesus Symbolically

Joseph and Mary were in no hurry to return to Nazareth. Mary needed time to rest after giving birth, so Joseph found work as a carpenter. Before long they moved into a little house where Mary nurtured her son and played with him. They liked it here in Bethlehem. She treasured the memory of the shepherds' visit, and all the events that had accompanied that night and the days that followed.

One of those memories came to her mind now. When Jesus had been eight days old, Mary and Joseph presented Jesus at the temple to be circumcised, in honor of the Abrahamic covenant. Two months later, "when the days of her purification according to the law of Moses were accomplished, they brought him to Jerusalem, to present him to the Lord" (Luke 2:22). Traditionally a lamb or kid would be brought as a sacrifice on the day of purification, but a couple who could not afford a lamb could bring turtledoves or pigeons instead (Leviticus 5:7); the Lord looks upon the sacrifice of the heart, not the costliness of the offering.

Mary and Joseph, still poor in earthly belongings, brought turtledoves to the temple. But they carried the true Lamb in their arms. A devout old man named Simeon had been watching at the temple and asked to hold the baby in his arms. Joy lit the man's face as he prophesied loudly, "With my own eyes I have seen the salvation that God has prepared for all people. He will be a light to the Gentiles, and the glory of the Jews." Then he turned to Mary and said quietly, "The Lord promised me that I would see the Messiah with my own eyes. Now it has happened. I can die in peace. But know this: His will not be an easy life. He is destined for the fall and rising of Israel. Even you will feel the pain, as though a sword pierced your own heart" (see Luke 2:27–35). Mary kept this moment and cherished it in her heart. The man *knew*. The Holy Ghost had told him through the spirit of discernment that her Son was the Messiah.

Next an old woman followed after Simeon with the same passionate desire to behold their little baby. Anna was known as a "prophetess, the daughter of Phanuel, of the tribe of Aser" (Luke 2:36). She, too, recognized the Messiah in His cherubic face. Anna had been a widow for eighty-four years, yet the glow of rapture as she held the child and gazed into His face made her appear as young as a new mother. Mary pondered all these things in her heart as she nurtured and cared for her baby boy. Kings and queens had not bowed down to Him, but those who nurtured the Spirit of God in their hearts had recognized Him.

These were happy days for the new couple. Jesus had grown chubby and strong as He laughed and toddled about the house, bringing a constant smile to the faces of Mary and Joseph. They did not know the danger that loomed in the palace not far from their house. But God knew. And He also knew how to protect them.

Now Mary peeked out to see the cause of the gathering commotion she heard in the streets outside their little house. It was already evening, yet the street glowed with a strange light from the sky. She could scarcely believe her eyes. Outside she saw a group of men dressed in brightly colored silk robes with upturned shoes and strange caps on their heads. Their entourage included brown-skinned servants and a variety of local urchins who skipped along and jostled for position to see these exotic visitors. Suddenly the men pointed into the bright sky above Mary's home. A look of joy, mingled with relief, covered their faces. The men nodded to one another and strode toward the door of their humble home.

Mary pulled back. "Joseph! Come see!" she called out to her husband. These were the Magi who had received a revelation about the birth of the Savior. Later generations would give them names: Caspar, Melchior, and Balthazar. But in the scriptures they are unidentified except by the direction from which they had come.

They had traveled hundreds of miles from the East to worship the Messiah and bring Him gifts, following a star that seemed to move until it rested right above Bethlehem. This star had caused the bright light Mary observed.

Upon arriving in Bethlehem, the Magi had looked for the Messiah by asking, "Where is he that is born King of the Jews? for we have seen his star in the east, and are come to worship him" (Matthew 2:2). These Wise Men naturally assumed that an event so profound would have been welcomed and celebrated in the community. But Jesus was born in obscurity. No one knew His messianic mission except His parents and a few sensitive souls, such as Zacharias, Elisabeth, Simeon, and Anna. When the Magi asked for the whereabouts of the king, they were mistakenly directed to the palace of King Herod, who feigned interest in worshipping this "new king." But Herod was secretly threatened and angered by the idea of a usurper. Was not Herod himself king of the Jews? Cunningly he said to the Magi, "When you find this king, come and tell me where he is, so that I may worship him too" (see Matthew 2:8). His real intent was to kill this potential enemy and usurper of the throne.

The Magi were unaware of Herod's evil plan as they found their way from his luxurious palace to the humble house where Mary and Joseph were living. They entered it not with the pomp of kings, but with the humility of servants. Immediately they fell to their knees in reverence and worshipped the child. Then they presented the gifts they brought with them, including gold, frankincense, and myrrh.

These valuable gifts were worth more than money. They represented the three key roles that Jesus would play during His earthly ministry. The gold symbolized royalty and His role as the King of this world. Frankincense was a spice burned in temple ceremonies, and symbolized His priesthood. Myrrh was a fragrant gum extracted from the rockrose and used as a holy ointment in purification ceremonies and embalming. It foreshadowed the day that myrrh would be brought to the tomb by His mother and the other women who would come to anoint His body for burial after His crucifixion.

The myrrh also united Mary and Jesus symbolically. "The Rock" is one of the Savior's appellations. He is called "the Rock of Ages," because He is that solid immoveable source of strength where the grieving and the penitent can "hide themselves" for comfort. Similarly, the rose would become a common symbol for Mary in paintings during the Renaissance. It represents beauty, love, and sorrow. Thus the rockrose from which myrrh is extracted foreshadowed both His death and His eternal relationship with His mother.

Immediately after the gifts were delivered, an angel warned the Magi of Herod's treachery and told them to leave Bethlehem by a different path. However, when the Magi slipped away without returning to him, Herod was furious that this infant usurper had evaded his murderous grasp. He devised an even more villainous plan: he would send out a dragnet to kill all the baby boys in Bethlehem and the surrounding coasts who had been born within the past two years, when the Magi had first seen the sign of the baby's birth. The anguished voices of those mothers whose babies were ripped from their arms during the ensuing "slaughter of the innocents" can still be heard in the heavens. The best of times had been followed quickly by the worst of times.

Baby John, Elisabeth's son, escaped the slaughter, probably hidden in the wilderness with the Essenes where he was raised on "locusts and wild honey" until it was time to begin his mission as the forerunner of Christ. Sadly, his father, Zacharias, would not fare so well; he was slaughtered "between the temple and the altar" (Matthew 23:35; Luke 11:51), during the massacre of the innocent children as he refused to reveal the whereabouts of his little son, according to Christian tradition.[7]

Jesus escaped the slaughter as well. An angel appeared to Joseph that same night, warning him to take his little family and escape into Egypt. Joseph did not have to be told twice. They departed immediately, probably using the gold provided to them by the Magi to pay for their journey. Thus the baby Jesus, King of the Jews and Savior of the world, began His young life as a fugitive. The holy family would stay in Egypt until the angel told them that Herod was dead. Even then, Joseph worried that it was not safe for them in Bethlehem because Herod's son, Archelaus, ruled in his place. They would move back to Nazareth, a sleepy village one hundred miles away, where no one would suspect they had evaded the heinous decree. Joseph and Mary would take no chances where this precious child was concerned.

And yet . . . just a few years later, they lost Him.

MARY'S PANIC

Mary enjoyed the fresh spring sunshine as she walked with the other women back toward Nazareth. Nearly twelve years had passed since their harrowing escape into Egypt. Mary still shuddered when she thought of the tragic edict that had befallen so many families. After King Herod's ignominious death, Joseph was told by an angel that it was finally safe to come out of hiding in Egypt. For safety's sake they had bypassed Bethlehem and returned to a simple carpenter's life in Nazareth, where Jesus learned His stepfather's craft. As the oldest son in the family, He was expected to take over His father's business. Mary and Joseph were about to learn just how literally that would come to pass.

As often as they could, they traveled to Jerusalem to celebrate the Passover. It was such a happy custom. Mary chatted with the women as they walked, and Joseph enjoyed conversing with the men. Their children played with their cousins and friends along the way, alternately running ahead or lagging behind, but always managing to stay nearby. "Typically, on such a journey, women traveled with the younger children, separate from the men and older boys. Jesus was twelve years old—a pivotal year in the life of a young Jewish boy as he transitioned into manhood, moving from the care of his mother to the tutelage of his father."[8]

Suddenly Mary realized that she hadn't seen Jesus for quite some time. She scanned the groups of children behind her and in front of her, but she could not see her eldest son anywhere. *Maybe He is with Joseph*, she thought, trying to calm her rising fear. *He enjoys listening to the men's conversations.* And He had just turned twelve. It was time for Him to be with His father and the other men. Still, she hurried to where her husband was walking.

"Joseph—Joseph! Have you seen Jesus?" Mary called, willing herself not to panic. Joseph's smile of convivial camaraderie instantly changed to soberness. "Isn't He with His friends? When was the last time you saw Him?"

"I can't remember," Mary replied. "Maybe a few hours? Maybe early this morning—I don't know. I don't know! Oh, Joseph! What should we do?" They questioned all their family and friends, but the conclusion was clear: Jesus was no longer with the group. No one remembered seeing Him since they left Jerusalem—and they were already a full day's journey toward Nazareth. Leaving their other children in the care of relatives, they hurried back to Jerusalem.

Mary and Joseph searched frantically for their son. What agony they must have felt. Could He have fallen and hurt himself? Had He been bitten be a scorpion, whose sting could be deadly? Had He been kidnapped? Killed? Where could He be? Their panic rose as they searched and searched. The Messiah had been entrusted into their care, and they had lost Him.

Three long days passed, mirroring the three days that He would be lost to the world inside the tomb. And then, finally, they found Him. No harm had come to Him. He was simply "in the temple, sitting in the midst of the doctors, both hearing them, and asking them questions. And all that heard him were astonished at his understanding and answers" (Luke 2:46–47). This was the magnificent temple King Herod had built just thirty years earlier on the very spot where King Solomon had built the first permanent house of the Lord. It was fit for the Son of God and built just in time for His use.

Jesus's mother and stepfather had taught Him well. He knew the scriptures. In fact, He understood their meaning far beyond what His parents or the rabbis had taught Him. But Mary was too frightened to appreciate the profound nature of what her Son was doing. "Son, why have you dealt with us this way?" she cried. "Your father and I have searched for three days. We have been beside ourselves with worry!"

Jesus answered calmly. "How is it that ye sought me? wist [knew] ye not that I must be about my Father's business?" (Luke 2:49). Mary was puzzled by this response. Joseph had no carpentry business in Jerusalem; that was back in Nazareth. She did not realize that Jesus spoke of His Eternal Father. Mary had not needed to scour the city looking for Him. Jesus expected her to know that He would be in the temple, His Father's house, preaching the gospel. That was His Father's business. He was twelve years old, the age when young Jewish boys entered manhood. It was natural and good that Jesus had expounded the scriptures and answered the questions posed by the rabbis in the temple. But He might have told His mother where He was going.

Jesus returned obediently with His family to Nazareth, but Mary could see that He had changed. He had "increased in wisdom and stature, and in favour with God and man" (Luke 2:52). Mary kept all His sayings and pondered them in her heart.

JESUS'S FIRST MIRACLE FORESHADOWS HIS ATONING SACRIFICE

Mary looked at the empty wine pots and wondered what they would do. The weeklong marriage celebration at Cana was far from finished, and already the wine was gone.

Jesus was now thirty years old, the age at which a man could become a rabbi. Mary was aware of the special powers that her Son possessed. She might not have understood the fulness of His ministry, but she knew that His words had power, a power as invisible and as tangible as gravity or electricity. She had been watching for the time when He would begin revealing His powers to others. He had been baptized; He had selected His Apostles. His ministry had begun. The time was now.

Mary sent for Jesus. Before she uttered a word, Jesus looked at the empty pots and said to His mother, "What have I to do with thee? My hour is not yet come" (John 2:4).

Mary turned to the servants and told them simply, "Do whatever He tells you to do." Then she backed away.

Jesus told the servants to fill six water pots with water. These were not household containers used for drinking water; they were "water-pots of stone, after the manner of purifying of the Jews, containing two or three firkins apiece" (John 2:6). The Jews used clay pottery for kitchen purposes. These stone pots were designated to catch the water that would be used for ceremonial washing. A firkin was equal to about nine gallons, so these were heavy pots, able to hold at least twenty gallons each. Jesus told the servants to fill the water to the brim. When they had finished, He told them to draw out the liquid and take it to the host of the feast who, after tasting it, declared it to be the best wine of the party. The host was surprised, saying, "Thou hast kept the good wine until now" (John 2:10). Ordinarily the best wine was served at the beginning of a feast, when guests could taste the difference, and cheaper wine was served at the end of the party, when guests were already somewhat inebriated and less able to discern good wine from bad. Thus the host was startled to taste such fine wine at the end of the wedding feast.

Why did Jesus perform His first miracle and "manifest forth his glory" (John 2:11) for such a seemingly trivial and superficial event as a local wedding? In fact, symbolically there was much more to this miracle than providing wine for a party. Wine is a symbol of Jesus's atoning blood. By changing the ceremonial water from the stone pots into wine, He symbolically demonstrated that the cleansing water of the Mosaic law was being transformed into the saving blood of Jesus Christ. The best—Christ Himself—had indeed been kept for last.

Mary Watches as Jesus Fulfills His Mission

Mary's personal time with Jesus had come to an end. For thirty years she had loved Him as a son; now she would worship Him as a Savior. As Jesus began His ministry, Mary traveled with Him, listening to His sermons and sharing in the joy of His disciples. She marveled at the miracles He performed, especially as He healed the sick and raised the dead. She gained insight from the parables He taught. But He belonged to the world now. Matthew, Mark, and Luke all record the experience when Mary and His brothers stood outside, wanting to speak with Him, but the crush of the crowd made it impossible for them to reach Him. All three Gospel writers report Jesus's words: "Who is my mother, and who are my brothers? My mother and my brothers are all those who hear God's word and obey it" (Matthew 12:46–50; Mark 3:33–35; Luke 8:20–21).

It may have been that Mary "and her younger sons became concerned for his welfare. He was so consumed by his ministry that he wasn't taking proper care of himself."[9] Others suggest that they were worried about Jesus's physical safety when they called out to speak with Him privately. After all, the scene occurs "when opposition to Jesus was becoming open."[10] Jesus had been accused of performing miracles through "an unclean spirit," and in turn He had accused His detractors of blasphemy (Mark 3:29–30). Jesus's response may have been a gentle rebuke toward His brothers, "for neither did his brethren believe in him" (John 7:5).

Whatever had been the catalyst, Mary's relationship with Jesus had clearly changed. "As a mother, she had once provided all His needs, but in the ultimate and eternal sense, He was *her* Savior and provider."[11] This appears to be the underlying point of the scene—not that He did not appreciate and respect Mary as His mother, but that He had more to offer her through their eternal relationship. "Jesus zeroed in on two sacred institutions for women—motherhood and family—and redefined them both. According to Jesus, a woman's life is truly blessed *not* when she becomes a mother, but when she hears and obeys his Word."[12] Mary and His siblings, special though they were, needed to approach Him in the same way we all do: as Mediator and Savior. Mary's relationship with Jesus would be strengthened as she became a true disciple of Christ.

In sum, Mary realized that Jesus was not rejecting her with these seemingly harsh words, but expanding the circle of His love to embrace all humankind as His family. Nevertheless, it must have been hard to accept that their daily mother-and-child relationship had changed. This is true for all mothers. If we do it right—if we teach our sons and daughters to be wise, strong, and self-reliant—we have to be willing to let go as they spread their wings. Every person comes to earth with a particular mission. The wise mother prepares her children to discover and accept that mission, and then she sends them on their way. This often means fading graciously into the background when the time comes. Mary supported Jesus throughout His earthly life. But she recognized that for now, He had work to do that might not include her.

It was not to His mother's home that Jesus walked each night during the last week of His life, but to the home of His friends Mary and Martha and their brother Lazarus. It does not appear that His mother was with Him at the Last Supper, nor in the shadows of Gethsemane, nor in the courtyard where Pilate ordered Him scourged. But she stood near Him at the cross in the final moments of His mortal life, encouraging Him and supporting Him. At the moment of His deepest agony, Jesus's heart turned once more to the woman who had loved Him first, and loved Him best: His mother.

Heavenly Father had been watching too. In the Garden of Gethsemane, when the burden of the world's sin—*our* sin—weighed so heavily that Jesus sweat "great drops of blood falling down to the ground," God sent "an angel unto him from heaven, strengthening him" (Luke 22:43–44). But as Jesus hung upon the cross, there came an awful moment when God the Father had to withdraw His Spirit from His Son. This separation from the spiritual lifeline that had never left Him in all His mortal days was essential to the Atonement; Jesus had to do it alone in order for His sacrifice to be complete. It was almost unbearable, worse even than the spiritual anguish of Gethsemane or the physical agony of crucifixion. It caused Jesus to cry out in surprise, "My God, my God, why hast thou forsaken me?"

But He was not entirely forsaken. His mother was there. We can only imagine the grief she experienced as she watched her beloved Son hanging in agony, His hands and feet bleeding from the nails driven through their tender nerves, and His naked body exposed to the mockery of those who despised Him. Yet she did not turn away. With the courage and love of the woman who jumped into the roiling sea so that her child who had been swept overboard would not die alone, Mary stayed with Jesus to comfort and sustain Him in His final moments.

Nearby stood Jesus's beloved Apostle John. The other Apostles had scattered, unsure of what they should do or where they should go. But John remained, and he was bereft. Despite His agony, Jesus saw it all. To speak in His condition required "the most desperate physical effort. . . . Jesus could only speak while exhaling, and, to do this, He had to lift Himself on those cruel, nerve-shattering spikes in His feet."[13] Nevertheless, looking down from the cross and motioning toward John, Jesus whispered tenderly, "Woman, behold thy son!" Then He turned to John and repeated, "Behold thy mother" (John 19:26–27). From that moment John treated Mary as if she were his own mother, and Mary loved John with all the maternal tenderness she had felt for Jesus. Tradition suggests that she eventually traveled with John to Ephesus, where he built her a little house. They comforted and sustained one another until her death. But there would be no comfort for her on this horrifying evening. Still, she did not turn away.

Crucifixion was a common form of execution in the ancient Roman Empire. Usually the convicted criminal was tied to the cross by ropes, and the weight of his body would drag him downward, making it impossible to fill his lungs with air unless he could straighten himself up. A little platform was attached to the cross under the feet so that the person could lift himself up to breathe. Eventually the person became exhausted and died from suffocation. But if it took too long, the impatient soldiers would break the legs of the criminal, making it impossible for him to stand. He would then die from the shock of the broken bones or from the lack of oxygen, or both. Jesus suffered longer than the Romans had expected. Despite the damage to His feet that would have made it agonizing to push up from the platform and fill His lungs, He continued to live for several hours.

Night was coming on, and with it, the beginning of the Sabbath. Mary watched in horror as the Roman soldiers prepared to break her Son's legs to hasten His death. But instead of breaking His bones, they thrust a sword into His side, upward toward His heart. Thus, unwittingly, the Roman soldiers fulfilled the prophecy foretold by David that "he keepeth all his bones: not one of them is broken" (Psalm 34:20). Jesus was the Passover Lamb, of whom it was commanded, "neither shall ye break a bone thereof" (Exodus 12:46). But this exquisite symbolism may have been lost on Mary in that excruciating moment as she felt the sword pierce her own heart, just as Simeon had foretold those many years before on the day of her purification after Jesus's birth (see Luke 2:34–35). As the sun went down, water gushed from His chest. He did not move. He was dead.

Mary's eyes were wet with grief as they pulled down the cross that would soon become a symbol not of criminal execution but of divine Atonement. She watched as the nails were wrenched from the bloody, swollen flesh of His hands and feet. There was no time for proper burial, no time to anoint His body with the precious spices and ointments that were part of the Jewish ritual. She mustered a grateful smile as Joseph of Arimethea, a wealthy disciple, offered his own nearby tomb as a burial place for her Son. Weeping, she hurried to her room to wait out the Passover and the Sabbath. Only when the holy days were finished would she be able to return to her Son's grave and anoint His body with the precious myrrh that had been fore-shadowed in the gift of the Magi—the ointment made from rock-rose that united mother and Son symbolically as well as physically. It would be a long, dark wait, but Mary would be at His tomb when the sun rose. And when her Son arose.

MARY'S LEGACY FOR JESUS CHRIST

Humility and *humiliation* are words that are often used inter-changeably, but while they share the same root, they are far from the same in meaning. Humiliation is a debilitating debasement inflicted by others. It is imposed from without. Humility is a serene under-standing of one's true nature and relationship with others. It comes from within. There is nothing demeaning about humility. In fact, it can be majestic. One of Jesus's greatest traits was His humility, and there is nothing humiliating in that statement. He knew who He was: the Son of God. That knowledge gave Him strength as well as meekness. He could endure all that was demanded of Him because He knew who He was. There was simply no need for hubristic pride.

Similarly, people who are secure in knowing who they are feel no shame in acknowledging what they do not know. They are confident in their strengths, and they recognize their weaknesses. They seek help when they need it, and they repent when it is necessary. There is nothing false or weak about true humility. It does not puff itself up to mask insecurity or inadequacy, but it is not self-debasing either. People who are humble are teachable, and as a result, they become stronger and wiser, more skilled and more confident. Humility is one of the noblest of traits.

Jesus learned humility from His mother's own example. Mary's humble faith and her unswerving obedience are her greatest lega-cies for Jesus Christ. With humble faith she bowed her head and said, "So be it unto me" when the angel Gabriel announced that she would be the mother of the Messiah. She accepted her role humbly, not as a queen but as a handmaiden in her earthly life. She taught her Son that meekness. Similarly, her Son would teach His competitive Apostles, "If any man desire to be first, the same shall be last of all, and servant of all" (Mark 9:35). Then He explained further, "For even the Son of man came not to be ministered unto, but to minister, and to give his life a ransom for many" (Mark 10:45). Jesus could have spent His earthly sojourn in the palace of a king, but He chose instead the role of a servant, reared in the home of a humble and faithful young mother.

During His great Intercessory Prayer in Gethsemane, when the guilt of all the sins of the world burned deeply into His conscience, it took every ounce of His strength to endure. The agony was more than even He expected, "which suffering caused [Himself], even God, the greatest of all, to tremble because of pain, and to bleed at every pore, and to suffer both body and spirit—and would that [He] might not drink the bitter cup, and shrink" (D&C 19:18). "Father, if thou be willing, remove this cup from me," He pleaded. But the words of His mother's humble acceptance of the Father's will those many years before echoed in His own as He added, "Nevertheless not my will, but thine, be done" (Luke 22:42). Giving all glory to the Father for His sacrifice, He "partook and finished [His] preparations unto the children of men" (D&C 19:19).

Mary Inherits a Great Legacy

Mary did not mother Jesus all by herself. She had the legacy of her foremothers to sustain and guide her. Generations of women stood before her—noble and courageous women with a shared goal of caring for their children and rearing them to become righteous leaders. From Eve, she gained the confidence to exercise the gift of agency and the courage to sacrifice her own comfort for the good of all humankind. From Noah's wife, she learned the importance of always being in the right place at the right time. With Sarah, Mary shared the intimate truth that there is not "any thing too hard for the Lord" (Genesis 18:14). From Rebekah, she gained the insight to listen to the Spirit and ponder its message. From Leah, she learned to nurture her own relationship with God, even when she felt alone and misunderstood. Like Leah, she learned "precept upon precept; line upon line" (Isaiah 28:13), and she taught her Son in the same way. From Tamar and Rahab, Mary developed the courage to act boldly. From Ruth, she inherited the tremendous traits of kindness and loyalty. And like Bathsheba, Mary recognized her Son's great mission as the future King and helped Him to grow in wisdom, humility, leadership, and love.

Think. Ponder. Pray.

Choose. Accept. Act.

This invitation is extended to all. "Both Old and New Testaments define women in terms broad enough to encompass every woman's life, from start to finish,"[14] not just those who become mothers. Each of us, no matter who we are or what we do, is called by the simple words, "Come follow me." As Mary learned, even more important than being His mother was the role of becoming His disciple. This is true for all of us. In learning His word and doing His will, we are adopted into His family and become joint heirs with Christ. This is the great legacy that all women, and indeed all humans, inherit from the strong, valiant women who are matriarchs in the lineage of Jesus Christ.

NOTES

1. "Jesus" is the Greek form of the Messiah's name. In His village He would have been called "Joshua," which means "God is help," or more literally, "Savior" in Hebrew. Similarly, Mary is the Greek form of the Hebrew name "Miriam," which means "star of the sea" or "sea of bitterness."

2. John MacArthur, *Twelve Extraordinary Women: How God Shaped Women of the Bible and What He Wants to Do with You* (Nashville, TN: Thomas Nelson, 2005), 116–19.

3. W. Cleon Skousen, *Days of the Living Christ* (Salt Lake City: Ensign Publishing, 1992).

4. Joseph Fielding Smith, *Teachings of the Prophet Joseph Smith* (Salt Lake City: Deseret Book, 1938), 261.

5. Skousen, *Days of the Living Christ*, xliii.

6. Christmas is celebrated on December 25 because it corresponded with the pagan celebration of solstice, or the birth of the sun. However, according to the Book of Mormon, Jesus died on the fourth day of the first month of the thirty-fourth year after the sign of His birth—that is, four days after His birthday. Since He died during Passover week, He was also born during Passover week (3 Nephi 8:5–23).

7. Smith, *Teachings of the Prophet Joseph Smith*; see also the Protevangelium of James.

8. Carolyn Custis James, *Lost Women of the Bible: Finding Strength and Significance through Their Stories* (Grand Rapids, MI: Zondervan, 2005), 170–71.

9. Ibid., 175.

10. Lawrence Richards and Sue Richards, *Women of the Bible: The Life and Times of Every Woman in the Bible* (Nashville, TN: Thomas Nelson, 2003), 132.

11. MacArthur, *Twelve Extraordinary Women*, 126.

12. James, *Lost Women of the Bible*, 177.

13. Skousen, *Days of the Living Christ*, 746.

14. James, *Lost Women of the Bible*, 178.

MARY MAGDALENE:
THE MORNING BREAKS,
THE SHADOWS FLEE

"The dawning of a brighter day majestic
rises on the world" (Parley P. Pratt).[1]

OR MANY YEARS our family celebrated Easter with a sunrise service all our own. In the early morning darkness my husband and I would wake the children gently, wrap them in quilts, and guide them out the back door to our little boat on Lake Virginia in Winter Park, Florida. Quietly we would motor to the middle of the lake, waiting for the sun to rise, just as the women had waited anxiously on that first Easter morn for the sun to signal the end of the Sabbath. Only then could they go to Christ's tomb to perform their final act of service for Him.

As the sky lightened our lake, birds would call to each other and fish would splash as they snapped at the insects. We listened to sweet hymns on the boat's stereo system, and I read my favorite part of the Easter story, John 20. I have read that chapter aloud at least a hundred times, but I can never get through it without a catch in my throat when Mary recognizes the Savior's voice as He speaks her name and she responds with the humble, joyous, "Master." It is perhaps my favorite story in all of the scriptures. At its center is a theme of Christ's deep, tender, and abiding love for His friends. May we all be counted among them when He comes again.

The Morning Breaks[2]

Mary Magdalene watched anxiously for the first rays of dawn to break through the shadows and signal the end of the Sabbath. She had hardly slept through the long hours of this interminable night while her Lord's body lay in the tomb. When Jesus was arrested, she had hoped He would do something to save Himself. Yet she knew in her heart that His time had come. Most of His Apostles had scattered, unsure of what they should do. But Mary had stayed with Him, watching with the other women from afar off until finally she moved with John to the foot of the cross, supporting Jesus with her adoration and comforting His mother. What exquisite agony she must have felt!

It hurt her terribly to remember how His body was rushed so quickly from the cross. Even in death He had "not where to lay his head" (Luke 9:58), she thought sadly. She remembered how, at the last minute, they had taken His body from the cross and laid it hastily in the tomb of a disciple, Joseph of Arimathea. There had been no time to anoint His body with sweet spices and prepare it properly for burial. The Sabbath had arrived.

Finally the morning broke through. The first day of the week had begun. Carrying the precious ointments of myrrh and other spices that had been foreshadowed by the gifts of the Magi at His birth, Mary Magdalene moved hastily toward the tomb that stood just outside Jerusalem's city walls. Several other women accompanied her to the tomb. All of them had waited reverently but impatiently for daylight to come. In her grief, Mary Magdalene barely saw them. She was aware only of her own sorrow, and her determination to express her love and respect through this final act of sacred service.

This was not the first time she had anointed Jesus with precious ointment. The tears of her current grief mingled with the memory of those tears with which she had bathed His feet, and the aroma of the ointment with which she had anointed Him then. How she longed to feel the warmth of His skin again, and to wash the dust from His weary feet! He had freed her soul from seven demons (Luke 8:2), and from the moment the demons went out of her, the Spirit of Christ had come in. She felt it. She knew it. She had followed Him from that moment forward as He traveled and taught throughout the countryside. His words spoke peace to her soul. Now, as she hurried to the tomb, that same peace gave her strength in her darkest hour.

The women wondered how they would move the massive stone that had been placed at the opening of the tomb. Jesus's enemies had demanded it be placed there, for fear that Jesus's followers would remove His body and then declare that He had risen from the dead. Two Roman sentries stood guard at the tomb throughout the Passover and the Sabbath.

But when the women arrived, the sentries were gone. The stone had been moved. And the tomb was empty.

Almost.

Inside sat a young man dressed in a long white robe who seemed to be waiting for them. "Don't be afraid," he told them gently. "You are looking for Jesus of Nazareth, who was crucified. He is not here. He is risen!" Then he added, "See for yourselves," directing their attention to the roughly hewn burial shelf. "Behold the place where they laid Him" (see Mark 16:5–6). Two thousand years have passed since Mary Magdalene walked out of the beautiful Garden Tomb that sits below the Hill of Golgotha, just outside Jerusalem's city wall. Many travelers have visited the Garden Tomb and "beheld the place where they laid him," and they have felt the same thrill of realization: "He is not here. He is risen. Behold for yourselves."

But at that moment, the women were confused. The angel continued, "Now go your way, and tell His disciples and Peter that He will meet them in Galilee," he instructed them (see Mark 16:7).

The other women fled in fear, and told no one what they had seen and heard. Others also resisted believing the story (Mark 16:11–14). Mary Magdalene was perplexed and troubled too, but she did as she was told. Quickly she ran to the house where the disciples were staying, calling out in her grief, "They have taken away the Lord out of the sepulchre, and we know not where they have laid him" (John 20:2). So focused had she been on her task of anointing His body that she had completely missed the point of the angel's message: *He is risen.*

Stunned, Peter and John raced to the tomb, with Mary close behind them. As they approached, Peter and John stooped to look inside. No one was there. Nothing remained except the burial shroud, neatly folded and placed upon the shelf. Peter and John did not know what to make of this, for they did not yet understand the scripture that said "he must rise again from the dead" (John 20:9). They returned to their own home, leaving Mary alone in the garden.

And then it happened.

Weeping inconsolably, Mary looked once more inside the tomb, perhaps thinking that she had simply overlooked the body—the way we often look again and again in the same place when we are desperately searching for something precious that is lost. Two angels appeared inside the tomb, but she was so focused on her search that she was not even surprised by their sudden presence.

"Why are you weeping?" one of them asked.

"Because they have taken away my Lord, and I know not where they have laid him," she answered, as though it were perfectly natural to see two personages dressed in white, sitting inside a tomb that had been empty moments before.

Realizing once again that His body was not there, she turned away from the tomb, anxiously scanning the garden for someone else who might help her. A man stood nearby, and He asked her the same question: "Why are you weeping?"

Thinking this man was the gardener, she begged, "Sir, if you have taken Him away, please tell me where His body is laid, and I will take it."

Then, using the voice she knew and loved, the man uttered her name.

"Mary."

As simply as that. And she knew. She turned around and looked into His face.

"Rabboni; . . . Master," she cried, as she burst into tears of joy. The risen Lord had appeared to her. To her alone.

THE SHADOWS FLEE

Who was this woman, Mary Magdalene, whose name is mentioned only once prior to the Crucifixion and Resurrection scenes of the New Testament? What is the source of her great devotion to the

Savior and her ultimate selection by Him to be the first witness of His resurrected body?

Luke is the only Gospel writer who mentions the name "Mary Magdalene" prior to the Crucifixion, and it is a minor mention at best. He simply says that she had been "healed of seven devils" and lists her among several women who had "ministered unto him of their substance" (Luke 8:2–3). She and the other women apparently shared what material goods they had with Jesus and His disciples. Nothing else is written of Mary Magdalene specifically until the Savior's Crucifixion and Resurrection, when suddenly she becomes the central figure, staying near Him during His agony on the cross, arriving first at the tomb, announcing His Resurrection to the Apostles, and being the first witness of His resurrected body.

Unless . . . Could it be that she appears more frequently in the record under a different name? After studying and teaching the Bible for decades, both as scripture and as literature, I am convinced that Mary Magdalene and Mary the sister of Martha are the same person. I believe that "Magdalene" refers not only to Mary's supposed town of origin (Magdala), but also to her family relationship: her sister, Magda. The Greeks Hellenized the names by which we know the characters in the New Testament: Jesus's Hebrew name was Joshua; Mary's Hebrew name was Miriam. And the name "Martha" is the same as the name "Magda." They both mean "maiden" or "lady." Thus Martha was the "lady of the house" in which Mary was the younger sister, and perhaps even the *wayward* or headstrong sister. Mary Magdalene—or Miriam the sister of Magda, perhaps also from Magdala.

Jesus spent the final evenings of His mortal life in the home of Mary and Martha and their brother Lazarus in what was most assuredly a haven of domestic peace for Him. The familial relationship was clear; these two women not only cooked for Him, they felt close enough to send for Him when their brother was dying, and to chastise Him for taking so long in coming. "If only you had come, our brother would not have died," they both lamented when they saw Him. Clearly Mary and Martha were His closest friends. Yet it was to Mary Magdalene that Jesus appeared first in His resurrected state. Inexplicably, Mary and Martha seem to disappear at this point from the story. But not if Mary Magdalene is actually Mary, Martha's sister.

Each of the four Gospels was written by a different narrator, each with a specific theme, tone, and voice. Moreover, while the Gospels are in harmony with one another thematically, they include many chronological and factual differences. For example, Matthew records a "sermon on the mount," while Luke refers to a "sermon on the plain." John says that Mary Magdalene went alone to report Jesus's missing body to the Apostles, while Luke says that "Joanna, and Mary the mother of James, and other women" (Luke 24:10) accompanied her, and Matthew says that it was "Mary Magdalene and the other Mary" who told the Apostles (Matthew 28:1, 8). Mark agrees with John that Mary Magdalene went to the Apostles alone, but Mark says that she saw the resurrected Lord first, before going to get them, while John reports that Jesus appeared to her after the Apostles had already come to the tomb. These differences actually serve to strengthen the veracity of the four Gospels, not weaken them. Humans have a tendency to get their stories mixed up in their memory, but a made-up story has no such flaws.

JUDAH'S REMNANT, CLEANSED FROM SIN

With this in mind, we can see how stories reported separately by the writers of the four Gospels might contain different details, and yet be the same story. Let's begin with the three stories about a woman who anointed Jesus with costly ointment, bathed His feet with her tears, and dried them with her hair, all to the disapproval of certain disciples who complained about her wastefulness. These are traditionally interpreted as three different events, but I am convinced that they are simply different versions of the same remarkable experience.

John provides the most details. The incident he describes occurs in Bethany, at the home of Mary and Martha, six days before the Passover on which Jesus would be crucified. Jesus went to their home every night during the last week of His life. It is apparent that they were very special to Him. Martha served the supper while Lazarus sat at the table with the men. Mary took "a pound of ointment of spikenard, very costly, and anointed the feet of Jesus, and wiped his feet with her hair: and the house was filled with the odour of the ointment" (John 12:3). Judas Iscariot, who is identified in this telling as "Simon's son," complained that the ointment could have been sold for three hundred pence and given to the poor. When one considers that a day's wages at this time was a penny, we can see that the ointment was very costly indeed—equal to ten months' wages. Jesus, however, recognized the symbolic significance of Mary's action; "Let her alone," He said to Judas. "Against the day of my burying hath she kept this" ointment (John 12:7).

Mark appears to be telling the same story, although the details are different. The story is still set in Bethany, but now it is in the home of Simon the leper, and it is just two days before the Passover. An unnamed woman brings an alabaster box of spikenard, but she pours it onto Jesus's head rather than massaging it into His feet (Mark 14:3). The complainer is not mentioned by name, but his complaint is the same: "Why was this waste of the ointment made? For it might have been sold for more than three hundred pence, and have been given to the poor" (Mark 14:4–5). Once again Jesus says to let the woman alone. "She is come aforehand to anoint my body to the burying" (Mark 14:8).

The most moving and significant telling of the story occurs in the book written by Luke, who reports that Jesus was dining in the home of a Pharisee named, again, Simon. Although this woman is unnamed, we can know something of her character through her actions and her emotions. She was a sinner who stood behind Jesus "weeping, and began to wash his feet with her tears, and did wipe them with the hairs of her head, and kissed his feet, and anointed them with the ointment" from an alabaster box (Luke 7:38). The host complained not because of the cost of the ointment this time, but because of the sinful background of the woman. It shakes his confidence in Jesus, and he thinks to himself that a prophet "would have known who and what manner of woman . . . touche[d] him; for she [was] a sinner" (Luke 7:39). Reading His host's thoughts, Jesus responded aloud by telling a parable.

"There was a certain creditor which had two debtors," He began. "The one owed five hundred pence, and the other fifty. And when they had nothing to pay, he forgave them both." Then He asked, "Tell me therefore, which of them will love him most?"

Simon thought for a moment. "I suppose that he, to whom he forgave most," he said.

Jesus nodded. "Thou hast rightly judged," He agreed. Then, in a moving and heartfelt rebuke of His host's critical judgment, Jesus said, "Do you see this woman? When I entered your house, you gave me no water for my feet, but she has washed my feet with tears, and wiped them with the hairs of her head. You gave me no kiss, but from the time she arrived this woman has not stopped kissing my feet. You did not anoint my head with oil, but this woman has anointed my feet with ointment. This is why I say that her sins, which are many, are forgiven: Because she has loved me much."

Then He added pointedly, "But those to whom little is forgiven, love me little." Simon had judged this woman for her sinful past, but Jesus loved her for her sincere devotion. Then Jesus turned to the woman and declared, "Your sins are forgiven" (see Luke 7:44–47). Significantly, this woman's story appears in the middle of a list of miraculous healings, indicating that to be forgiven is indeed to be healed. Jesus is so consistent in His forgiveness! It is not where we start but where we finish that counts, and there are many paths that can take us there. This woman had sinned, but she was no longer a sinner. She was forgiven. And she was loved.

Traditionally this unnamed devotee is thought to be Mary Magdalene, because she is named in the very next story as one of Jesus's followers, a woman who had been "healed of evil spirits" (Luke 8:2). This is also where the idea originates that Mary Magdalene had been a sinner.

It is unlikely that the women who followed Jesus had enough money to pour pounds and pounds of costly ointment into Jesus's feet again and again. It is much more likely that all three of these accounts are different versions of the same story, performed by the same person—and that would make the sinful woman who is generally identified as Mary Magdalene, as recorded by Luke, the same Mary who was the sister of Martha, as recorded by Matthew. Significantly, these two Marys never appear together, but they share nearly identical experiences. Whenever either of them is mentioned, it is always in relation to the great love and concern she felt for Jesus, and that He felt for her.

Moreover, it doesn't make sense that Jesus's devoted friend, Mary the sister of Martha, at whose home He spent each night of the last week of His life, would suddenly abandon Him on the days of His Crucifixion and Resurrection. It is much more likely that, with so many Marys in the story at the tomb (Mary the mother of Jesus, Mary the mother of James, Mary the sister of Martha, Mary the wife of Cleopas, and "the other Mary"), John simply began to identify her as we do in modern times, by her family relationship: Mary the sister of Martha, or Miriam Magdalene.

To Bring Her Ransomed Children Home

This gives us greater insight into the woman who had the privilege of being first to see the resurrected Christ. We first meet her as Mary the sister of Martha, in Luke's account. Jesus was visiting in their home, which is actually described as belonging to Martha. Martha was "cumbered about by much serving" and complained that she was doing all the kitchen work while her sister Mary was listening to the men's conversation. Jesus responded, "Martha, Martha, thou art careful and troubled about many things: but one thing is needful: and Mary hath chosen that good part, which shall not be taken away from her" (Luke 10:38–42). Note that Jesus did not say, "We don't need food," but that Martha was worrying over less important things when compared to the opportunity to sit with the Savior and feel His healing Spirit. In modern parlance, we might compare it to worrying over table decorations and cute little handouts while neglecting the opportunity to sit in on a lesson, read the scriptures, or spend quality time with one's children or visitors. Good meals and clean houses are important, but we should spend most of our time doing things that have lasting consequences. It is also important to note that Jesus welcomed women into the discussions, even though He lived in a time and a culture that expected women to remain socially isolated from the men.

Shortly thereafter, we read the parable of the prodigal son, in which a younger brother leaves home and "waste[s] his substance with riotous living" (Luke 15:13). The young man falls more and more deeply into poverty and degradation until finally, while living in a pigsty, he remembers how well his father treated their servants. "I will arise and go to my father," he decides, "and will say unto him, 'Father, I have sinned against heaven, and before thee, and am no more worthy to be called thy son: make me as one of thy hired servants'" (Luke 15:18–19).

This young man is no longer a proud, boisterous, demanding and profligate sinner; he is humbled by experience and fully repentant. He makes no demands on his father, nor does he make excuses for himself. He does not ask to be accepted back home as a son. He simply asks if he may have the same opportunity as other strangers at the door—the opportunity to work and to serve. It is the father's own decision to "bring forth the best robe, and put it on him; and put a ring on his hand, and shoes on his feet: and . . . be merry" (Luke 15:22–23). Just as Jesus rejoiced in the genuine repentance of the woman who wept tears of gratitude for the forgiveness He showed her, the father rejoiced, "For this my son was dead, and is alive again; he was lost, and is found" (Luke 15:24).

In Prokofiev's ballet "The Prodigal Son," choreographed by George Balanchine for the Ballet Russes, the prodigal son returns wracked with shame and sorrow for his riotous living. As he approaches his father's home he prostrates himself on the ground. Then slowly and agonizingly he crawls to where his father stands waiting for him. The father yearns for him to return, but the son must do it on his own. He kisses his father's feet and bathes them with his tears. Then he drags himself painstakingly up till he wraps his arms around his father's neck and curls himself up against his father's chest, lifting his knees into a fetal position until the father reaches his own arms around and cradles his son like a baby. Their tears mingle. It is a beautiful, poignant moment. Through sincere repentance, the prodigal son is no longer a sinner, but has become as innocent as a child.

As we can see through the melding of the three stories about anointing Jesus's feet, the repentant woman most likely was Mary the sister of Martha. Thus the parable of the prodigal son may have been a veiled lesson directed at Jesus's two dearest friends. It is also possible, though purely speculative, that Mary had spent time as a wayward and prodigal daughter, especially if she is indeed the Mary who was freed from "seven devils." This idea gives greater emphasis to Jesus's statement that she had "chosen that good part" after having experienced the bad part. She may have returned home sadder, wiser, and filled with joy and gratitude for having been forgiven. For all these reasons Mary fully recognized the comparative values of domestic occupation and spiritual feasting.

And Martha, bless her heart, was like the elder brother, the responsible one who owned the house, served the meals, and took care of their older brother, Lazarus. By her own choice, she was working in the kitchen while her sister experienced the greater joy and love of listening to the Savior. Jesus taught Martha the same lesson that He taught Simon the Pharisee: By worrying so much about kitchen things, she missed out on the opportunity to sit at the Savior's feet and feel His love. Mary loved Christ deeply, while Martha, because she had less need of forgiveness for serious transgressions, had missed out on the great joy that comes from gratitude.

This story about the prodigal son is tucked inside a chapter about finding precious things that have been lost. First Jesus told the parable of the shepherd who left his ninety-nine "good" sheep to look for the little sheep that was lost. Then He told the parable of the woman who lost one of her ten pieces of silver and searched high and low until she found it, rejoicing and telling all her neighbors of her great joy for having found the missing coin. In each case, the other sheep and the other coins were just as valuable, but they were safe.

Similarly, it's the children we worry about the most who cause us the most joy when they repent and return to the family fold, because the possibility of losing them forever had been so real. The father did not reject his elder son; the shepherd did not reject his faithful sheep; the woman did not throw out her nine silver coins; and Christ did not reject Martha's friendship. All continued to receive love and protection. Yet there appears to be a special bond between the Savior and those who need His saving grace the most. "There is joy in the presence of the angels of God over one sinner that repenteth" (Luke 15:10).

The Dawning of a Brighter Day

Telling them these parables seems to have had the desired effect, because when we read of Mary and Martha again, they are completely united in their support of one another, and in their testimony of Jesus Christ. But it was a sad occasion. Their beloved brother Lazarus had fallen ill, and they wanted Jesus to bless him and bring him back to health.

Jesus loved these three siblings dearly. Nevertheless, when He heard the news of Lazarus's dire illness, He waited two days before going to Judea. His disciples thought His delay was motivated by concern for His own life. After all, the Jews had threatened to stone Him if He returned to Jerusalem. His disciples cautioned Him against going, especially when He said, "Our friend Lazarus sleeps. I am going so that I may wake him from this sleep." Why should He risk His life, they argued, if Lazarus was simply sleeping? Didn't that mean he was getting over his illness? (see John 11:5–15).

Of course, Jesus was using a common euphemism. Lazarus wasn't merely sleeping; he had died. In fact, his body had already begun to decompose. Jesus had delayed His coming on purpose, not to protect Himself from His enemies, but to perform a great miracle and teach a powerful lesson. When our hearts are broken, our spirits are full. Jesus used this opportunity not only to comfort Mary and Martha, but also to strengthen their faith.

When Martha heard that Jesus had come, she ran out to meet with Jesus privately. She knew it was not safe for Him to be so near Jerusalem. Still, in her grief, she cried out against Him. "If only you had been here, my brother would not have died!" she wept. Surely we can forgive Martha's outburst. Who of us has not railed against God in a moment of anguish? Who has not felt a sense of abandonment during a time of great testing? But even in her anguish, Martha had hope. "I know that whatever you ask of God, He will give it to you," she said (see John 11:21–22).

Jesus promised her that Lazarus would rise again, and in her simple faith she responded, "I know that he shall rise again in the resurrection at the last day" (John 11:24). But this gave her little comfort as her beloved brother lay in his tomb. Anyone who has lost a child, a sibling, or a spouse knows how empty the promise feels: "You will be together in heaven someday." She missed him *now*.

Jesus challenged her once more. He would need the power of great faith in order to accomplish the miracle He was about to ask of God. Then He proclaimed the most profound and powerful message in world history. "I am the resurrection, and the life," He said. "He that believeth in me, though he were dead, yet shall he live: And whosoever liveth and believeth in me shall never die." Then He asked Martha, "Believest thou this?" (John 11:25–26).

With a powerful testimony Martha responded, "I believe that thou art the Christ, the Son of God, which should come into the world" (John 11:27). Her words rang with sincerity. Jesus was satisfied. Martha too had "chosen that good part, which shall not be taken away from her" (Luke 10:42). Her faith was now strong.

Then Martha went back into the house and whispered to Mary that Jesus was standing outside in the shadows. Mary hurried to find Him. As soon as she saw Him she fell down at His feet and, as her sister had done, cried out in her grief, "If only you had been here, our brother would not have died!" (see John 11:32).

Jesus did not challenge Mary or teach her the way He had tested Martha. He simply wept with her. Watching her grieve, hearing her sobs, He felt tremendous compassion. Jesus "groaned in the spirit, and was troubled" (John 11:33). In the shortest verse of scripture we read, "Jesus wept" (John 11:35).

Those around Him said, "Behold, how he loved him!" (John 11:36). But there was more significance to Jesus's weeping and compassion than grief over Lazarus's death. He knew that He was about to bring their brother Lazarus back to life. He knew the great joy and relief they would shortly feel. But He also knew of the great grief they would again experience in just a few short days. The time had come for His own great sacrifice. Jesus Himself was going to die. How much He had loved His time on earth! How much He had loved His friends and followers! How much He would miss this life, and these two women in particular. He groaned to think of their inconsolable heartache when He died. He wept for them.

But for now, He could give them this gift. "Jesus lifted up his eyes, and said, Father, I thank thee that thou hast heard me" (John

11:41). Mary and Martha would not be left utterly alone at His death. Lazarus would be there to comfort them.

ISRAEL'S BLESSINGS ARE AT HAND

As Jesus accepted the agony that awaited Him in Gethsemane and at Golgotha, it was the women who comforted and supported Him. Each day of that final week He walked the dusty road from Bethany to Jerusalem to face His accusers. He challenged the Pharisees and Sadducees, cleansed the temple once more, cursed the fig tree for its hypocrisy. He sat on the hill overlooking Jerusalem and foresaw His triumphal return in the last days. He lamented, "Oh Jerusalem, Jerusalem, thou that killest the prophets, and stonest them which are sent unto thee, how often would I have gathered thy children together, even as a hen gathereth her chickens under her wings, and ye would not!" (Matthew 23:37).

Early on the Sunday morning following His Crucifixion, Jesus stood within the shadows of the garden, waiting for the proper time to reveal His resurrected body. Several women arrived at the tomb at dawn, including His own mother, for whom He had shown such tender concern as He hung, dying, on the cross. Two of His disciples would also arrive: Peter, His first and chief Apostle, and John, "the other disciple, whom Jesus loved" (John 20:2). He would watch as they looked inside the empty tomb and then hurried away to find the other Apostles. Only one person would remain: Mary Magdalene, who had come to perform a final act of devoted service, that of anointing Christ's body for proper burial. Jesus chose this woman to be the first person to view His resurrected body, and to carry the message to His disciples that He had truly risen from the dead. This woman was very special.

Throughout the scriptures Jesus is referred to metaphorically as "the bridegroom," and the Church as His bride. In his Epistle to the Ephesians the Apostle Paul wrote, "Husbands, love your wives, even as Christ also loved the church, and gave himself for it . . . that he might present it to himself a glorious church, not having spot, or wrinkle, or any such thing; but that it should be holy and without blemish" (Ephesians 5:25–27). In the parable of the ten virgins Jesus said, "While the bridegroom tarried, they all slumbered and slept" (Matthew 25:5), right after He explained that "of that day and hour [when He would return] knoweth no man, no, not the angels of heaven, but my Father only" (Matthew 24:36). This close juxtaposition suggests a connection between the two events, the great wedding and His return, a suggestion made even clearer in the book of Revelation: "John saw the holy city, new Jerusalem, coming down from God out of heaven, prepared as a bride adorned for her husband" (Revelation 21:2); "Let us be glad and rejoice, and give honour to him: for the marriage of the Lamb is come, and his wife hath made herself ready" (Revelation 19:7).

Mary Magdalene is the symbolic personification of the Church itself. She represents that sanctified bride, redeemed through His blood. Just as Orpheus in Greek mythology enters Hades's Underworld to rescue his beloved Eurydice, Christ descended in the Garden of Gethsemane to the very depths of hell to redeem His Church and sealed that sacrifice in the agony of the cross. Similarly, in Norse mythology, the hero Siegfried battles a dragon and enters a ring of flames to rescue Brunnhilde, who has been chained to a rock for her disobedience. Through the Atonement, Christ loosens the chains of death and hell to rescue the Church, whom He loves.

Some might be troubled by the idea that a self-proclaimed sinner would be chosen to represent the Church and bride of Christ. Wouldn't He have chosen someone more "worthy"—more perfect? This notion suggests that a sinner cannot be truly forgiven—that only those who have lived a completely righteous life deserve to be raised to the celestial kingdom. However, such thinking limits the power of the Atonement, rendering it finite rather than infinite. It suggests that the repentant sinner may come into the room, but not eat at the table. This is the elder brother's argument, and nothing could be more false, "for all have sinned, and come short of the glory of God" (Romans 3:23). Jesus Himself taught that those who are forgiven most love Him most (Luke 7:41–43). What better way for Jesus to demonstrate the infinite power of the Atonement than to choose Mary Magdalene as the representative of His Church at the Tomb? Thus the story of the Bible, which begins in a Garden with a woman who fell, ends in a Garden with a woman who is redeemed.

Now, as Mary Magdalene stood in the garden beside the tomb, she recognized His voice as the Savior called her name. Her agony of sorrow was over, and she clung to Him with joy. It would not be necessary for her to anoint His body with spices for its burial after all. His body would never decompose. Through His great sacrifice at Gethsemane and on Golgotha, His body had become immortal and incorruptible. Here, standing beside her, was the First Fruits of the Resurrection.

Their embrace lasted only a moment, but it was enough. "Hold me not,"[3] He told her gently, "for I am not yet ascended to my Father: but go to my brethren, and say unto them, I ascend unto my Father, and your Father; and to my God, and your God" (John 20:17). Through His atoning sacrifice, humankind had been redeemed and restored as joint heirs with Christ. He could now say to all who would accept His gift, "All that I have is thine." That which was lost had been found, forever.

NOTES

1. Parley P. Pratt, "The Morning Breaks," in *Hymns of the Church of Jesus Christ of Latter-day Saints* (Salt Lake City: Church of Jesus Christ of Latter-day Saints, 1985), 1.

2. The section titles for this chapter are taken from the lyrics of the hymn *The Morning Breaks,* written by Parley P. Pratt.

3. The King James Version uses the phrase "Touch me not," suggesting that Christ would not let her touch Him, perhaps because His body was not yet tangible. But according to noted linguist Royal Skousen, the original Greek is more closely translated as "Stop clinging to me." I believe it was said gently, and with a sense of reluctance on His part. He had work to do.

VALIANT WOMEN FOR TODAY

"Can a woman forget her sucking child, that she should not have compassion on the son of her womb? yea, they may forget, yet will I not forget thee. Behold, I have graven thee upon the palms of my hands" (Isaiah 49:15–16).

THE BIBLE IS a story of families torn apart by jealousy, bitterness, and sorrow, then brought together again through the healing power of forgiveness and family devotion. It is a story of sibling rivalry, but also a story of siblings who made amends. As a boy, Ishmael teased and disrespected little Isaac, but as a man he remained close to Father Abraham, gave his daughter to Esau to be his wife, and stood beside Isaac at the burial of their father. When Jacob used a cunning plot to secure the birthright blessing from Isaac, Esau vowed to kill him. Yet twenty years later, Esau embraced Jacob with a brother's welcome. Jacob's son Joseph was so hated and resented by his older brothers that they sold him into slavery. Nevertheless, more than twenty years later, Joseph rescued those same treacherous brothers from famine and restored the love that should always exist among siblings. Women stand firmly at the center of these stories, using their feminine strengths to encourage, support, plot, and guide.

As we have seen, there is no single blueprint for womanhood or for motherhood. Each woman is an individual, motivated by her own hopes, talents, weaknesses, and responsibilities. And each is an *ezer*, endowed by her Creator with the innate power to become a rescuer and savior within her community. M. Russell Ballard wisely observed, "There is nothing in this world as personal, as nurturing, or as life changing as the influence of a righteous woman."[1] This is true of women in their relationships not only as wives to their husbands and mothers to their children, but also as teachers to their students, neighbors to their friends, and leaders to their constituents.

Jesus is the Messiah and the King, yet He chose the tender mother-child relationship to demonstrate His relationship with His disciples. In Isaiah we read, "Can a woman forget her sucking child, that she should not have compassion on the son of her womb? yea, they may forget, yet will I not forget thee. Behold, I have graven thee upon the palms of my hands" (Isaiah 49:15–16). First Isaiah acknowledges the absurdity that a nursing mother could forget her baby, and then he reminds us that Christ bears the imprints of His love within the nail prints of His sacrifice. He cannot forget us. We are part of Him.

A mother knows how completely in tune one person can be with another. I have a distinct memory of putting my firstborn into her crib one night and thinking, "She will be hungry in about three hours." Such a small thing, yet it struck me in that moment that I was no longer a separate individual; I would always be connected to this child and acutely aware of her needs. As more children came into our home, my capacity to be constantly aware of them expanded. It was an invisible line connecting our spirits. I felt it with each birth. Perhaps it stems from the need to communicate soul to soul rather than with words in the first months and years of a child's life. Fathers and mothers alike are willing to lay down their lives for their children, but "a mother, whose antennae are acutely attuned to her child, picks up signals that pass undetected by others."[2] A mother is privileged to have that constant awareness, if she nurtures it. The connection is both spiritual and physical. We ache when we are away from our babies. The longer they are away from us, the more we ache. They are engraved in our stretch marks and in our hearts, just as we are engraved in the palms of Christ's hands. Even when we stray, as we often do, "His anger is not turned away, but his hand is outstretched still" (Isaiah 9:8–12). A mother knows that feeling.

Jesus's maternal ancestors knew that feeling too—as mothers and as daughters. Like most of us, they experienced hardship, sacrifice, sorrow, and even sin, but by reaching for His outstretched hand, they also found the joy of spiritual peace. Their experiences and backgrounds were diverse, yet they have much in common with today's women—and men—as we face obstacles, seek guidance, and make choices. Leah knew the heartache of watching her children lose their way, but she found peace by nurturing her relationship with God. Rahab was a single woman walking a worldly path in a worldly city, but she became a noble and virtuous wife and mother. Bathsheba, too, gave in to sexual temptation, but through repentance she became a righteous queen whose son was known for his great wisdom. Tamar and Ruth, both childless widows, found happiness as they helped their father- and mother-in-law overcome sorrow and regain the right path. Sarah reminds us that it is normal to grieve for the path not taken, even when the path we are taking is correct.

In sum, readers of today can find profound guidance by following the example of these valiant women in the lineage of Jesus Christ. Endowed by their Creator with feminine strengths, they had the audacity to change the world.

Notes

1. M. Russell Ballard, "Mothers and Daughters," *Ensign*, April 2010. https://www.lds.org/general-conference/2010/04/mothers-and-daughters?lang=eng.

2. Carolyn Custis James, *Lost Women of the Bible: Finding Strength and Significance through Their Stories* (Grand Rapids, MI: Zondervan, 2005), 174.

ACKNOWLEDGMENTS

"In every thing give thanks: for this is the
will of God" (1 Thessalonians 5:18).

ONE OF THE profound joys of writing a book such as this one is retracing the steps that led to this point and thanking those who helped along the way. My journey began when I was given a set of W. Cleon Skousen's *Thousand Year* series, which recounts the thrilling and poignant stories of the Old Testament. From him I learned the importance of telling the story and providing the doctrine. I hope that he would be pleased with my writing style as well as my perspective on these women. Through him I not only fell in love with the scriptures, but also with his nephew, Mark Skousen, who has been my husband and partner for more than four decades.

Dr. Maurice O'Sullivan, chairman of the English Department and my mentor at Rollins College, challenged me in classes to embrace the Bible as a piece of beautifully written literature aside from its power as a religious document. I learned to recognize literary archetypes from him. Dr. David Leverenz, who directed my master's thesis at the University of Florida, taught me how to use close-reading techniques to analyze literature, and this skill was immensely useful as I teased out the often-overlooked details in these accounts and reflected on their implications to gain a deeper understanding. Both these men have guided my reading, writing, and teaching styles, and each has become a treasured friend.

A teacher learns alongside her students, and my students throughout the years have influenced me in many wonderful ways. I am also grateful for my mother and my sister, who have been *ezerim* throughout my life, and for my children, who made it easy to live by the dictum, "The most important of the Lord's work you will ever do will be within the walls of your own home."[1] I have treasured every minute of being their mother.

Several people read the manuscript and provided valuable feedback. I am grateful to Chris Schoebinger of Shadow Mountain, whose conversation on a plane convinced me that this was a book worth writing; to Emily Chambers, McKell Parsons, and the staff at Cedar Fort, who recognized the inspirational and educational value of the manuscript; to Mandy Williams for the beautiful art, "Valiant Women," that graces the cover; to Claudia Bushman, Stephen Cox, Steve Forbes, and Daniel Peterson for their written endorsements; to my friend Gary Burnett, who read an early draft when I was feeling discouraged and gave me the confidence to move forward; to my sweetheart, Mark Skousen, who endured what I imagine every husband of a writer endures during the course of bringing a book to print; and to Dr. Stephen Cox, my colleague, editor, and friend, who read each chapter carefully and challenged me to get it right.

Most of all, I am grateful for these valiant women who have been in my heart for so many years and whose stories are now recorded in this book. I hope they look down from the heavens with an approving nod.

NOTES

1. Harold B. Lee, *Teachings of Presidents of the Church: Harold B. Lee* (Salt Lake City: The Church of Jesus Christ of Latter-day Saints, 2000), 135.

WORKS CITED

Alexander C. Jensen, Shawn D. Whiteman, Karen L. Fingerman, and Kira S. Birditt. "'Life Still Isn't Fair': Parental Differential Treatment of Young Adult Siblings." *Journal of Marriage and Family*, 2013: 438–52.

Ariel, David. *What Do Jews Believe? The Spiritual Foundations of Judaism.* New York: Shocken, 1995.

Ballard, M. Russell. "Mothers and Daughters." *Ensign*. Salt Lake City: The Church of Jesus Christ of Latter Day Saints, 2010. https://www.lds.org/general-conference/2010/04/mothers-and-daughters?lang=eng.

Bellis, Alice Ogden. *Helpmates, Harlots, Heroes: Women's Stories in the Hebrew Bible.* Louisville, KY: Westminster/John Knox Press, 1994.

Bryan Holmes, ed. *Bulfinch's Myths of Greece and Rome.* New York: Viking Penguin, 1979.

Bulfinch, Thomas. *Myths of Greece and Rome.* Edited by Bryan Holme. New York, NY: Penguin.

C. Winsper, M. Zanarini, and D. Wolke. "Prospective study of family adversity and maladaptive parenting in childhood and borderline personality disorder symptoms in a non-clinical population at 11 years." *Psychological Medicine*, 2012: 2405–20.

Carmichael, Calum M. *Women, Law, and the Genesis Traditions.* Edinburgh, Scotland: Edniburgh University Press, 1979.

Cartmell, Todd. *Keep the Siblings, Lose the Rivalry.* Grand Rapids MI: Zondervan, 2003.

Chapman, Annie. *The Mother-in-Law Dance.* Eugene OR: Harvest House, 2004.

Dew, Sheri. *Are We Not All Mothers?* Salt Lake City: Deseret Book, 2011.

Ebeling, Jennie R. *Women's Lives in Bliblical Times.* New York: T & T Clark International, 2010.

Emerson, Ralph Waldo. *Emerson in His Journals.* Edited by Joel Porte. Boston, MA: Belknap Harvard, 1982.

Evans, Richard Paul. "How I Saved My Marriage." *Deseret News.* Salt Lake City, UT: http://www.deseretnews.com/article/865621517/Richard-Paul-Evans-How-I-saved-my-marriage.html?pg=all, February 9, 2015.

Feiler, Bruce. *Walking the Bible: A Journey by Land through the Five Books of Moses.* New York, NY: William Morrow, 2001.

Feld, Merle. "At the Crossroads." In *Reading Ruth: Contemporary Women Reclaim a Sacred Story*, by Judith A. Kates and Gail Twersky Reimer. New York: Random House, 1994: 166–81.

Fishman, Sylvia Barack. "Soldiers in an Army of Mothers." In *Reading Ruth: Contemporary Women Reclaim a Sacred Story*, by Judith A. Kates and Gail Twersky Reimer. New York: Random House, 1994: 273–83.

Frankiel, Tamar. "Ruth and the Messiah." In *Reading Ruth: Contemporary Women Reclaim a Sacred Story*, by Judith A. Kates and Gail Twersky Reimer. New York: Random House, 1994: 321–35.

Frost, Robert. "The Road Not Taken." In *Robert FRost: Collected Poems, Prose & Plays*, by Richard Poirer and Mark Richardson. New York, NY: Literary Classics of America, 1916, 1995: 103.

Frymer-Kensky, Tikva. *Reading the Women of the Bible.* New York: Schocken, 2002.

Givens, Terryl Givens and Fiona. *The God Who Weeps.* Salt Lake City, UT: Ensign Peak, 2012.

Gordon, Charlotte. *The Woman Who Named God.* New York: Little Brown and Co., 2009.

Graham, Elizabeth. *Mothers-in-Law vs. Daughters-in-Law.* Kansas City: Beacon Hill Press, 2010.

Henry, Matthew. *An Exposition of the Old and New Testament.* Peabody, MA: Hendrickson Publishers, 1706, 2008.

James, Carolyn Custis. *Lost Women of the Bible: The Women We Thought We Knew.* Grand Rapids, MI: Zondervan, 2005.

Johnson, Paul. *The Quest for God.* New York: Harper Collins, 1996.

Klagsbrun, Francine. "Ruth and Naomi, Rachel and Leah: Sisters under the Skin." In *Reading Ruth: Contemporary Women Reclaim a Sacred Story,* by Judith A. Kates and Gail Twersky Reimer. New York: Random House, 1994: 261–72.

Kristen E. Kvam, Linda S. Schearing, and Valarie H. Ziegler. *Eve & Adam: Jewish, Christian, and Muslim Readings on Genesis and Gender.* Bloomington, IN: Indiana University Press, 1999.

Landers, Ann. "Message for Siblings: Learn to Get Along Now." *Reading Eagle/Reading Times,* August 21, 1996: C2.

Lee, Harold B. *Teachings of Presidents of the Church: Harold B. Lee.* Salt Lake City: The Church of Jesus Christ of Latter-day Saints, 2000.

MacArthur, John. *Twelve Extraordinary Women: How God Shaped Women of the Bible and What He Wants to Do with You.* Nashville, TN: Thomas Nelson, 2005.

McConkie, Rebecca Lyn. "Rahab the Harlot: Her Place in the Hebrew Bible." *Selecgtion from the Religious Education Symposium 2004* (Religious Studies Center, Brigham Young University), 2004: 79 91.

Melissa L. Sturge-Apple, Michael A. Skibo, and Patarick T. Davies. "Impact of Parental Conflict and Emotional Abuse on Children and Families." *Partner Abuse,* 2012: 379–400.

Meyers, Carol. *Rediscovering Eve: Ancient Israelite Women in Context.* Oxford: Oxford University Press, 2012.

Neil, James. *Everyday Life in the Holy Land.* London and New York: Cassel and Co., 1913.

Nielsen, Donna B. *Beloved Bridegroom.* Salt Lake City, UT: Onyx Press, 1999.

Owens, Virginia Stem. *Daughters of Eve: Seeing Ourselves in Women of the Bible.* Colorado Springs: NavPress, 1995, 2007.

Ozick, Cynthia. "Ruth." In *Reading Ruth: Contemporary Women Reclaim a Sacred Story,* by Judith A. Kates and Gwail Twersky Reimer. New York: Random House, 1994: 211–32.

Pagels, Elaine. *Adam, Eve, and the Serpent.* New York: Random House, 1988.

Pratt, Parley P. "The Morning Breaks." In *Hymns of the Church of Jesus Christ of Latter-day Saints.* Salt Lake, UT: The Church of Jesus Christ of Latter-day Saints, 1985: no. 1.

Reimer, Judith A. Kates and Gail Twersky, ed. *Reading Ruth: Contemporary Women Reclaim a Sacred Story.* New York, NY: Ballantine Books, 1994.

Richards, Lawrence Richards and Sue. *Women of the Bible: The Life and Times of Every Woman in the Bible.* Nashville: Thomas Nelson, 2003.

Robinson, Robert. "Come Thou Fount of Every Blessiong." *Come Thou Fount of Every Blessing: Vocal Score.* Edited by Mack Wilberg. Oxford: Oxford University Press, July 23, 1757, 1998.

Scott, Richard G. *21 Principles: Divine Truths to Help You Live by the Spirit.* Salt Lake City, UT: Deseret Book, 2013.

Skousen, W. Cleon. *Days of the Living Christ.* Vol. 2. 2 vols. Salt Lake City, UT: Ensign, 1992.

Smith, Joseph Fielding. *Teachings of the Prophet Joseph Smith.* Salt Lake City, UT: Deseret Book, 1967.

Terrien, Samuel. *Till the Heart Sings: A Biblical Theology of Manhood and Womanhood.* Grand Rapids MI: Wm B. Eerdmansn, 1985, 2004.

Top, Brent L. *A Peculiar Treasure: Old Testament Messages for Our Day.* Salt Lake City, UT: Deseret Book, 1997.

Webb, Diana. *Forgotten Women of God.* Springville, UT: Bonneville Books, 2010.

Wordsworth, William. *Ode: Intimations of Immortality.* 1804.

Ziglar, Zig. *Courtship after Marriage.* Nashville, TN: Thomas Nelson, 1990.

ABOUT THE AUTHOR

*J*O ANN SKOUSEN has taught English literature and writing at Rollins College in Florida, Mercy College in New York, Chapman University in California, and Sing Sing Correctional Facility up the river from Manhattan. She holds a BA in American Literature from Rollins College and an MA from University of Florida.

Jo Ann is also the entertainment editor of Liberty Magazine, the founding director of the Anthem Libertarian Film Festival, and associate editor of Mark Skousen's *Forecasts & Strategies*, a financial publication. She speaks frequently at conferences across the country and around the world. An avid traveler, she has led groups through the Mediterranean from Athens to Rome, relating the myths and Bible stories that took place in each location.

For over twenty years Jo Ann served as a seminary teacher and a gospel doctrine teacher while also teaching Classic Mythology and Bible Literature in her Honors English courses. Both of these teaching experiences, one focusing on religion and the other on literary archetypes, have given her great insights into the hearts and lives of the people who inhabit the scriptures. She has come to know and love the women of the Bible.

Jo Ann has been married to her husband, financial economist Mark Skousen, for over forty years. They have lived in Washington, DC; the Bahamas; London; Florida; New York; and California. In addition to collaborating on twenty-five books, two investment newsletters, and a large conference business, they are the parents of five children, who genuinely like each other. Jo Ann is never happier than when reading aloud to her grandchildren or teaching them to catch a wave at the beach.